Critical Acclaim for *C*

"Part *Love Boat*, part *Mutiny on the Bounty*, *Cruise Confidential* does for cruising what *Animal House* did for higher education."
—J. Maarten Troost, author

"Spray crashing, thunder blasting, bo
floor. Ship on the rocks? Nope, just a
'under-the-waterline' world of the wor
hum. The funniest travel book I've rea
breaks down the water-tight doors th
the really wild times at sea."
—Peter Mand
Across the Atlantic

"*Cruise Confidential* is a deliciously addictive read, much like *The Nanny Diaries* or *The Devil Wears Prada*. Only this book offers a blistering kiss-and-tell about the dysfunctional life working on cruise ships. Bruns is uniquely over-educated for his job, yet he seems to have a penchant for abuse and becomes the only American to survive a full contract working on the service side of the business. We've heard stories about what it's like, and we've assumed there's a good reason the only ones willing to do it are seemingly desperate citizens from the world's poorest countries. The reality is worse than whatever you imagined, and Bruns suffers through it first hand as the ultimate insider. It began as a quest to be together with his girlfriend, but he gets roped in along the way and, as a result, we get a good look into the orgy-like crew parties, a frightening management style that's a mix of Old Testament and Mafia, and a unique view of how cruising Americans are viewed by the patient foreigners who have to pamper them day and night (many of the international staff refer to the American guests as cows since they're easily placated, constantly grazing, and have about the same size waistline)."
—Doug Lansky, author of *Last Trout in Venice* and *Signspotting*

"These hilarious misadventures at sea will shock and delight any buffet-ready cruise traveler."
—Jen Leo, editor of *Sand in My Bra* and *The Thong Also Rises*

Travelers' Tales Books

Country and Regional Guides
America, Antarctica, Australia, Brazil, Central America, China,
Cuba, France, Greece, India, Ireland, Italy, Japan, Mexico, Nepal,
Spain, Thailand, Tibet, Turkey; Alaska, American Southwest,
Grand Canyon, Hawai'i, Hong Kong, Middle East, Paris,
Prague, Provence, San Francisco, South Pacific, Tuscany

Women's Travel
100 Places Every Woman Should Go, The Best Women's Travel
Writing, A Woman's Asia, A Woman's Europe, Her Fork in
the Road, A Woman's Path, A Woman's Passion for Travel,
A Woman's World, Women in the Wild, A Mother's World,
Safety and Security for Women Who Travel, Gutsy Women,
Gutsy Mamas, A Woman's World Again

Body & Soul
Stories to Live By, The Spiritual Gifts of Travel, The Road Within,
A Mile in Her Boots, Love & Romance, Food, How to Eat Around
the World, The Adventure of Food, The Ultimate Journey, Pilgrimage

Special Interest
Not So Funny When It Happened, The Gift of Rivers,
How to Shit Around the World, Testosterone Planet, Danger!,
The Fearless Shopper, The Penny Pincher's Passport to
Luxury Travel, Make Your Travel Dollars Worth
a Fortune, The Gift of Birds, Family Travel, A Dog's World,
There's No Toilet Paper on the Road Less Traveled,
The Gift of Travel, 365 Travel, The Thong Also Rises,
Adventures in Wine, The World is a Kitchen, Sand in My Bra,
Hyenas Laughed at Me and Now I Know Why,
Whose Panties Are These?, More Sand in My Bra

Travel Literature
A Sense of Place, The Best Travel Writing, Marco Polo Didn't Go
There, A Rotten Person Travels the Caribbean, Kite Strings of the
Southern Cross, The Sword of Heaven, Storm, Take Me With You,
Last Trout in Venice, The Way of the Wanderer, One Year Off,
The Fire Never Dies, The Royal Road to Romance, Unbeaten
Tracks in Japan, The Rivers Ran East, Coast to Coast, Trader Horn

CRUISE CONFIDENTIAL

A Hit Below the Waterline

CRUISE CONFIDENTIAL

A Hit Below the Waterline

Brian David Bruns

Travelers' Tales

AN IMPRINT OF SOLAS HOUSE, INC.

PALO ALTO

Travelers' Tales and Solas House are trademarks of Solas House, Inc., 853 Alma Street, Palo Alto, California 94301. www.travelerstales.com

Cover Design: Brian David Bruns
Interior Design and Page Layout: Patty Holden, using the font Sabon
Production Director: Christy Quinto

Library of Congress Cataloging-in-Publication Data

Bruns, Brian David.
 Cruise confidential : a hit below the waterline / Brian David Bruns.—
1st ed.
     p. cm.
   ISBN 1-932361-60-X (pbk.)
   1. Ocean travel—Anecdotes. 2. Cruise ships—Employees. 3. Cruise
ships—Humor. I. Title.
   G550.B78 2008
   910.4'5—dc22   2008019496

First Printing
Printed in the United States of America
10 9 8 7 6 5 4 3 2 1

Dedicated to my parents,
Marty and Audrey,
for their endless support
and enthusiasm

Contents

PART I

Trainee
(The Plunge)

The only thing worse than being talked about
is not being talked about.

—Oscar Wilde

1 *Strange Bedfellows*

THE SHOWER WAS, PERHAPS, THE MOST LUXURIOUS OF all time. The pressure was just shy of pummeling and the temperature was one grunt away from scalding. I lowered my head to let the water caress my shoulders and stared at the generous array of gifts nearby. There were tiny bottles of shampoo, conditioner, and body wash; little bars of hand soap and face soap, a courtesy disposable razor, and even a shower cap wrapped in a tight little waterproof bundle I had to steal for Mom. Steam billowed up to hide the ceiling, and my mind shared its carefree drifting.

I deserved this shower of bliss. I had been nearly manic with preparations to get here, and stressed beyond all reasonable measure by those two evil airline gods: Delay and Flightswap. But finally I had arrived in Miami and found myself exiting a taxi at the Marriott. Carnival Cruise Lines provided a surprisingly nice room for employees, and covered meals generously. They allowed $12 for lunch and an unprecedented $25 for dinner at the restaurant, called the Veranda Grill. I couldn't remember the last time I had eaten. Sometime yesterday, lunch maybe. But I was only interested in getting into my bed: it was late and tomorrow I had a 5:15 A.M. wake-up call.

Just me and my glorious shower. I listened to the whir of the fan overhead, diligently collecting steam. I became one with the cascading water swirling at my feet. I smiled at the telltale sounds of sexual ecstasy.

I blinked.

Sexual ecstasy?

In a flash I cut off the water and stood dripping, straining to hear what I surely had not heard. Someone was in my hotel room! I ripped the towel from the rack and wrapped it hastily around my middle even as I stormed out of the bathroom.

I looked into the bedroom to realize it was not in darkness. I had left the heavy curtains closed, but they had been thrown open while I showered. Thinner, sheer curtains silhouetted the likely culprits in the far bed, a bed that should have had no occupant at all, let alone two. From the doorway I stared incredulously. There was a strange couple in my room... having sex!

They weren't just making out, or petting, or in any sort of preview. They were heavily in the act. I don't know how long I stood there, gawking in disbelief. Surely it was a mere moment before I gave in to decency and prepared to depart. As quickly as possible, of course, without watching at all. I was planning without delay my exit when the woman's eyes, which had been screwed shut, opened in leisurely bliss...only to fly wide upon seeing me.

She barked a warning in a foreign language, and the rhythmic bouncing of the bed ceased. The man, who had been intent on his work, reluctantly turned to regard me.

"Can we have some privacy?" he asked casually.

"P-Privacy?" I blurted. They both were astonishingly composed as they regarded me. Obviously European, they were pale-skinned and slender. His reddish hair was shaved nearly to the scalp, matching his unshaven chin. He was not an attractive man. The woman, on the other hand, was phenomenally beautiful. Her slight waist flared where it should and she was bumpy in all the right places. I don't recall ever seeing so slender a woman with such large breasts. Natural, that is.

He frowned, suddenly taken aback. "You American?"

"Oh my God!" she shrieked, clutching the sheets to her chest. "There's an *American* in our room!"

"Ah," he continued. "America's latest invasion. I never thought it would be my bedroom, but you never know."

"Huh?"

"After a month on the ships, you'll understand."

"What the hell are you doing in my room?" I demanded, finally coming to my senses, now that she was covered.

"You not Carnival?" he sat up in bed, concerned.

"Yes, I am."

He seemed greatly relieved. "For minute I thought there was mistake."

"You think?" I retorted.

He chuckled. "Typical American. You thought the room was just yours?"

"I...well, yes."

"Is not. Pay no attention to Paula, but I tell you now: Bring no men here."

"What do you mean?"

"You are obviously dancer."

"Why do you say that?"

"You look like. No Americans on board unless they entertainers."

"What does that have to do with Paula?"

"Don't play me. You are obviously gay."

His look was so seriously distressed at the thought that I suddenly began laughing. At this point, how could I take anything seriously? "Why do you think I'm gay?"

"All American dancers are gay. And no normal man has eyes that pretty."

"Is this some kind of a joke?"

"You management?"

"Yes, I am management training."

"Ah, that explains it. Look, I just never met dancer on ship who's not gay. No matter. I am Alexandro. Croatia. You know where that is?"

He rose and approached to shake my hand...still completely naked and sweaty. I guess his worries about my sexual orientation were over.

"Uh, yeah. Used to be Yugoslavia."

"Hey, Paulina," he said, turning to the woman. "An *educated* American! Paula's from Serbia. You bombed her, but she doesn't mind."

"We never bombed Serbia...NATO bombed Serbia."

Alexandro sat back on the bed and patted Paulina on her shoulder. "Sorry, babe. I want to show you good time, but this guy only talks politics."

"You brought it up!" I protested.

"Whatever. Where you from?"

"I'm from Iowa."

"Ah, potatoes farmer."

"That's Idaho."

"Whatever. Which ship?"

I felt uncomfortable with this ugly, naked, foreign man questioning me. "*Carnival Conquest.*"

"Ah, of course. The most big, most new ship for the American. Look, we have to start over now. You aren't going to read in bed, are you? That would distract."

"I'm going to...to the restaurant."

"Good idea. Ciao."

"Yeah, O.K.," I said as I mechanically dressed and shuffled past them. Just as I was leaving I overheard him say, "Ship life will eat him alive."

2 *Global Warning*

I HAD BEEN WARNED REPEATEDLY THAT THERE WERE NO Americans working on the ships. I reflected on this as I wandered through the open-air courtyard of the Marriott. The Jacuzzi bubbled with the laughter of a dozen men and women. Even if they weren't speaking a foreign language, I could tell they were Europeans. They were all so slender. Each and every woman could have been a model. I hoped they were all assigned where I was going.

I moved past the pool, noisy with a group of Indian men playing volleyball. Small chain-smoking Asians drooped from the pay phones. The tables held scattered people with books and magazines in their native cultures. The strange lettering on the familiar titles fascinated me, from John Grisham's *The Pelican Brief* in Cyrillic to a *Cosmopolitan* magazine in Vietnamese.

For sure I was the only American here...I was in Miami!

Before I went to the restaurant, I stopped at the bulletin board hidden in a narrow passageway beneath the building. A throng of men and women from all over the earth jostled to read the lists displayed. I patiently waited for my turn to view the information, content with the knowledge that I was assigned to the *Fantasy* for Carnival College, then would join my girlfriend on *Conquest*.

I relinquished my place in line to a superlatively attractive woman with raven-black hair. Her sharp features could only be described as sultry and passionate. She was quite trim, and wore a snug black sweater and even tighter blue jeans. I could not fathom how she had possibly gotten into those pants. Unfortunately I could not fathom how *I* could get into them, either.

"Beautiful, isn't she?"

I looked up at a huge man who spoke the words. I am six foot one, but this man was easily two inches taller than I and very broad-shouldered. He had skin of a light cocoa color, black hair parted to the side, and was quite handsome. He spoke crisply correct English with a delicate cadence. We watched the petite beauty stride away.

"She certainly is," I replied. "You are Indian?"

"Yes, I am from Bombay. Where are you from?"

"I wish I was from wherever she is. Instead I am American."

He smiled. "India has the most beautiful women in the world. However, where I come from, we would say that woman has the exquisite beauty of a flower gently clasping the final drops of morning dew as the sun drenches it with brilliant love."

"That's nice," I replied sincerely. "Where I come from we would say she has an ass that would make a grown man cry."

Ahh...women. A woman was the reason I was undertaking this crazy business. I had vowed to do anything to be with my new girlfriend Bianca, a crew member aboard the *Conquest*. While she vacationed, visiting a friend who happened to be my business associate, Bianca and I met for a few whirlwind days. We hardly slept, talking until the sun came up and then spending the day adventuring together. After two earth-shattering days she left for Las Vegas to see another old friend. Yet rather than finish her U.S. stay in Sin City, she flew back to see me for her last day. Then she was truly gone, leaving for Transylvania for her last few weeks of vacation before another eight-month contract at sea. Within days I was flying to Europe intent on every day together we could get. Later, when she left for the sea, I did too.

The *Carnival Conquest* was built in the fall of 2002, the world's largest cruise ship at the time. Her maiden voyage was from the shipyards at Montfalcone, Italy to the Big Easy herself, New Orleans. The entire crew was approximately one thousand one hundred, including my girlfriend who had been slaving in the restaurant all week to get the ship ready for action. What that entailed is difficult to explain to the uninitiated: the two dining rooms served 3,500 guests in a single evening. Now imagine finding the lost salad tongs that were delivered to the wrong cargo hold.

When *Conquest* arrived in New Orleans, Bianca was already exhausted. The stress of the maiden voyage was far more than merely planning, preparation, and practice. It also entailed serving the company's owner, president, CEO, and other upper echelon corporate staff. Bianca was granted the dubious honor of taking care of such VIPs. Despite the stresses, she miraculously managed to obtain an interview for me.

I only wish she had warned me of the man's magnitude *before* the meeting.

"First you'll get questioned by Cedric the Mean Indian," Bianca had said as she puffed on her cigarette the day I flew in for the interview. She chose to prepare me in the crew bar, taking advantage of its relative emptiness. Smoke from the previous evening still smothered the air and my eyes watered. Her eyes were immune to the sting of smoke, but they were far from unaffected by her environment: the purple circles beneath them made her look like a panda.

"Cedric is an Indian name?"

"I don't know. But he's really important and tough as hell. He's usually not very friendly."

"Well, all good companies have their bad guy. I'm sure he's good at what he does."

"Oh, there's no doubt about that. If you can make it past him, you'll see Mladen."

"Great!"

She looked me in the eye. "Do you have any idea what you're getting into?"

"It will be fine."

"These foreign guys are going to tear you up. Things are harder elsewhere in the world."

"Oh, I see. You are an expert on the softness of corporate America now?"

"Just don't say I didn't warn you."

"Fair enough."

My interview with Cedric was in a commandeered office. He was a very small, dark-skinned man of few words. As soon as we sat he began flaying me with sharp, masterful strokes of his tongue. This brutal elective surgery lasted about two minutes, during which I said perhaps ten words. Then he simply got up and left.

I was confused, most certainly, but mostly I was angry. What kind of an interview was that? I had flown all the way to New Orleans and was barely allowed to speak! I stumbled back to Bianca's cabin feeling dejected, awaiting the order to leave the ship.

Apparently I had, in fact, made a good impression upon Cedric. I can't imagine how. I'm sure none of my lethal charm, quick wit, and staggering intelligence got past my modesty. It must have been based solely on my good looks. I wondered if he thought I was applying to be an entertainer. Regardless of his reasons, he informed Bianca an hour later that I should report to the dining room for a further interview.

At the appointed time I found myself sitting at a corner table in the massive rear restaurant of the *Conquest*. Though the Monet dining room was not yet open, the blur of activity from the waiters made it look like a beehive. Tonight the ship was moored on the Mississippi River and was receiving special dinner guests. I noticed that the waiters took pains to show their respect for soft-spoken Mladen. I did not know who Mladen was, other than the man who would decide if I was to be allowed on the ships or not.

"And why do you want to do this again?" asked the trim, middle-aged man before me. He was average in size, dark-haired, and wore glasses. He had a kind face and a kinder bearing. Mladen spoke gently, completely unlike the Mean Indian who sat with us.

"A woman."

"Ah, that's right. Bianca's with you now. It all makes sense."

Something about the way he said that made me feel awkward.

"You have no experience on ships at all."

"No, but I have a decade of restaurant experience, mostly fine dining. I have a college degree. I'm smart."

"Yes, you co-founded a software company?"

"Yes."

"And now you want to work on ships."

"I would follow that woman anywhere."

"Well, you aren't the first," Mladen replied amiably. I was a little unnerved by his statement, but he moved on with a glance to Cedric. "Well, Cedric liked you. But I cannot start you as management. It is very different on ships. The employees will devour you."

"I'll do my due diligence. Start me on the bottom, let me learn the system."

"You will do the dishes?"

"Of course. I have to work up from the bottom. When I was a busboy I learned how to spin dishes on my finger, and I still can."

He leaned back and regarded me.

"You know," he finally said, "I do not know of a single American in the dining rooms. Do you, Cedric?"

"No."

"In fact, in the thirty years Carnival has been running, I only know of one American working the dining room without quitting. He transferred to a different department before his contract was completed, though."

Mladen leaned forward and stared at me intently. I suddenly grew nervous.

"Do you not wonder why no American has *ever* survived a *single* eight-month contract in the dining room in Carnival's thirty-year history?"

"Well," I replied as coolly as possible, "I'll tell you in eight months."

He chuckled, then added, "All right. As long as you know that everyone else has failed before you. I will give you the chance, too. Good luck."

"Thank you."

"But it is against my better judgment."

After Mladen uttered his cryptic words, I strode out of the dining room with a bounce in my step. Dan, the maitre d', stopped me.

"Welcome to the team," he greeted, apparently aware in advance of Mladen's decision. "You were awfully casual with Mladen. I would be careful with that, if I were you."

"Oh?"

"Either you got balls of solid rock, or your head's made of it."

"What do you mean?"

"Didn't you know he's in the top tier of Carnival? He's got 30,000 people working for him. Either you're unflappable under pressure, or just stupid as hell. I guess we'll find out."

I dismissed the New Orleans interview from my mind as I approached my hotel room with trepidation. Fortunately the show was over between Alexandro and Paulina, though truthfully I would have preferred it to his snoring. Several hours passed before I could sleep with his constant sawing of logs. The phone rang and I hung it up before actually answering it, assuming it was my wake-up call.

Moments later the phone sharply reprimanded me with an emphatic ring. Croatian words were flung at me from the other end of the line. Though I couldn't understand the content, the tone was an exact copy of my former mother-in-law's.

At 5:30 A.M. I gathered my suitcase and trudged down to the passageway with the bulletin boards. I noted the tall, handsome Indian was among the crowd of trainees. More importantly, the raven-haired beauty was also assigned to the *Fantasy*.

The bus driver hurriedly opened the luggage compartment below the bus, then casually wandered off for a cigarette. Being the two largest men present, the Indian and I handled the luggage. After ten minutes we joined the others, followed by the driver and his loyal cloud of smoke.

There were only two seats left, and by pure chance one of them was beside the brunette beauty. The Indian flung himself into the seat before I could get there. My sour look earned me a grin from him.

The bus rumbled onto the highway to take us to Port Canaveral.

3 *Under the Water*

THE BUS DROVE ONWARD, AND WE WERE CAUGHT UP in amazingly dense traffic. To my surprise, this happened far out of the cities as we were driving northward along the coast. The Indian turned in his seat and handed me a muffin he had purchased earlier from the Marriott's vending machine. I was quite surprised, and truly touched. I was a complete stranger, and he just bought me breakfast.

"Well, that's extremely kind of you," I said earnestly.

"You're my first American," he said, grinning with huge, white teeth. "I'm Ravi." (pronounced Rah-WEE).

"Brian," I replied, shaking his hand. His grip was so delicate I suddenly felt bad about crushing his hand.

"Today your space shuttle *Columbia* is launching. It's so exciting, but I don't think we'll be able to see."

"Really? I love that stuff."

"Oh, yes. My son told me all about it last night on the phone. Imagine being at Port Canaveral the same morning as a space shuttle launch!"

"You have a son? You look awfully young to me."

"Thank you. I have two children," he said, beaming. "Here, look."

Like all fathers everywhere, he instantly produced photographs of his children. To my surprise, the sexy Euro-vixen beside Ravi suddenly spoke up.

"May I see?"

He handed her the photos and she practically melted. "Oh, they are so small and brown!"

Ravi grinned from ear to ear and puffed up like a blowfish.

"I have a nephew," I said hastily. "He's white at the moment, but he can be brown. He can be any color you want. I'll even dye him like an Easter egg."

"Don't listen to him," Ravi suggested as he took back the photos.

"I like listening to him," she answered. "I like his accent. All these other accents are hard to understand."

"Yes," I said, cutting off Ravi. "His sing-song accent is far too complicated. You just stick with me, my dear. I'm Brian, by the way."

"My name is Liezle."

"The mute Indian here is Ravi. He's happily married, so he's embarrassed to say how pretty he thinks you are."

Now it was Ravi's turn for a sour look. He retorted, "Oh, and you don't think she's pretty?"

Liezle looked up at me with dark, intense eyes.

"Uh, me?" I replied, suddenly on the defensive. "I, uh, I plead the Fifth."

Ravi frowned. "I do not understand."

Liezle smiled for the first time. "He means the Fifth Amendment of America. The Bill of Your Rights."

I stared incredulously at her. "How on earth did you know that? Half the Americans I've met don't even know that."

"Slovakia is a democracy now," she replied. "We studied America's government."

"But India is the world's largest democracy," Ravi piped up, not to be outdone.

"Yeah, well, America was the first," I rebutted.

"That's true," she agreed. "We studied your government and your short history. We were even required to learn all fifty-three states."

"Fifty," I corrected.

Liezle and Ravi both frowned, then looked at me like I was an idiot. "There are fifty-three states."

"We only have fifty states," I defended. "Perhaps you think the District of Columbia is a state, but I don't know what the others are. Puerto Rico, maybe? But how can you get fifty-three?"

"Puerto Rico isn't a state?" Ravi asked.

"No, it's a territory," Liezle said. "America has a lot of territories."

"We do?"

"Liezle, I suggest you stay close to me," Ravi said. "I am married and harmless. Brian is not. He's dangerous. He may attempt to teach you the International Language in his cabin."

"International language?"

"Love," he answered smoothly. "It goes beyond borders."

"Yes, I would love to learn your geography," I added. "Wait, are you blushing? Oh, no. I don't think I could bear to be around a woman still capable of blushing. You are safe with me after all, darling."

The three of us bantered idly until the bus finally pulled up to Port Canaveral. The weather was surprisingly cold and nasty. Being from Iowa, I was subject to the common misconception that Florida was always warm and sunny. But today, January 15th, the sky was dense with clouds and wicked with wind from the ocean.

The bus parked far away from the ship in the center of a vast concrete lot. A murmur arose from the people on the bus. Many onboard had never seen a cruise ship before. It was impressive, looking up at the immense hull so far above. The *Fantasy* was fairly old for a Carnival ship, and by modern standards small. She still towered above the port facility, which reminded me of a huge airplane hanger.

In the middle of the vast concrete desert was the check-in area. A small section of Carnival security guards clustered around a table where the purser gathered passports. Many were justifiably uncomfortable handing over such an important personal document, and I received a few annoyed looks when I, as American, did not have to.

Once processed, Ravi joined me and said, "I hope you can behave. Those security guards are dangerous."

I glanced over at the handful of guards. They wore black sweaters with epaulettes to signify their status. The four Indian-looking men were all distinctly smaller than me.

"They don't look so tough."

"So American!" he chided. "Bigger does not mean better. Those are ex-military, Ghurka soldiers from Nepal. Fight for the British. Very, very tough."

"Really? They look harmless. Let's say I was wildly drunk at a bar and some hot blonde throws her strawberry daiquiri in my face and screams at me to leave her alone...and stop following her...and to pay her back the fifty bucks I owe her. Just for the sake of argument, of course. I don't think they could throw me out. Bouncers are supposed to be huge black men that can twist you into a pretzel, don't you think?"

"I think you are very white," he replied. "Do not be fooled, my friend. They may look gentle, but I assure you they are not. Those men are trained killers. I had heard that Carnival hired a lot of them."

"Well," I replied thoughtfully, "That would be very smart. They don't intimidate the guests but can still protect them. And they are cheaper than Americans."

"Probably smarter, too."

"Ha ha."

We were fully processed and then ordered aboard. The gangway was a long, slender metal bridge with evenly spaced slats that served as steps when it was angled. I glanced down as I crossed over. Huge rubber fenders between the hull and the concrete protested mightily as the *Fantasy* gently inched up and down with the surge of the sea. The squeaking was horrendous. We entered at the bow of the ship.

We were only given fifteen minutes to find our cabins and report to the crew bar for a meeting. The pursers warned us the crew bar was hard to find, so be careful. They made no attempt to direct any of us anywhere. But then, when did I need help finding a bar? I had a natural compass for such things.

"Ground floor" was even with the waterline and called deck zero. A nicely ornamented area near the elevators indicated they were not for us, but for the guests. Separating the oasis of sophistication from the crew area were heavy plastic flaps hanging from the ceiling.

Beyond the dirty flaps was a long, undisturbed hallway that ran the entire length of the ship, known as the I-95. I assumed this label was a reference to an Interstate, but only later did I discover the name also cleverly referred to the I-95, the document foreign workers were required to carry in the United States. The floor was painted rich blue, but was horribly mauled by having countless pallets pushed along it. The deck, or floor, was all metal, with those little raised bumps shaped like Xs.

Having never been on a ship before, I was fascinated with the little things. Yellow arcs were painted on the floor everywhere to identify the space required for doors to close. Blocking a door from closing on a ship, especially near the waterline, was a huge no-no. Many of the doors to hallways had a lip almost a foot high, while others did not. I could detect no rhyme or reason for it yet.

I pushed back against the wall as a forklift blasted down the corridor hauling several hundred melons. I nearly fell down a narrow metal staircase on which sat a dozen coffee cups overflowing with smashed and mangled cigarette butts. The whole area smelled rank. An Asian waiter sat on the steps enjoying the last few puffs of his cigarette. He was a small young man with dark skin and amazingly smooth features.

His hair was so black and spiky it looked positively dangerous.

"Hey," he called, "Don't lean on that wall."

I looked at what I had been leaning against. A network of hydraulics led to a thick red lever rising from the floor. Beside me was a huge doorway, over a foot thick, across the I-95. The door extended a full foot above and below the deck. A metal plate obviously designed to push up and out of the way covered the gap while the door was open.

"That's a watertight door, my friend," he continued in sharp, choppy yet easy-to-understand English. "Once that starts closing, nothing can stop it. Not even Captain."

"Sections off the lower decks in case of a flood?"

"That's right. If those lights flash and the horn sounds, run like hell. Those doors cut through anything that blocks them. If the ship is going down and a desk falls to block it, the door cuts right through. People get cut in half, too. Last cruise an engineer fell asleep holding the lever and cut off his fingers."

"Come on," I scoffed. "How can you fall asleep standing up?"

The waiter looked at me strangely.

"Where you from?" he asked, but then suddenly disappeared without waiting for an answer.

Along the I-95 were most of the crew areas. The crew mess was there, as was the officers' mess. The human resources offices were located there, and the offices of the purser, security, and the restaurant management. In the center of deck zero was a huge area known as the marshalling area or the dock, where the hull of the ship opened on either side to admit forklifts and pallets of food and materials. Beyond the dock were the refrigerators and dry storage for many, many tons of food, as well as access to various engineering areas.

There were three decks below the waterline. The lowest was for the water tanks and the engines, while the other two hid the crew cabins in an insane labyrinth of metal corridors and steps. The walls, floor, and ceiling were all coated with a quarter-inch of paint. Everything was cold metal and alien. Though the paint was white, the area felt old and dirty. Tucked into every nook and cranny was a cabin or a communal shower.

Each section was separated by watertight doors and host to one stairwell. When in port, the watertight doors below decks were always closed. To move from one section to another required that you ascend above the waterline, cross over, and descend again. I had very little time to find my cabin and grew exasperated by the strange numbering system. Only later did I learn that odd numbers were always on starboard, on the right side of the ship, and evens to port, on the left.

Finally I found my cabin, the door horrendously scratched, on B deck, twenty feet below the waterline where there was a constant vibration in the metal all around me. I could hear clearly what sounded like a Chinese martial arts film coming from inside.

With a breath of anticipation, I opened the door.

The cabin was larger than I expected. I had visited Bianca's cabin on *Conquest* and had been horrified at how small it was. However, here I could actually do a push up on the floor were I so inclined. I would have to move the chair, some boxes and two suitcases, but it was possible. The desk was completely covered by a thirteen-inch TV. The space beneath it was filled by a small refrigerator, forcing the single chair into a corner to hold a Nintendo. The cabin was stifling hot.

The narrow path that led past the two lockers to the bunks was blocked by my new roommate. He lay sideways across the cabin with his legs splayed wide open, and propped onto two boxes. His rear was on a third box, and his head rested on the feet of a huge teddy bear that occupied his bunk. The controls of his gaming consol sat comfortably on his lap. Though the Nintendo was hooked up to the TV and the controller was in his hands, the screen blasted a very loud, very obnoxious Chinese movie with Asian subtitles.

And, of course, he was completely naked.

Within my first twelve hours of Carnival life I had already encountered two naked men in my bedrooms. This was not in any of the brochures I had seen.

My roommate woke up with a snort. He shook his head and regarded me skeptically.

"You're American!" he said.

"How can you tell? You're the naked one."

"You're my roommate? Are you crazy, or just stupid? Why are you here?"

"A woman," I explained.

"Oh…" he said, nodding understandingly.

"I'm Ben," he said as he rose and brushed himself off. He made no effort to clothe himself.

"Brian," I answered. "How can your name be Ben?"

He smiled roguishly. "My real name is too hard for you Americans, so I say Ben. My last name has eighteen letters, so forget it."

"That's probably best."

"Look," he began as he shut off the TV. "I'm easy to get along with. I keep things simple. Just don't touch my spicy shrimp and we will be O.K. I'll know if you do anyway, because you'll probably be screaming on the toilet for the rest of the day. I like it hot."

"I see. Well, I'm easy too. I would say don't touch my razor, but you don't seem to have a hair anywhere except on your head."

He grinned again. "Yeah, I never shave ever."

"What was on the TV?"

"Oh, that's a forty-part Chinese movie with Thai subtitles."

"You're Thai? You have awesome English."

"Thanks. I watch a lot of movies. Yours is good, too. Not from Texas, then?"

A knock sounded at the door. "Oh, that's Amy. Can you open that?"

I opened the door to admit an amazingly small woman. She was pretty without looking glamorous, with luxurious black hair that ran down her back. She looked up at me with great surprise, then asked me something in what I thought was German.

"I'm American," I said to her.

"Oh! I'm sorry," she said in unaccented English. "You look German."

"My family is from there originally."

"Say, can we sleep together?"

"Of course! But try Ben first, he's already naked. I'm uncomfortable with the idea of making a naked man angry."

Amy slipped around me and embraced Ben. "We just got engaged last week."

Visions of Alexandro and Paula came to mind.

"Look, we won't make any noise. No cheeky-cheeky with you here. We just want to be together."

"Yeah, of course. Look, I have to run anyway. I need to find the crew bar."

"That's deck four. Go all the way to the front, near the laundry. Take the crew stairs. Deck four."

"Thanks!"

Knowing I had almost no time left, I threw my suitcase on the top bunk and rushed off. All the meetings of the trainees were to take place in the bar, the purser had said. Rampant nudity and classes in the bar...ship life sounded great already!

4 *Denizens of Babel*

THE FORWARD CREW STAIRS COULD MORE ACCURATELY be described as an angled ladder than a staircase. Each step was so narrow that the word "rung" seemed most appropriate. The backs of the stairs were open so that my toes dangled in the air. Going up those four flights could be considered cruel and unusual punishment. Yet descending was downright terrifying. I feared for my life should I leave the crew bar drunk some night.

The crew bar was not overly large. To the right was the window to the bar, but it was gated shut. A number of small café tables were pushed to the corner and some two-dozen chairs were arranged on the tiny dance floor facing a retractable movie screen. In the far corner were a ping-pong table and a heavy weather-resistant door that led to the open deck. There were no windows at all. The monotony of the walls was only broken by a few posters and a Nintendo that competed with the dart board for space.

A small Indian man in a neat, crisp white uniform invited us in. He had exceptional boyish good-looks, with thick black hair in a distinctive wave that reminded me of James Dean.

"Come on, folks, let's go."

About two dozen men and women from all over the world sat down on the banquet-style chairs. I sat in the front row in the corner, careful to sit closer to Liezle than Ravi. He was happily married and I was madly in love, but it was already a game that made the three of us more comfortable. I found great relief in being taken, because the beauty quotient of the female personnel was staggering! Without exception the women of the class were raven-haired and, if not pretty, at least they had stunning bodies. Had I been single I would have been overwhelmed.

"My name is Boota," he announced. "I am from India. I'll be your lead instructor for the next four weeks. Welcome aboard the *Fantasy*. This ship carries 2,000 guests on ten decks and has over 900 crew. It is 70,000 tons, which makes it almost twice as big as *Titanic*. We do three- and four-day cruises from Port Canaveral to Nassau, the capital of the Bahamas. Every cruise will have a sea day and will otherwise overnight in port, which is unusual. Enjoy it while you can.

"We are going to have a lot of fun, and we are going to do a lot of work. I can tell you now that this will be a new experience for all of you, and it will not be easy. Please be patient with me: I hope to have all your names memorized within a day or two, but for now it's hard. Not all your names are familiar to me. For example, we have a Biljana, Egle, Rasa, Martina, Yhasmina, Sylwia, and Medea. I won't even get into last names, like Mrzljak.

"Now," he continued. "I will be training you most of the time. The little guy over there is Srinivas. He's from Sri Lanka and yes, he is in fact shorter than I am. Please mock him at every opportunity. We also have one other trainer who isn't here. You'll know him because he looks like Elvis. We trainers are all here for the same reason: for you. And you are all here for the same reason."

He flashed his boyish grin. "For money."

"We are all here for money," he repeated. "Except for this man."

To my surprise he was referring to me. "This crazy man is here for a woman."

I couldn't help but laugh with the others. My reputation preceded me, apparently!

"Now, we are here to learn about serving Americans. I don't know what things were like where you are from, and it doesn't matter. The vast majority of cruisers will be American, so we need to learn what they like and what they don't like. Now, has anyone here worked in America before?"

I raised my hand. I was alone.

"We have a real treat this time around," Boota continued. "We actually have an American with us. I have been serving Americans for years, but we can all learn from this guy. I'm sure he'll be very open to answering questions any of you ladies might have. Privately, of course."

"I am a fountain of knowledge, ladies."

"Americans are the easiest people to serve in the world," Boota continued. "They don't care about anything except having a good time. They are not interested in fine service. They are here for fun. These are the Fun Ships, after all. They are extremely friendly, and will ask about you and your family. Where I am from, and in Europe, for example, a waiter is rarely even acknowledged. Certainly you would never ask his name or details about his family. In America, though, they will ask about everything. They want a friend, not a servant. They'll ask about your family, where you're from, everything. Of course, they probably won't *know* where you are from, so don't be surprised about that."

Boota smiled at me. "It's probably weird for you hearing about your country in the third person."

I chuckled. "Sort of. But I have nothing to compare America to. I guess you can't understand it really until you leave it."

"Very true. So, anyway, even if they *have* heard of your country, don't ask them to find it on a map. Most importantly, though, is that Americans want to know you are trying. They eat out almost every day there, so they want something different, something fun. Being in the dining room is not a special occasion for them the way it is for most of us.

"I'll tell you all right now, you must abide by American standards. That doesn't mean you must eat hamburgers all day, but you must follow some of their basics. Ah, here's Paul with the list. Good."

An Indian with surprisingly white skin entered the room. He did look like Elvis's twin Indian brother. He had the same thick sideburns and the same black hair with the wave. It was uncanny. He began handing out papers listing dress codes and hygiene regulations.

"I'm Indian," Boota said. "And some Indians, for example, smell bad. When here, we do what the Americans do. That means soap and water every day.

"Now," Boota continued with a sly smile, "what do you call a person who speaks three languages?"

"Trilingual," somebody answered.

"That's right. And someone who speaks two languages?"

"Bilingual."

"And someone who only speaks one language?" There was silence. "American," Boota revealed to a chorus of laughs. I chuckled, lamenting over my four years of Spanish lessons in school that amounted to absolutely nothing.

"I speak five languages and ten dialects," Boota continued. "But let's ask the expert. Brian, how many languages do you speak?"

"One," I admitted, suddenly feeling sheepish as the room laughed again.

"But a very important one," Boota consoled. "American also means English. I don't care what you say below decks, but in the guest areas you must always, always use English. Even if you are talking about cricket scores, Americans will assume you are talking about them if they can't understand you.

"Now let me tell you a story. This is no joke. I worked with a guy for years from the Philippines. One day a couple of little old ladies refused to leave after lunch. They had completely ruined his whole afternoon and were in danger of ruining his evening as well. He needed to leave to set up his station for dinner before all his silverware was pinched. Finally the lady called him over, he assumed to say goodbye. Instead she ordered more coffee, which he would have to brew because it was long gone. He was so angry that he stormed across the dining room swearing in Tagalog the whole way. Not just little things, but really ugly, nasty words."

He paused for emphasis, his eyes glinting. "The lady was married to a military man who had been stationed in the Philippines. She understood every word he said. She got up and walked straight to the hotel director. The waiter was forced to apologize and was sent home at the very next port.

"Carnival Corporation has over sixty nationalities, and we are all far from home in a very strange place. Yet we all get along very well. If we don't, we get sent home. That means no money. If you fight with anybody because he's different, you will be sent home. No money. Even if someone hits you and you don't fight back, you are both going home. Carnival takes it that seriously. Revel in learning about the world, but don't forget why we are here. We are here for the money."

Srinivas, the assistant trainer, suddenly stood up and took the stage. He was an extremely short man, but not a small man because his shoulders were very broad. He was the first man I had ever seen with jet-black skin who did not look African. He looked fantastic in his pressed white uniform against that amazing skin.

"Let me add to this, Boota," he said. "We do not talk about religion or politics for a very specific reason. There is a big difference between people and their government. Not all of us are from democracies, after all, and even a democracy does not necessarily reflect its people. For example, never mention all the military actions of the U.S. It's completely against policy, but more importantly the guests won't know what you're talking about and will probably be offended.

"It's best not to talk about military actions anyway. Boota is Indian and he works with several Pakistanis. You think they talk about the war in Kashmir? No way. My country of Sri Lanka has been in civil war for thirty years. You won't see me talking to myself."

"No," interjected Boota, "but that does explain your suicidal tendencies."

"Anyway," Srinivas finished. "It's just not worth it. Politics are dangerous enough, but we all know how religious talk can really cause problems. Don't even go there."

"Very true," Boota agreed. "Now, we are going to begin by going around the room and introducing ourselves. I want you to say your name and your country. We'll learn a little about each country later. By the end of the week you will be closer to all these foreigners than you ever thought possible. We will all be family. You'll see. Let's start over here."

Boota gestured to an extremely tall woman. She was paper thin and easily six and a half feet tall. Her hair was black and straight and rushed directly down to her waist as if in a hurry to get there. She had a non-exotic, girl-next-door beauty and slightly crooked teeth, but her smile was genuine and engaging. She was obviously nervous.

"My name is Philippa," she said. "I come from Czech Republic, the heart of Europe."

She dropped into her seat so quickly that Boota had to laugh good-naturedly to keep her at ease. His smile was extremely disarming. Next rose the raven-haired beauty.

"My name is Liezle. I come from Slovakia: the heart of Europe. *Not* Czech Republic."

"Humph!" Philippa retorted but with a smile.

Boota stepped forward and introduced me to the class. "Ladies and gentlemen, we have a very special attendee here. This is Brian. He's from a place called...*America*." A groan actually swept through the room, but I didn't mind. I love notoriety. Usually I had to do something drastic or stupid to get special attention. Here, as the minority, it was built in.

"Hello, everyone. I am Brian. I am from America, the heart of Europe."

The outrages commenced, but Boota merely smiled. "Typical American!"

The crew mess was quite a place during meals. The room was large enough to accommodate dozens of people, and offered a buffet set-up. The line of hungry crew wound around the coffee station, which also featured soft-serve ice cream. The coffee, which reminded me of turpentine with black oil paint in it, was frequently augmented by the crew with a dash of ice cream. Men and women of all ethnicities rifled through a huge bin of plastic coffee mugs in search of the few that were properly cleaned.

There was no limit to the amount of food you could order. Half of the buffet was always allocated to Asian tastes: two whole sections were continuously filled with steamed white rice. The majority of the crew was Southeast Asians, mostly Indonesian and Filipino. Both groups typically ate huge plates full of white rice with every meal.

I was very pleased with the crew mess because they offered strip steak nearly every day. On this, our first lunch, I sat with my assigned training group. There were six in the group, but only five at the table: myself, Philippa the Czech Giantess, Anjana a Serbian, Hila an Indonesian and, happily, Liezle.

"So," the spunky red-headed, large-bottomed Anjana asked as we all sat down, "are you crazy, or just stupid?"

"I can tell you, Anjana," I replied as she snatched the salt-shaker from my hand and rapidly unscrewed the top. "I am *not* crazy."

"It's pronounced Anyana, not AnJana. Where I come from *J* is pronounced like your Y."

"Same in Slovakia," Liezle added.

"So," Anjana continued, "you didn't want the job your government gave you?"

She began liberally topping her roast beef with a thick layer of salt. I had never seen anything like it. She rocked her head back and forth excitedly, her bobbed hair bouncing.

"I don't know what you're talking about."

"They give everyone a job in the States, don't they?"

"Hardly. They don't do much for us, actually, except create an environment that allows us to do everything for ourselves. That's pretty cool."

"So *are* you crazy, then? Why are you here?"

"I am following a woman."

The ladies at the table all shared a silent but meaningful glance. I had absolutely no idea what they communicated with that look, but they were all on the same page. Suddenly nervous, I browsed the condiments on the table. I understood condiments far better than I understood women. There were industrial-sized bottles of both red and green Tabasco sauce, spicy Cholula, and a sweet chili sauce from Thailand called Mae Ploy.

Liezle quietly began stuffing her pockets with green tea bags.

"What are those for?"

"For later," she replied. "I like green tea when I drink."

"I like tequila, myself," I quipped, trying to be funny. "Though I don't think it would mix well with green tea."

"Oh, no," she replied gravely, "only Jack Daniels."

I blinked in surprise. She was serious! Any woman who drinks green tea and Jack was a woman for me, even if she *did* blush occasionally.

"How about you, Hila?" I asked, trying to bring her into the conversation. "What's your favorite? I somehow picture you drinking mint juleps on the porch of an antebellum mansion on the Gulf Coast."

Hila was a tiny woman from the island of Bali, and was Carnival's first female Indonesian, according to Boota. Her hair was so long it almost reached her behind, and it was the deep black of most Asians. Her smile was huge and so quick it was almost intimidating. Yet she was extremely shy.

"Oh, no, I do not drink," she answered. "I am Muslim."

"Oh, I didn't know that. Wow, so that means no pork, either, right?"

She shook her head.

"You are stronger than I. I could never be Muslim or Jewish because life without bacon would make me jump overboard. I couldn't be like Ravi either: no beef! How can he get so big and never have had a rare New York steak? The world is a fascinating place."

For the first time I reviewed what everyone was eating. Anjana and I were the only ones with any meat at all. The other European ladies all had nothing but fruit. Huge towers of sliced melons and pineapple graced each plate, along with at least one orange and a dash of strawberries. Hila had a loaded plate of steamed white rice which she had topped with one ladle of fish soup.

"Holy Cat! No wonder all you women are so tiny! Anjana, I'm so glad you are here with me to enjoy something manly. By the way, would you like some beef with your salt?"

"Ha ha," she retorted sarcastically. "The salt in your country is so weak compared to mine back home. I have to use four times as much for the same flavor."

"I believe salted meats went out of style with the feudal system."

"You are so odd."

"That's what my ex-wife always said."

All the women abruptly stopped and stared at me. Once again I was suddenly nervous and self-conscious. I struggled to recall what I had said. Had I gone too far again?

"You were married?" Philippa asked, looking down to me.

"Of course. I'm American. Don't we all have at least one ex-wife?"

"How can you joke about it?" asked Hila, shocked. Her brown eyes were wide.

"Well, why not? I loved being married. My ex-wife didn't, though. I don't know what I'm like to live with, but I think I was all right. I'm actually a nice guy when I'm not drinking and whoring and stuff. I did all the cooking, cleaning, and laundry and she didn't even have a job. That's gotta count for something."

"So you hit her too much?"

"Of course not! I never hit her, or lied once, or cheated. I probably worked too much, though. Anyway, we shouldn't have gotten married in the first place, so the divorce was no big deal. It was only a drive-through wedding chapel in Nevada."

"You're not serious!"

"Yes, I am. Like I said, it was a mistake."

"Do you have any children?"

"Oh, no. Can you picture me as a father? Perish the thought."

"So you were in Las Vegas?"

"Close. We lived in Reno. Much prettier, and the divorce capital of the world, you know. Couples used to walk onto the bridge over the Truckee River and ceremoniously drop their wedding rings in. Of course, the river is only a meter deep, so the homeless people quickly snatched them up. Lots of cool history in that area. The largest silver rush in the history of the world, gambling, prostitution, cannibalism...all the good stuff. Nevada is cool. By the way, Anjana, if you drive just one hour east from Reno you would be very happy. You'll find whole deserts of solid salt."

My roommate Ben and his fiancé Amy walked past us. Ben carried two trays with a total of four plates of food. Two were filled with rice, and the others with several steaks and a pile of vegetables. A jar of spicy Thai shrimp rose near a glass of water. I called out to them.

"Hey, Ben! Holy Cat, when did you last eat?"

As they passed by, he responded, "I want to be as big as you."

"He eats like this every day," Amy added. "We'll see you later, O.K.?"

They disappeared into the crowd, leaving me stunned. If I ate that much food, I would weigh 300 pounds.

"Brian," Philippa asked, "why do you say 'holy cat'?"

"Well, we aren't supposed to be religious and all that."

"You were just talking about Jews and Muslims and bacon, Indians and beef."

"Yeah, well, O.K. You're right. It's just my cat obviously thought I should worship her. In the end I guess I did. It's habit now."

"Who was that, anyway?" asked Liezle.

"That's my roommate."

"How can you tell? Don't they all look alike to you?"

There was silence for a moment, then we all burst out laughing.

"Trust me, Liezle," I finally answered. "If you had met him the way I did, you would never forget his face, or anything else."

5 Nobody Parties Like Sailors

I AWOKE THE NEXT DAY NOT FEELING AT ALL RESTED. We had finally been released at 10 P.M. after non-stop activities beginning at 5:30 in the morning. At 10:00 we weren't free yet; we had to wash our trainee uniforms for the next night. These were leftover rags from previous training classes passing as pants and vests. I was terrified to try ironing the stuff, lest it dissolve before my very eyes.

There was a mad dash to the tiny laundry in the bow, but I finally managed to get my wash in a load with Liezle and Philippa. I was disappointed that only uniforms were involved, no panties or anything exciting.

When I finally returned to my cabin, the walls were thumping with hip-hop music from the next cabin. The base was so powerful I felt every beat in my breastbone. Trying to ignore it I crawled painfully into bed, but my feet and head were pressed against the walls, so with each beat I got squeezed. Nevertheless I finally began to drift off despite the noise until the Indians across the hall began competing with *their* music.

The bathrooms, to my horror, were at the end of the hall. On the newer ships a single shower and toilet were shared between two cabins. A little light even politely revealed if it was occupied. Unfortunately the *Fantasy*'s was a communal system. The showers were rather unkempt but mostly clean, but I vowed never, ever to use the toilets. Of the half-dozen stools at the end of our hall, I never saw a single one flushed. The task of pressing the lever seemed beyond the residents of my hallway, who were all Caribbean or Asian.

I had one great environmental advantage over the other residents, though. The air so far below the waterline was entirely supplied by vents and air conditioning, and almost every resident fell ill from it. Fortunately, as an American, I was used to oppressive, artificial air conditioning. Overall, I was appalled at my new home and by the filthiness of those I lived around. But I knew this was only temporary so it never even occurred to me to let it bother me. The only thing that wore me down was the apparent requisite six daily queries if I was crazy or just stupid.

Class began in the crew bar at 8:30 A.M. and lasted until roughly 4:30. Lunch was around a half hour in there some-where, and in the evenings we had restaurant practicals, where we learned in a real environment, from 5:45 until 9:30 P.M. After this we had homework for an hour or two. This schedule, of approximately fourteen hours a day, lasted the entire month, seven days a week. No time was allocated for laundry, occasional runs to the store, haircuts, or anything else. I could not imagine working eight months straight with-out a single breakfast or dinner off, but such was ship life.

While the classes were relaxing and even fun, they crammed our poor little heads with so much information we were all constantly exhausted. Subjects varied from intense training on separation of garbage to ship safety procedures.

All solid waste was separated from food waste which was separated from bones. Any whole food was ground up and released into the sea once *Fantasy* was several miles offshore. The water, too, was classified and managed. There was gray water from the sinks and showers, and black water from toilets. All crew were trained in such things.

We were educated about the inflatable life rafts: how many there were, how to offload them, how to inflate them, and how many liters of water per person they held. For cryin' out loud, we even had to learn the scientific measurement of energy that every person was allocated daily. Ten thousand kilojoules, by the way.

Though twenty-five people were supposedly able to fit on a life raft, the illustration of such was quite shocking. I was one of the last to get in, and the groan emanating from the others was quite amusing. I weighed nearly double the average Asian weight, and even with such small folks it was still like stuffing fifty clowns into a Volkswagen Beetle.

I was fascinated with the hydrostatic release of the rafts on deck nine. They were designed to make human assistance unnecessary if the ship sank. The raft canisters would automatically release and pop to the surface. The pressure required to trigger the release was equivalent to only five feet of depth. I guess Carnival figured if deck *nine* was already under water, perhaps it was time.

We also had boat drills twice a week. This meant standing in the Bahamian sun for half an hour in several layers of polyester. The United States demanded one of the highest levels of nautical safety in the world, if not *the* highest. A U.S. Coast Guard inspection was a serious issue that was prepared for diligently weeks in advance. But above and beyond this, Carnival took safety very, very seriously. They were professional as can be with their preparations, procedures, and training. Their lifeboats cost over $100,000 apiece and were designed to float even if flooded. No one was going to be hurt on Carnival's watch.

Boota was a phenomenal instructor. He was charming and interesting, extremely knowledgeable, aggressive with his schedule and yet still able to empathize with everyone's situation. Even when he was covering a subject I thought I knew already, such as the American food courses, I learned a great deal.

One rarely reflects upon his own culture if he has nothing to compare it to, but now I did. For example, I was surprised at the universal reaction to American salads. Everyone, from every corner of the globe, was horrified to learn Americans intentionally destroy the *entire* nutritional value of salads by smothering them in thick condiments made of buttermilk and sugar. They had great difficulty differentiating between ranch and blue cheese dressing, and were genuinely surprised we didn't add chocolate syrup to the list. To them it was just as absurd.

I mistakenly thought I had it much easier than anyone else because English was my native language. The situation we were in was as alien to me as it was to everyone else. None of us was comfortable about anything. But at the end of yet another consecutive fourteen-hour day, over a drink in the crew bar I could speak my native language…for those three minutes before I passed out from exhaustion. The others were still forced into their second or even third language. Only later did I realize how wrong I was — in fact, I was the one with a severe disadvantage.

At the beginning of our seventh day of this grueling schedule, Boota casually sat beside me before class and said, "Today will be a good day for you."

"Oh? Why is that?"

"Your team is unloading supplies."

"Well, that sounds fabulous. Thanks!"

He smiled. "I know you. You work very hard. Everyone thought you would be leaving this morning now that we are back in home port. I knew you wouldn't. I know Americans actually work harder than most people on earth. You have everything because you work for it. And you, Brian, have a great attitude. It will shine today when put to the test."

I cocked my head and regarded him seriously for a moment. "Thank you, Boota. That's very kind of you. Why am I suddenly nervous?"

"Look," he admitted quietly. "Training is designed to be harder than the usual life here. It's a rough life at sea, but not this bad. You'll see how much better it is when you are out there. But you had to know it was hinted that I should break you in particular if I could. Not in so many words, of course, but we don't want to waste our time and money on you if you'll just leave like all the others. So I have been intentionally placing you where you don't want to be. That's why you haven't even worked in the dining room yet."

"I was wondering about that. Hey, I actually enjoyed doing the dishes. Seriously, I did. But I don't ever want to go behind the chef's line again."

"No, you're done with all that. I think it's a problem there aren't more Americans on the ships. You will find management usually thinks the other way because the track record speaks for itself. You'll get a hard time from most managers, I'll tell you right now. But I see how much you help the others in your free time."

I was truly pleased, but took pains not to show it. "Thank you, Boota."

"So," he continued, "that is why you are working the late shift at the crew party tonight."

"I knew it!"

"Look, we just passed a USPH inspection. You will learn what that means. That is the most stress you will ever see on a ship."

"Shy of an iceberg, perhaps."

"The crew deserves this party, and you new trainees don't. This ship is a party ship much more than even the others. Anyway, there are three shifts working the party, and I want you and Ravi to be the clean-up guys. You two are the most responsible here, and I know you won't be drunk by the time your shift starts. Enjoy the party, but be ready to work at midnight tonight."

"Yeah, O.K."

"Be ready," he warned caustically. "You've never seen a party like a sailors' party. Now, go get into something that can get dirty for the dock!"

Ten minutes later I stood with my training team in the I-95, aft of the dock. Being a home port day, the dock was insanely busy with loading. The amount of food a cruise ship devoured within a week was staggering. The *Fantasy* averaged roughly 25,000 pounds of fresh vegetables weekly, and 100,000 eggs. But loading involved far more than merely perishables; it covered everything. A cruise ship was a complete hotel, fully self-sufficient and afloat. There were bars to bottle, restaurants to feed, staterooms to launder, a daily paper to deliver, a stage to prop, and far, far more. On top of this there were engine room parts, safety equipment, wardrobes for 1,000 crew members, cases of condoms for the crew...the list was exhaustive.

"Anjana," I called sharply, pronouncing her name phonetically to annoy her. "Get that salt shaker out of your pocket! Unless there's room for a bottle of rum, too."

"Look, American Boy, I am out of here. I've already done the bar college, and I'm not going to unload a million loaves of bread today. In fact...I'm staying!"

She looked past me and suddenly stood taller. Her usual contemptuous look was replaced with a sly smile. I assumed it was Boota was behind me, but in fact it was someone else entirely.

"Hello!" a deep voice called. "My name is Jordan."

His name tag revealed that the *J* in his name was pronounced as a Y, just like Anjana's. Jordan was an extremely powerful-looking man, just shy of six feet in height and densely muscled. His unshaven features were heavy and dark, with a solid, wide nose. He looked rugged and very handsome in a short-sleeved blue boiler-suit that revealed arms thickly corded with muscle.

"I'm Brian," I said, shaking his hand. He had a grip that would have destroyed poor Ravi.

"He's American," Anjana chimed in as she bounced up to his side where she clung to his arm and gazed up at him. "But I'm Serbian, much closer to home."

Jordan frowned at me. "You American? I Bulgarian! You look strong. Good! We move!"

Within minutes Jordan had the group organized. With his broken English, he directed us into a line to transfer boxes of melons from the forklift to the walk-in refrigerator. My job was to pull boxes off pallets and hand them to Philippa, who handed them to the small, portly Timea, who handed them to Liezle. Hila was the last in line, arranging the boxes on the shelves in the refrigerator. She wore a thick coat designed for the men who work in the freezer. She never uttered a single word of complaint, but you could tell she was already missing her tropical home.

Anjana flitted in and out of sight like a phantom. She would always materialize when Jordan was around, however.

It was hard work, but I loved it. I had not been able to exercise for a full week and, despite my fatigue, I had missed it. I was whistling as I hauled cantaloupes, honeydews, and pineapples.

"Come on, Anjana, start humping those melons."

"Screw you, Yank. Where's Jordan?"

"Running from you. I told him you were going to suck the salt from his body. I saw that in a movie once."

"Shag off."

For three hours, non-stop, we hauled melons. The ladies were overwhelmed by the brutal labor. Most of those boxes held anywhere from six to eight melons, which was a heavy burden for women who weighed less than one hundred pounds each. They were learning firsthand the way things were in America: to be the equal of men, women had to do the same work. There were more than a few grumbles from the corners of the giant refrigerator.

Then Jordan brought in a forklift loaded with pallets of watermelons.

"O.K., American," he called cheerily as he slipped on some work gloves. "We have watermelon. They very heavy, and go high on shelf. Just you and me, O.K.?"

"Stand back and behold American power!"

The ladies gratefully took a break and sat in the corners of the dry storage and snuck handfuls of grapes. Anjana hovered to watch Jordan in action. The boxes each held four watermelons and the shelves allocated to them were over our heads. We had a great time hauling those melons almost fanatically, laughing and even singing the whole time.

"I know American song. We sing," Jordan offered with a smile. "You like Michael Jackson?"

"Uh, not really. He's kind of weird, don't you think?"

"All English singers are weird! American Kiss, English Boy George? How you not like Michael Jackson? Everyone like Michael Jackson!"

"What else do you know? I'm sorry, I don't know any Bulgarian music."

He suddenly began singing, "Oh, Suzanna," and to my great embarrassment I had to stumble through many of the lyrics. We worked for another thirty minutes. Finally, dirty and exhausted, Jordan delivered the last case of watermelons.

"O.K., you free, ladies."

"Oh, I'm definitely free," Anjana gushed. He ignored her and reached his hand out to me. I took it and he shook it vigorously.

"American," he said, looking me in the eye. "I respect you. You strong and faster than all others. I respect you."

That was my proudest moment with Carnival Cruise Lines.

The crew party that night was the most intense party I had ever seen, or even heard of.

The forward area of the ship, all the way up front, is set aside for the crew. Yes, that most famous of spots immortalized by the incredible kiss in the movie *Titanic* is off-limits to guests. The reason is very simple: no lights are allowed up there. Because the bridge is directly over the bow, lights have to be out at night so the officers' eyes can adjust to the dark. With America's litigious society, the company's fear was that someone could trip and sue the cruise line for not properly lighting the area, regardless of the big picture. The crew, of course, could not sue anybody.

The *Fantasy* was docked in Nassau, Bahamas. The city lights rippled over the warm Caribbean waters around us and flooded over the mass of sweaty, writhing bodies dancing on the open deck. It was a magical setting: the clear sky above with its twinkling stars so bright, and the majestic Atlantis Resort and Casino floating nearby on Paradise Island.

It was a humid, sultry night of intense energy. The discs were spun by the chief officer, a bald Italian with a thick middle and a wicked gleam in his eye. Several gorgeous ladies clung to him as he danced behind his equipment. The techno was pumping, the crew was wildly drunk, and the air crackled and thumped with liquor, sex, and the knowledge that we all would return to work in just a few short hours.

Ravi and I observed the scene from above the Empress deck. He was thoroughly uninterested, while I was fascinated. The energy was incredible and I wanted to hurl myself into the orgy below. And I don't even like to dance! We had begun our shift at midnight doing simple duties, mostly cleaning up paper plates of food or abandoned drinks or empty beer bottles. At just after 3 A.M. we were informed we were nearly finished.

"I have to wake up in four hours," Ravi lamented as he sipped his Coke.

"We don't start until 8:30. The safety test is first on the list, isn't it?"

"Yes. I think Boota did that to keep us from partying too

much. I need a good hour to wake up and get ready. I need to shave, have my coffee, meditate."

"Wow, you meditate? Is that why you're so close to beating me in class?"

He smiled. "It won't be long."

"I know, I know. You're far more deserving than I."

We had been competing for first place on the college's tests. Because we weren't on the same training team, we didn't see each other as much as before, which I regretted. I found him inspiring.

"Isn't it amazing?" I commented on the dancing crowd on the open deck below us. "Not one person is dancing with another of the same race."

"That's true."

"I think that is exceptionally cool. It's like a crime here to date anyone of your own color. I am glad that so many people are viewing this as an opportunity."

"But you have all sorts of races in America, don't you?"

"Well, yeah, but not really. I come from a place that has a small black population, but it's mostly white folks. Our idea of ethnic diversity is a Mexican restaurant run by an Irishman. It's called Carlos O'Kelly's, for Cat's sake."

"Really? I always thought America was the 'melting pot.'"

"Oh, we used to be. I don't know what it's like in the big cities or anything, but I come from the Midwest. It's all white bread there, if you know what I mean."

"No, I don't."

"Anyway, you can tell that a lot of these women have never had any freedom. Check them out. They come from second- or third-world nations and are probably completely dominated by their men. Here they can make the same amount of money and do what they want."

"They are all acting like men," Ravi observed with disapproval. "They sleep with anything that moves."

"God love 'em."

"You support this?"

"Well, actually no, because none of them have found me yet. But seriously, I support that they are no longer held to the double standard that makes men cool and women sluts for the same behavior."

"Behavior *neither* should participate in," he harrumphed. "Are you ready for the last round of cleanup?"

"Indeed I am, my fine brown friend, champion of monogamy."

We descended to the Empress deck and immediately pressed Boota to release us. He told us we had one final duty. "Guys, I need your help. Security is too busy to handle them all, so help me over here."

He led us through the crew bar and into a service hall. There a young woman was sitting on the steps, or rather she had been until she had passed out and slid partway down. The slide had hiked her shirt up. As a gentleman, I didn't even spare a glance for her black lace bra with the little red rose stitched into the clasp, which was happily in the front.

"This woman is drunk!" Ravi observed. "Look at her! She has…she has soiled herself!"

We regarded the Eastern European woman. Even though her short hair was plastered to her forehead with sweat and her eyeliner ran in jagged streaks where her spastic dancing had flung it, she still looked pretty. And as Ravi observed, she had urinated in her skin-tight jeans after she passed out.

Boota shrugged. "I warned you guys it was going to be a party. Look, Brian, help me get her up and we'll hand her off to security on the I-95. Ravi, call housekeeping."

After handling the situation, I returned to the Empress deck. Ravi had already retired, and Boota said I was free as well. The music had stopped and the crowd had dispersed into dozens of fragmented groups. The energy was still high, and the magic was still in the air. It was calling to me, taunting me. I felt like a hungry man looking through a restaurant window.

I recalled that Ravi and I had left our aprons and notes for the safety test on the upper deck. Near the top of the steps I slowed when I heard recognizable sounds from above. Visions of Alexander and Paulina popped into my head.

A Moldovan woman lay upon the cart where we had left our items, using our aprons as a pillow. Her head was to the side, her state far closer to unconsciousness than sexual ecstasy. A slavering Caribbean man was standing between her legs, his pants around his ankles. The cart rolled back and forth with each thrust. The scene was so pathetic that even a natural voyeur like me was revolted. I was grateful Ravi was not here to see it!

The man paused in his work and gradually managed to turn his bleary eyes to look at me. His face actually drooped from the excess of alcohol. I couldn't believe he was capable of standing, let alone his other activity. As soon as he paused, the cart rolled a few feet away from him and, suddenly no longer occupied with action, he slowly crumpled to the ground. The woman rolled her head back onto my apron, her eyes glazed over and she, too, passed out.

I stared at them, wondering what to do. I had a strong desire to take our things and leave them the way they were, slobbery and disgusting and completely exposed. Her tube top was relatively unscathed, but her pants were wound around one of her legs and there was no sign of her panties. The man was shirtless and flat on his back, pants down saluting the Bahamian moon.

Finally I just had to laugh. Welcome to ship life!

6 *The Midnight Bahamian Toga Bash*

"**B**RIAN," TIMEA ASKED, "ARE YOU GOING TO THE toga party tonight?"

Timea was from Hungary, but had worked in England for several years as a nanny. Her ease with English was very impressive, especially considering how very different her native Magyar was. She was a dumpy, decidedly average-looking woman who was one of my favorites.

"No, not after seeing that party last time. You know I love to party, but that was ridiculous."

"Did you hear that after 10 P.M. the aquarium in Atlantis is free for crew?"

My eyes widened. The Atlantis Resort and Casino is the world-class entertainment complex just a few miles from where *Fantasy* docked in Nassau. It was reputed to have one of the finest aquariums on earth. While most cruise ships did not spend the night in a port, but left early, we were lucky that *Fantasy* spent two overnights a week in Nassau.

"I say let's do it," I cheerfully answered. "I don't need more than my four hours of sleep anyway. I've been running on that so long I don't feel it anymore. Isn't that amazing?"

She chuckled and nodded in agreement. "I'm asking Diana to join us."

"Please, get as many women as you can. This is my golden opportunity for bragging rights."

When 10 P.M. struck, we were miraculously ready to leave the ship. Timea and Philippa from our training team were going, as well as Timea's paisana, Diana.

Chronic shyness rendered Diana virtually mute, but she had an amazing, regal beauty. Her skin was pale as fresh cream, and her jet-black hair was cropped short with just a hint of spikiness. The lips beneath her almost Roman nose were very expressive and naturally reddish, so she never wore lipstick.

The four of us rushed off excitedly into the humid Bahamian night. The checkpoint to exit the port was crawling with taxi drivers. They all perked up at the sight of us and a surge of tall, skinny men rushed toward us. We chose a driver at random, but in hindsight we should have first asked if he had any family. No man with a wife and child at home would drive so suicidally!

Our driver introduced himself as Tobey as he rushed in and out of the opposite lane. I presumed he failed to recognize that the vehicles were in fact moving *toward* us. An exceptionally tall and slender bridge separated our destination, Paradise Island, from Nassau. The span was high enough to allow sailboats to pass beneath with ease, though two unfortunate vessels still had somehow managed to crash. Their two mysterious hulks lay half-submerged in the dark waters below, provoking my imagination. I had a particularly good view of them as Tobey drove across the bridge on the sidewalk. The side mirror had long ago been ripped off, so I was mere inches from the edge.

The drive took only a few minutes, so it was unclear why he had to risk our lives to shave off sixty seconds.

The Atlantis Resort and Casino was staggering in scope and splendor. It consisted of a wide structure dominated by two thick towers with a connecting span at the uppermost levels. The towers and edges of the building were flared strangely to create a distinctive look, with gargantuan seahorse sculptures hugging the corners. Despite having lived in Las Vegas, a city world-renowned for taking splendor over the top, I still found Atlantis humbling.

Once inside, we staggered through the lobby, still shaky from the drive, and stood on the mezzanine overlooking the dining room. Three of the four sides of the room, easily fifteen feet high and a hundred feet long, were in fact the giant glass walls of a massive saltwater aquarium. While guests dined on escargots, a ten-foot manta ray cruised by to supervise.

A labyrinth of halls meandered around dozens of tanks devoted to sea jellies, sea horses, and moray eels. One particularly fascinating section was packed with hundreds of lobsters above and on both sides, so viewers could observe their alien-like undersides and backwards propulsion. The maze continued through the gigantic lagoon and offered constantly changing views of the entire shining, healthy saltwater ecosystem.

Behind each glass wall was a scene evoking a lost, sunken Aegean-like civilization. The halls were lit only by the light that filtered through the waters. Because it was night, huge stone sculptures reminiscent of Minoan bulls were silhouetted, as were the thick schools of giant fish. It was an amazing amalgam of real and imagined Mediterranean cultures. Several areas were obviously designed for the viewer to look up through the aquarium at the brightly lit towers above.

It was mesmerizing! We were all left speechless after seeing displays that would make Sea World blush. We wandered for nearly half an hour before we were through, and reluctantly returned to the casino.

Philippa, being a head taller than the rest of us, noticed a sign for the shark tank and led us toward it. I stumbled along behind deep in thought until I saw something that froze me in my tracks.

"That's a Chihuly!"

I rushed ahead of the ladies and into the casino where I stopped before an information kiosk and nearly dropped to my knees in reverence. A massive globe of flat glass plates in seductive blues and silvers and whites revolved above.

"What's that?" Philippa asked.

"That, my dear, is an original Dale Chihuly sculpture. It must be worth half a million dollars easily."

"Who is Chooly?"

"Chihuly," I corrected. "He is probably the world's leading glass artist. You should see what he did for the lobby of the Bellagio in Las Vegas. He did a whole garden of glass flowers that cost something like one hundred grand each and...Holy Cat! There's another one!"

I sped through the casino to genuflect before a huge orange-and-yellow sunburst. It was easily ten feet in diameter and glowed brilliantly. We discovered four of these masterworks that night. The Atlantis was world-class indeed! Alas, the ladies were not interested in art worship at such a late hour and they dragged me kicking and screaming outside.

High above us towered dozens of palm trees mingling with light posts. The Bahamian night greeted us with its damp embrace. Though the temperature was high, the night was strangely energizing. The last time I had been outside at this hour, I had assumed the vigor was caused by the crew party. I realized now that it was, in fact, the vibe of the island itself.

This was the Caribbean! This was why we worked so hard. Sure, we were all here for the money or, in my case, to chase Bianca. But really, deep down, we all had a sense of adventure, a lust for life! This was a life that most people would never dream of. We were not rich or famous, but we had guts. Otherwise why else would we have come out here on such a pathetically small amount of sleep?

"I'm very glad to be here, ladies," I said seriously. "Did you ever think you would be in such a magical place? This is why we work so hard, and it's worth every drop of sweat and every hour of sleep denied."

The mood turned reflective for a few moments as the sea breeze shifted the palm fronds above us. As if to reward us, we all simultaneously saw the shark display, which was in the form of a Mayan-style pyramid.

We strode up to it awestruck. The huge pyramid towered above a tank filled with a dozen full-size sharks. Behind a series of pillars was a wall of glass offering a better view of the occupants. We watched them swim around for several minutes in silence.

"Did you know the first pyramid in Egypt was also a step pyramid?" I mentioned to no one in particular.

"It was?" Timea replied.

"Yes, built for Zoser long before the pyramids at Giza. That was at Saqqara, built by a guy named Imhotep. I was horrified to see them use his name in the movie version of *The Mummy*. I hated that movie. Of course, I watched it in the back of a bus driving through the Egyptian Sahara at midnight. It was dubbed over in Hungarian, but it had Romanian subtitles. You want stories, baby, I've got 'em."

"You are so odd."

"Hey," Philippa asked. "What's that clear plastic tube that cuts through the tank?"

Suddenly excited, Diana shouted her first words of the evening. "Look! It's a water slide! Look up above!"

The little steps running up the pyramid's front cleverly held dual waterslides that shot downward and into the shark tank. Clear tubes sent the slider safely through the waters, but not without a fright: the sharks liked to nap on top of the tubes!

"This place is amazing!" I said. "Look, there are no railings preventing people from jumping into the pool!"

"So?" asked Timea.

"Are you kidding? I could jump right in with the sharks!"

"Why would you do that? That would be stupid."

"You obviously don't understand America at all," I replied. "If there is no sign stating the obvious, someone will do it, stupid or not. Then, of course, he will sue whoever owns the property upon which he did his idiotic deed. If this were America I could jump into this tank, get my leg bitten off, and sue Atlantis because they didn't have a sign warning me of danger. I would be set for life."

"But it's a shark tank! *Obviously* it's dangerous. If you jumped in there, you would deserve what you got."

Sadly, I shook my head in resignation. How could I explain what I couldn't understand myself?

The four of us returned to the *Fantasy* at half past midnight. I felt we had achieved a grand success for the evening, and my desires for adventure had been sated. Yet despite my best efforts, the ladies convinced me to join the toga party in the crew bar. What little energy I had was nearly exhausted by climbing those awful forward crew stairs, but finally we entered the crew bar.

The sound blasted us as soon as we entered the small room. The dance floor was packed with nearly all of the college trainees circling Boota. Unlike any of the students, Boota wore a toga, which jiggled as he worked some crazy Indian moves. He was a tremendous hit. The bald Italian officer Renatto was once again DJ, and he was just as wild as ever. Spontaneously he clawed open his shirt and screamed obscenities in Italian.

Suddenly a cry rose up from everyone. I hurriedly glanced around trying to identify what had captured their attention. I could detect nothing in particular that would account for the ripples radiating throughout the party...until the chanting began.

"Yank! Yank!"

Both Boota and Srinivas pushed through the crowd to greet me. Grinning mischievously, the short but powerful Srinivas shook my hand heartily, then pulled off my shirt! Hands came from all directions to wrap me in a white sheet. I did not resist, flattered at the attention, until I felt a tug at my khaki shorts. The crowd jostled, the disco ball disoriented, and the music assaulted, as my shorts were removed by persons unknown and carried off into the dark.

The mob pulled back and I found myself in the center of the circle, wrapped in a makeshift toga, and expected to dance, something I had no idea how to do! I was struck numb with embarrassment. Why, this was the first time I had been embarrassed since I had discovered what girls were!

Laughing off my own discomfort, I just started wiggling like mad. Everyone cheered and the throng crushed into the circle. I took the first opportunity to sneak off to the bar and get a drink. Of course, I had no money as my wallet was making the rounds somewhere in the dark. Fortunately it held only a few dollars and my Carnival ID. Even more fortunately there was a ready supply of drinks from my classmates.

For a while I stood by the bar in my underwear and toga, watching the party. Yet the mood called for dancing, and I actually found myself taking a stab at it voluntarily. I wouldn't have said I had it in me, but without really knowing how, I found myself dancing with Yhasmina.

Yhasmina was a Bulgarian with, quite simply, the most beautiful face of any woman I had ever seen. From the waist up she could have been a supermodel although below she had a disproportionately large bottom. She was wearing an exotic blue dress with streaks of silver and a sequined silk scarf over her luxurious black hair. She looked like a gypsy, and moved like one, too. Only later did I realize that she was, in fact, a gypsy. Everyone paused to watch her work her dance floor magic.

The moment did not last long, however. As the techno music pumped ever faster, overcome with excitement I flung my hands up over my head and struck a light fixture, knocking it down directly onto Yhasmina's head! Fortunately it was just cheap plastic and weighed little.

I was aghast, but she merely shrugged it off. Before I knew it the hour was 3 A.M. and everyone was drunk and very sweaty. The dance floor was stifling, the mood energetic, and I decided to do my Italian officer impersonation.

I ripped off my toga and began screaming Italian obscenities. Of course, I did not know any Italian obscenities, so I substituted Italian food names. The crowd roared as I shrieked, "Parmigiana! Rigatoni! It's not delivered...it's DiGiorno!"

Too late I realized the crowd was, in fact, cheering because I was only in my underwear.

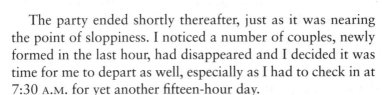

The party ended shortly thereafter, just as it was nearing the point of sloppiness. I noticed a number of couples, newly formed in the last hour, had disappeared and I decided it was time for me to depart as well, especially as I had to check in at 7:30 A.M. for yet another fifteen-hour day.

I stumbled from the crew bar in my underpants and sandals, and nearly fell down the steep stairs. I clung to the railing for dear life, recalling how difficult the steps were when sober. Finally I staggered along the I-95, surprised at just how many crew members were awake at 3:45 A.M. I received mostly startled looks, with the occasional mild applause as I descended toward B deck. The echoes of music rattled my brain. Only when I neared my hallway did I realize that it was not, in fact, an echo. The hip-hop music from my neighbors was thumping louder than ever before, and the Indian music blared in angry response.

Things were about to get ugly in my hallway.

The doors to my two neighbors' cabins were open, and I saw the music lovers for the first time. Blocking access to my cabin were two huge Jamaican men in their underwear facing off against three surprisingly large Indian men in chef's uniforms. I tried to sort out the overwhelming audio stimuli. I could hardly make out their words over the noise, but there was no mistaking the communication. I saw muscles tensing and fists flexing, eager for action.

Suddenly the door to my cabin burst open and tiny Amy

stormed out. She marched right up under the noses of all five massive men and began screaming. They tried to back away, obviously unsure about this new little menace, but she didn't give them an inch. She even poked one of the Jamaicans in his belly, which was about eye-level for her.

"It's four in the morning!" she shrieked. "You are ALL assholes! Where you from? You can't play any music after eleven, but I never said a word. But now I will! All of you get back in your cabins before I call security. And no, I won't call your paisanos the Indians. I'm calling the chief himself! He's Filipino, and he likes me a *lot* more than he likes you! Go to bed, NOW!"

She slammed the door as a perfect exclamation point. Within one minute the hall was empty and silent, except for a lone, stunned, half-naked American.

7 *Ship Life 101*

THE EVENING PRACTICAL LESSONS FINALLY BROUGHT me into the dining room as a waiter. Never again would I have to serve as a line cook, dishwasher, or wine steward. In a Carnival dining room there are always teams of two running a station: a head waiter and a team (or assistant) waiter. As a trainee, I was to assist two Asians. In this team the head waiter Made (pronounced mah-day) was a middle-aged and surprisingly heavyset Indonesian. His assistant was the small and energetic Rodante, a Filipino who never let his smile lose its glow.

We prepared our service station in one of the generously spaced pantries. The great advantage to working on a *Fantasy* class ship, other than that it was smaller and laxer with discipline, was the amazing pantries. On newer, larger ships the living facilities were orders of magnitude cleaner and more personal, but the pantries were far inferior. Less than six hours a day were allocated to sleeping and over twelve were spent in the dining room, so I preferred the better pantries.

Every team assembled its bus tubs in the same order for the same contents: one for waste foods or liquids; one for waste paper, plastic, or wood; and one for soiled linen. The dirty dishes were assembled on an oval tray if you could find or steal one. All silverware went into blue racks that were brilliantly labeled by their owners.

The shortage of materials was a serious issue. Each head waiter was assigned a specific amount of silverware, and he would guard the pieces fanatically. His rack would always be branded emphatically, and anyone caught "borrowing" from the soiled rack faced a severe reprimand. Anyone caught pinching *clean* silver risked decapitation. At the end of the first seating, each head waiter would rush his silver to the dishwasher, refusing to leave until the precious cargo was fully cleaned and accounted for. The dishwashers enjoyed healthy gratuities for protecting a waiter's silver should he be called away.

At first, I was disgusted with Carnival's apparent inability to supply their employees with proper equipment. Every station was required to have X number of saucers, water glasses, wine glasses, silverware, side plates, coffee cups, and so forth. Yet there was simply *never* enough of *any* of the items. Absurdly, a nightly inventory was required and all items were displayed upon the tables. Usually for a station to pass the inventory a waiter was *required* to steal from another. Highly prized items, such as bread tongs and butter dishes, were exposed for all to pinch. The latter were overwhelmingly stolen by the guests, by the way.

All good waiters arrived at their stations an hour before their shift began, to ensure they would have enough equipment to serve the guests.

Only after observing the restaurant staff did I begin to understand Carnival's policy. The attitude of most waiters was one of extreme indifference toward property. Breakage was exceptionally high because no one cared about the cost. Carnival was a billion-dollar company, so why should an overworked waiter worry if he dropped a cup? But twenty broken cups a night on each of twenty ships added up in a hurry. By demanding that each station be equipped completely and enforcing it nightly, Carnival threw the responsibility right back onto the waiters.

Any waiter serving twenty-six guests simultaneously demanding coffee, who only had ten cups and eight saucers, would take breakage much more seriously. Yet even legitimate accidents did not mean a replacement of necessary equipment. The system was brutal but effective—a metaphor for all things at sea. My problem was that it was completely inimical to the Restaurant College's demands for superior service.

Our pantry was shared by a Romanian couple, Dumitru and Lowena: paisanos and friends of my girlfriend Bianca. They were a husband and wife team who worked well together, but were hampered by their cultural principles.

Dumitru assumed that Lowena was incapable of carrying anything even remotely weighty because she was a woman, this despite her role as team waitress, which required heavy lifting. Certainly he would never have switched roles with her, for he wouldn't have dreamt of taking orders from a woman. Instead he obsessively made sure that he carried all the heavy trays, to the detriment of their team performance. What I at first assumed was gentlemanly behavior was in fact not. His efforts had little to do with Lowena, but were "preventive maintenance" for his future children.

On that particular cruise Dumitru and Lowena had a difficult station, while Made's was a little light. I therefore found myself assisting Dumi most of the time.

After serving the entrees, there was always a lull of five to ten glorious minutes for relaxation. During that leisure period the waiters had little to do except prepare coffee, organize the cups and pinch the neighbor's saucers, take loads of soiled plates to the dish line, and empty the nasty food garbage from the bus tubs. Such light responsibilities seemed like paradise.

One evening Dumitru called me over to him. He was a middle-aged man with a round face and round glasses. His hair was black and straight. He was significantly older than

Lowena, who was a very pretty, very petite home-wrecker, according to Dumitru. When he met Lowena he was so smitten that he abandoned his wife and children to chase after her.

"Hey, Brian, you want to have some fun?"

"Always."

"Watch closely, and don't try this at home."

Dumitru placed an empty coffee cup and a spoon on a saucer. The spoon he slipped through the cup's handle in such a way that at a glance all appeared normal. He looked at me to verify if I was following his activities. I shrugged.

Dumi casually strode over to one of his tables and suddenly bellowed in shock. He pretended to trip and flung the cup right into his guest's face! The spoon kept the cup safely in his hand, but the guest had already reflexively leapt backward and nearly soiled himself. I thought the poor man was going to have a heart attack. I was so shocked at Dumitru's stunt I stared, speechless, for several minutes before crumbling to the floor in laughter. To my astonishment the guest was surprisingly cool about the whole thing. I think the joy his family took in the prank made him swallow his pride.

"Dumitru," I stated gravely at the end of the second seating, "I must acknowledge that your balls are not only significantly larger than my own, but surely made of solid gold."

He frowned in confusion. "What are balls?"

"Eggs," Lowena answered in Romanian slang, with a roll of her eyes.

My group decided to indulge in a drink to celebrate our first dining room practical. The crew bar was packed with bodies of all shapes, sizes, origins, and colors. Needless to say, 99.9 percent of those present were non-American and therefore likely smokers. I could not see the ceiling, *literally*, because the smoke was so thick. At the table beside us were clustered eight Indonesians, all chain-smoking and drinking

Coronas. On the other side sat a boisterous bunch of Italian officers who made no effort at all to hide their ogling of the ladies at my table.

We five were smashed into a corner table. Timea, Anjana, and Philippa had managed to fit into the corner of a booth, while I was required to share a stool with both Liezle and Hila. The proximity to such divine behinds was wonderful, but was also proving to be quite stressful. The ship rocked like crazy in high swells and the stool maliciously had one shorter leg. I found myself after weeks of exhaustion, an hour of heavy drinking, powerful swells, and three butts on an uneven stool, quite simply unbalanced.

"Ladies, I'm afraid I don't believe you," I was saying. "You must know who has my khaki shorts from the party."

"So Brian," Philippa asked, changing the subject. "Do you drive a car?"

"Of course. I had a Jeep before I moved out of the apartment to join the ships. I loved my Jeep. Passionately. I would have made love to that car if I could. Well, O.K., that's creepy."

"You already had an apartment and a car?" Liezle asked with surprise. She mercifully set down her steaming mug of green tea that I had been eyeing warily during each shift of our stool.

"Of course."

"I didn't know you were rich."

"Are you kidding? I was flirting with bankruptcy for months when my software company split up."

"But you had a car and an apartment!"

"Everyone has that."

"My goal with Carnival is to buy a car."

"Mine, too," Philippa added. Anjana agreed as she fingered the salty rim of her margarita glass.

"Well, I didn't own the apartment. I just rented it. All Americans have a car and a place, more or less. That doesn't mean they own them. We all have the bills to pay. Credit cards and all that. It's stressful."

"But you had a car and an apartment! What more do you need in life? Did you have a television?"

"I took great pride in killing my TV five years ago, but almost everyone has a TV and a VCR or DVD and all that stuff, sure."

"We have a TV, but papa only watches football on it," Liezle sighed as she poured a shot of Jack Daniel's into her green tea. Hila was fairly hugging her Coke as we shifted yet again.

"Ah, it's all just stuff you buy on credit and pay for later. America has a great credit system. We have everything we want, but that doesn't mean we own it. When we buy a house we can live in it while we are paying for it. I know most of you guys can't do that, and have to pay all the money first. Not everyone has a house, but everyone has a couple of TVs and at least one car."

"When I was waiting at the Marriott," Timea suddenly fumed, "I was so angry. I asked a man for directions to the nearest mall, and he said it was only ten minutes away. It took me over an hour to get there! People here just assume you have a car, I think."

"Oh, you thought he meant ten minutes walking? Nah, he meant by car. I'm sure he didn't think about it."

"Wait a minute," Philippa interjected. "You said at least one car? Why would you have more than one?"

"Oh, lots of people have more than one."

"But you can only drive one car at a time! And you're trying to say they aren't rich."

"Well, some people have a car for play and one for daily use, but that doesn't mean they are rich. I mean, I come from a nice middle-class suburb where everyone's doing all right. Both my brothers have two vehicles, for example. Not me, but they are a lot smarter than me."

"I've heard of suburbs," Hila said. "They don't look real. Like little models of houses that all look similar, and never stores nearby."

"That's right. That's why you need a car. The nearest store is usually a few kilometers away. So, do any of you ladies drive?"

I was answered by a chorus of no's. Suddenly it was my turn to be interested.

"None of you? Really? In America kids are legal to drive at sixteen, boys and girls."

There were gasps around the table.

"We have to be eighteen in Slovakia, and then it's usually only the men."

Anjana nodded in agreement as she licked the salt from her glass. "My uncle gave me a car when I was eighteen, but it was stolen in the war."

"Well, you can get a permit at fourteen, but an adult has to be in the car with you. I'm telling you, life without a car is really, really tough in America."

"My husband," Philippa said, "earned his driving license at age twenty-three."

"You are married?" Timea asked, surprised. "You never said that. You aren't wearing a ring."

"I have been married for three years. I didn't want my ring to get lost, so I don't wear it at work. I'm...I'm worried though. My best friend worked for Carnival and when she came back, she split with her husband."

Timea looked shocked. "Why?"

Philippa shrugged, making her thin body shiver. "She didn't want to cook anymore. He said he waited two years for her to cook for him, and he wasn't going to wait any more. She said she would hire a cook. He said he couldn't afford that. But she said she could. And that was the end."

I sipped my drink, not knowing what to say. I suspected all these young women were going to have to face a collision of cultures. They would return with more money than their boyfriends or husbands could make in a year, and be used to being completely equal with men and free to make their own decisions. I didn't think they were all ready or willing for such a change.

"I think it must be nice living in America," Anjana said, breaking the silence.

"Oh, it's a great place to live. I love it. But we have our stresses, too. We work so hard. Americans average more working hours than almost anybody on the planet. I think Japan is the only one higher. You know why Americans don't know anything about the rest of the world? We don't have enough free time to go and see it. How can you get to know a place when you only get a week or two off a year, and to travel overseas takes a couple days. What can you learn from another culture in a few days? I won't even bring up the expense. So we focus on our stuff and stay at home. Even traveling within America is hard because it's so big. I mean, I have only seen a dozen states, and we have fifty!"

"Fifty-three," corrected Liezle.

"Anyway, having that stuff does not always mean personal satisfaction."

"Personal satisfaction?"

"Of course. I'll tell you ladies, I have more guests telling me how jealous they are of me *here* than you can possibly imagine."

"Jealous of *us*? I have not had six full hours of sleep in three weeks!"

"I'm serious. The adventure calls to people, the dream of traveling and working with exotic people. Many of us are unfulfilled because we have all this stuff and not always meaning. By meaning I guess I am referring to happiness and a sense of purpose. Stuff doesn't really make you happy. Of course, that's just my opinion and I am considered odd."

"*Very* odd," Liezle said, correcting me again.

The ship lurched as a wave hit us from the side. The pitch was always more acute near the bow and higher up, right where the crew bar was. Hila, Liezle, and I all spilled our beverages as we madly struggled to right ourselves on our crazy stool. I cringed when I got a lapful of Liezle's drink. I couldn't believe I was being called odd by a woman who drank green tea and Jack.

"I guess the grass is always greener on the other side."

8 *Creepy Conch Fritters*

FTER THREE WEEKS OF UNRELENTING TOIL, MANY of the trainees were given an afternoon to relax. The *Fantasy* was docked in Nassau again. No one ever got time off when the ship was at sea, for the guests had nowhere to go and they invariably ate all day. But during ports, sometimes you were allowed a little freedom. This was my first time free to wander the port alone.

Nassau is not a large city, though it contains the majority of the Bahamian population as well as the pirate museum which showcases the city's rich history as the ideal pirate hideaway for centuries. A former British colony, the evidence is everywhere, from the uniforms on the police to driving on the left side of the road. Most place names are British and references to their royalty.

I browsed through the markets and past countless t-shirt stands. These markets were densely packed with whatever they could fit under their tarps, whether it was leather goods, beads, necklaces, or woodwork. The vendors all wore loose-fitting, light clothing splashed with vivid shades of red and yellows.

The sky was clear and blazed as it only can in the Caribbean. Without the sea breeze it would have been uncomfortably hot. As it was, I overheard an inordinate number of American tourists loudly complaining it was too humid for their taste.

The weather was magnificent for the beach, so I had little desire to spend my precious time in a loud, close bazaar. I pushed past dozens of peddlers offering their obviously fake Cuban cigars at me, determined to find a real one now that I was outside the United States. After wandering a while in the pricier shopping areas, I discovered a British-owned cigar shop that appeared reputable. I was well aware that a high price in no way guaranteed authenticity, but I was satisfied with the Bolivar Belicosa I bought. The tobacco was so strong I was light-headed all day!

I noted a cluster of fellow trainees walking toward the beach, and went over to join them. There were half a dozen ladies from the Czech Republic and Slovakia, including Philippa and Liezle from my group, as well as a Czech man named Denis. I could not allow this man to enjoy the glory of a six-to-one ratio of women to men!

The public beaches were beyond the British Colonial Hilton, the ridiculously expensive landmark hotel at the port. The beaches boasted moderately clean sand with not too much broken glass. Though it took us nearly twenty minutes to walk there, the *Fantasy* was moored right across the bay from us and blocked our view of the sea. We spread out in a long line with our towels and soaked up the rays. The sun sank deep into my flesh, and I could instantly tell why everyone warned so repeatedly the need for sun block: the rays were far more intense in the Caribbean.

I made sure I was downwind as I finished puffing my divine stogie.

"Hey, Brian," Philippa said. "You said you were from Ohio?"

"Iowa."

"Where they make potatoes?"

"No," I said chuckling. "That's Idaho."

"Those are red Indian names? They all sound the same to me."

"Yes, they are. Anyway, yes, I am from Iowa. You know, my hometown was visited by the President of Czech Republic. There is a big museum in Czech town, near downtown."

"Wait," Philippa interrupted. "You know Cheddar Rapids?"

I started laughing and nearly choked as I accidentally breathed in some smoke. "Cheddar Rapids? It's not in Wisconsin! No, it's *Cedar* Rapids, like the tree."

The tall brunette shrugged. "In my language a *c* is like your *ch*. Yes, we know about that. Bill Clinton met our president there."

The group all excitedly began talking in their language. Slowly I became aware of something different. For the first time I was completely excluded from the conversation. This was not an intentional snub, they were merely all caught up in the comfort of their native language. I could see they were truly relaxing for the first time since I had known them. Even Liezle, who had clung to me so much in the beginning, forgot about me.

This is what paisanos meant.

I was not disturbed by their treatment, other than by my jealousy of Denis's getting all the female attention. I lay on the beach and reflected upon the conversations I had recently had with my fellow trainees. We all came from such completely different worlds. There were few enough points of reference even with the Europeans.

I could not discuss American movies because I deplored the mindless Hollywood films that usually circulated worldwide. My preference in books was non-fiction and of highbrow subjects that few Americans even cared to discuss. I had not watched television for nearly a decade, and the only series they knew were from before my time, such as *Dallas* or *The Partridge Family*. They had no concept of our working conditions, our credit system, what we did for fun. With the Asians I had even less in common.

That's when it struck me that I was truly alone. I had mistakenly thought that my native English would make relaxed conversation easier, but in fact I was the most isolated of all. Everyone on board understood English, yet no one else could possibly understand where I came from, what my motivations were, or what my fears were. We all got along fabulously and clung to each other tightly, but there was a barrier that would require serious effort and time to topple. My years at sea would teach me that ship friends are never really friends. But it fools you every time.

With such a heavy realization weighing me down, I said my goodbyes and returned to wandering the Bahamian streets. I was suddenly disturbed. Would I encounter this barrier with Bianca when I finally caught up to her? Somehow I doubted it because we had both been amazed by the lack of any barriers even in the beginning. But was a wall hiding deeper down than we had had a chance yet to go?

I discovered a conch stand as I passed an empty dirt lot beside an abandoned hotel. It was partially hidden behind a chain-link fence entangled with weeds and garbage. Scavenged planks and warped sheets of water-damaged plywood formed the semblance of a bar. The roof was rusted corrugated metal. The sign by the road was scrawled: conch fritters and beer.

I knew conch was about the only uniquely local food in the Bahamas. The meat came from those big seashells from which islanders make horns. If I wanted something authentic, I could hardly do better than a conch stand in an empty dirt parking lot.

I parked myself on one of the stools and glanced around. The kitchen counter was merely a few crates stacked up, and the sink was a jug of water and a large basin.

Working the stand were two men of completely opposite characteristics, other than their shared African heritage. The younger man was tall and broad shouldered, amazingly built, in fact. He was extremely handsome and had his hair tied in short braids. He was well groomed and wore the bright blue sports jersey of a soccer team I didn't recognize.

The older man was a wafer thin and short Rastafarian. Of his teeth I saw little evidence, though I had difficulty tearing my gaze from his hair and beard. Most of his long locks were coiled beneath the red, yellow, and green-striped hat, though several lengths had escaped. His beard was the most hideous thing I had ever seen in my short life. Where I expected to see the beard, namely the sideburns and the chin, only a few patches of hair were visible. Yet drooping from the underside of his chin and fairly sprouting from his neck were long and soiled loops that connected and split apart depending upon whatever filth held them together.

Both men completely ignored me, although I was the only other person present. I watched them continue to ignore me for several minutes. The Rastafarian sat on a crate and was apparently stoned. The young man didn't appear to be doing anything at all either, and after several minutes he simply left.

I chuckled to myself. I had not expected aggressive service, but I was certainly not ready for such a lapse. This was my first encounter with "island time." Life was going nowhere slowly, and so were they. It was obvious these men were not going to offer me service at all, so lesson learned, I asked the older man for a beer.

He did not respond.

I was loath to move any closer to the man, but I had invested five minutes already, and was determined to discover something truly local. After about fifteen minutes, the athletic man returned.

"Hello!" I greeted him. "Do you have any local beer?"

"Yeah, mon. We talk Kalik here."

"May I have one, then, and an order of conch fritters?"

"Yeah, mon. That what we do here. We no talk foolishness, but only talk truth."

"Uh, that's great."

He retrieved a bottle of the beer called Kalik from the cooler and thumped it on the bar for me. He then left again, walking toward the big, abandoned hotel with a small bucket. I watched him depart, then discovered the beer did not have a twist top. Usually I would improvise an opener with a key, but now that I was on ships I had none.

"Say, do you have a bottle opener?" I asked the old man. I think his jaw was a little slacker than before, but he was otherwise unchanged. "Bottle opener?"

He did not respond. I leaned over the bar and reviewed the jumbled contents inside the makeshift conch stand. I found absolutely nothing that would work: there were no utensils of any kind, no tools, nothing. I did not think I could open the bottle by hitting the cap against the edge of a counter, and all the wood was fairly rotten anyway. I enjoyed the absurdity of the whole encounter and mentally filed it away. Though tempted, I decided not to abandon the brew and catatonic Rasta Man.

Finally the young man returned. He had with him a small plastic bowl in which he was mixing some batter with a plastic spork from Kentucky Fried Chicken. He was very intent on his work, and seemed almost surprised when I spoke to him again.

"Do you have an opener for this bottle, chief?"

He set aside his labor and took up the bottle. With a movement that was excruciating to watch, he popped the beer's lid off with a set of beautiful white teeth. I couldn't believe he abused them so! Was he *trying* to look like the old man? I was still cringing when he handed the beer back to me and returned to his work.

Finally I received my conch fritters a full hour and fifteen minutes after ordering them. I was nearly ecstatic when he handed me a paper bowl lined with a MacDonald's napkin and filled with steaming fritters. The oil instantly soaked through everything to burn my palm, and the flavor was what one would expect from deep-fried corn meal. I was convinced there was no conch whatsoever in them.

I enjoyed my mild adventure, but was most pleased that the Rastafarian hadn't touched my food.

9 *Graduation*

NEAR THE VERY END OF OUR TRAINING, BOOTA arranged something special as a reward for our hard work: a trip to Kennedy Space Center at Cape Canaveral. He rightly observed that this was an opportunity of a lifetime for most of the students. I recalled how excited Ravi had been on the day we arrived when the space shuttle launched. We had since learned that we'd missed seeing it by a mere two hours. Unfortunately we also learned that it was the final, tragic mission of the space shuttle *Columbia*.

"Brian?" Ravi asked me eagerly. "You must accompany me to Kennedy Space Center. I want pictures of us by a space shuttle for my future children."

"Of course," I replied. "Wait a *minute...future* children? What about your sons?"

He grinned, then made sure Liezle was not nearby.

"Those were my nephews."

"You lying dog!"

"One month has passed," Boota said to the college trainees on February 13th. "Do you remember how you felt when you first sat in this room? You were all nervous and confused and overwhelmed. The person beside you was from another part of the world. And I told you that by the end of training this strange group would feel like family. Tell me, is anyone happy about leaving tomorrow for the real assignment?"

I leaned back and smiled. He was absolutely right.

"In this month you have probably worked harder than you ever have before, and you've learned a lot. You cleaned dishes, you cooked, you served. You learned how to present fine wines and you have learned dining room etiquette. Only you can measure how much about the world you have learned. Starting tomorrow, you are all going to be in the real thing. Congratulations!

"But first, who wants to know who is the top in the class?"

I was in the back row beside the giant Indian and the sexy Slovakian. Ravi and I shared a smile. We had been back and forth with the highest scores in class all month. The first two tests I had nudged up above him, but the results from the final test had not yet been presented. He had been a studying machine for days on end determined to ace this test, and was nervous that he had performed poorly.

Liezle and I had drifted slightly apart in the final week of the college as she grew more comfortable meeting her paisanos outside of the class. Ravi, although the only Indian in class, was nonetheless one of many from the Asian subcontinent on board. Just recently he had invited me to the after-hour Indian Republic Day celebration in the officers' mess. I had been honored to be the only white guest, posing in the pictures with the two dozen Indian officers on board. Since the chefs were mostly Indian, the food had been phenomenal.

"The winner by two points—and two points only—Ravi! Go India!"

Yeah, I had bombed the test. I never let on that I had not studied at all.

The class gave Ravi a warm round of applause, mixed with a few good-natured jeers about Indian preferential treatment. He was everyone's favorite, he was so incredibly kind and gentle. I was very proud to have called him my friend for that trying month. I believe strongly that you can judge a man by the company he keeps, because I appear much better that way.

"And in our number two spot," Boota continued with his sly grin, "Is the man we love to hate...Mr. America!"

Never one to let a moment pass, I rose and flexed my muscles. I smiled when I heard the words, "Typical American!"

"Now comes the part that everyone wants to know, the ship assignments."

The class instantly was silent and at attention. "I will begin with our champion. Ravi is assigned...the *Holiday*!"

Hoots, jeers, and laughter rose from the class. The *Holiday* was the oldest, smallest, and nastiest of Carnival's fleet of nearly twenty ships. It was well known that Carnival was planning on selling it within a year. I was disappointed that Ravi would be sent to such an awful ship. How could they reward such hard work with such an insult? Perhaps he had requested it, having friends or family onboard. I hoped so.

"Since we all know that Brian is here only to chase a woman, we shall now learn which ship she is on...*Conquest*!"

"Figures!" someone shouted. The *Conquest* was, of course, the newest and biggest and most glorious of Carnival's world-class fleet. I breathed a sigh of relief. My assignment had been promised to me, yet after a month with Carnival I had already learned how capricious such promises could be.

I had done it. I had proven to the whole ship that an American could not only survive on the ships, but excel. I had worked harder, faster, and more efficiently than almost everyone in class. The crew thought Americans were lazy because so many guests would literally wait ten minutes for an elevator rather than going up a single flight of stairs.

"I can tell you all something else, now," Boota added. "Some of you no doubt guessed this already. Brian is not training to be a waiter like the rest of you. He is going to be an assistant maitre d'. So I hope you all treated him well, because he's going to be your boss."

The class all began throwing their taunts my way, but Boota interrupted with a surprise.

"Also going to *Conquest* is Liezle."

"Aha!" I said, hugging her shoulder. "I knew you loved me. You can't help it, you'll follow me anywhere. All the love poems I asked your roommate to deliver paid off."

"She's been holding out on us," Boota continued. "Liezle has a boyfriend there. Those are the only two going to the new ship. Next we have Timea going to *Triumph*."

"Boyfriend?" I asked her. "I thought I was the man of your dreams."

"No, *you* are the man of your dreams."

"Yeah, well. O.K.," I finished lamely with a smile.

Boota finished naming the ship assignments and told us the afternoon would be allocated to a trainee party. Upon hearing those words all the men in the class formed a mob and carried him to the small pool on the open deck. He frantically emptied his pockets of important objects, and hollered before his dunk that he had computer disks in his pocket that couldn't be lost. He hurriedly tossed them to someone just as we tossed him into the water. During the struggle Srinivas quietly slipped out the side door to safety.

The party was short but sweet. I was shocked that they had an open bar. Several people were hitting the alcohol hard. While most of the trainees had no preference regarding their ship assignments, that was not always the case. Anjana had wanted to join her boyfriend on *Destiny*, but was instead assigned to *Elation*, the same ship she worked previously as a bartender and hated. All afternoon she licked the salt from at least two margaritas simultaneously.

The lights were lowered and the mirrored ball began its spin. The Gipsy Kings blasted over the speakers and soon everyone was dancing. I sat at a table and watched the ladies wiggle their magic. My eyes met Yhasmina's and she gave me a sly smile, adopting into her rhythm a move that protected her head from falling objects.

I discovered I was in a reflective mood, not a partying one. I was about to join my Bianca, whom I hadn't seen in three months. I couldn't wait!

I had to be honest with myself; I was enchanted by all the gorgeous women on the ships. They were from all over the world and experiencing life in ways they never had before. Despite their varying ages, most of them were exploring personal freedom in ways not unlike Americans do when they become freshmen in college. The energy and enthusiasm was arousing.

The ships were ideal opportunities for sexual adventure: most people were ambitious, young, attractive, and far from home. The job was so difficult, any distraction or quick pleasure was welcome. Condoms were handed out free to the crew along with the aspirin, band-aids, and seasick pills. And everyone was verified in perfect health before they were allowed onboard. My medical checks-ups had cost hundreds of dollars and were so extensive that my physician suspected I was joking. Carnival required tests usually allocated for men fifty years or older.

I watched Liezle and I mulled our situation over. She and I had been about as close as any two people this month. Though we did not take it seriously, there was real desire behind our light-hearted banter. Had I been single I would have been more aggressive toward her. I also knew she didn't really have a boyfriend on *Conquest*. She had obviously found someone to claim the role to help her get aboard. Too bad she wasn't just trying to follow me!

I was surrounded by dozens and dozens of beautiful women. It was a veritable smorgasbord! I had a heart for only one, yet I was nervous. Was I strong enough to handle all this temptation? More fundamentally, I wondered if I was foolishly wasting the opportunity of a lifetime.

Was I ready for the real Carnival? I resolved to avoid placing myself in situations where the temptation might be too much for me.

"Ah, Brian!" Boota called, joining me. "I have news for you. Carnival is sending you and Liezle to Mexico the night before you are to sign on to *Conquest*! You'll arrive at 8 P.M. and have the whole night to do, well, whatever you want. Enjoy!"

10 *The End of the Beginning*

WE HUNKERED IN PITCHERS, THE SPORTS BAR OF the Miami Marriott. Seven of us had signed off the *Fantasy* and been bussed down to Miami to await our ship assignments. The rest had all already been shipped off to their destinations.

Srinivas had joined us, having been assigned another ship on which to build a second restaurant college. Most of my training group was present: Timea, with a mild hangover; Anjana, with a crippling hangover; and Liezle. Also present were gentle Ravi and shy Diana. The mood was very subdued.

The partings had been surprisingly difficult. While I was truly close to no one in particular, I was also traveling with my favorite new friend. Those who had discovered and then depended upon their paisanos were truly distressed, and there were many tears. None of us wanted to let go of such an amazing experience. We had all learned how quickly you make friends, if shallow ones, on ships.

"So, Srinivas," I asked, "did I just overhear that you are divorced?"

"I wish!" he answered with a smile.

"What do you mean, you wish?" asked Anjana. She pulled open her roast beef sandwich and spread a thick layer of salt over it with her knife.

"In Sri Lanka divorce is just not done. I live in the same house as my wife, but we hate each other. But where else are we to live? The paperwork for divorce has taken eight years already. I even had to convince a friend to let me use his address to 'prove' that I lived elsewhere. You can't divorce unless you live apart, but we can't afford that. My working on ships ten months a year is not enough for them. My mother has not spoken to me since we applied eight years ago, and she never will again. That is the way things are there."

"What about you, Brian?" Srinivas asked. "You said you already were divorced."

"Yes," I answered, dropping my Cuban sandwich with disgust. I was loath to abandon food, but this was the worst sandwich I had ever tasted. How was it possible to have a bad Cuban in Miami? "It cost me $300 for the paperwork and was done in a few weeks. We didn't have any complications like children or a house. I did lose my Jeep, though, which I was not happy about."

"We had better ask for the check now," Timea suggested. "It took us two hours to get this lunch, just like it did when I arrived last month."

"Yes," Srinivas agreed. "The waitresses all know Carnival pays for the food, but not the tip, and none of us has any money. What Brian tips for a sandwich would pay for my whole family's meals all day back home."

"You should have seen my generosity before my divorce."

"Can we change the subject?" asked Timea. "It's Valentine's Day, you know."

Srinivas and I looked at each other and started laughing.

That evening Srinivas, Liezle, Timea and I walked over to a local liquor store and bought a bottle of gin and some tonic. It was a delicate night, balanced precariously between warm and chilly. The hot tub bubbled welcome, and we accepted its invitation. The mood was quietly optimistic.

Ravi and Diana, both non-drinkers, had said their goodbyes and retired early. They had a 5 A.M. wake-up call. Fortunately the *Conquest* shared the same home port as *Holiday*, so there was a small chance of our meeting again.

Near midnight we were all surprised to see Diana approaching us. She stood over the hot tub for a moment awkwardly, her hands behind her back.

"Hello Diana," Srinivas greeted. "You decided to join us after all?"

"No," she replied demurely. "I just forgot I had something I wanted to return."

"Oh?"

Nearly trembling with nerves, she suddenly hurled something at me and fled. I spilled my drink catching a pair of shorts. My shorts, taken from the toga party!

"I don't know what I'm going to do," Timea suddenly admitted as she sipped from her plastic cup. "I am terrified of escalators."

"How is that possible? They aren't enclosed, like elevators. They aren't spiders, or heights, or anything. You aren't speaking in front of a crowd of them and you're not naked on them." I sat on the edge of the Jacuzzi and leaned back, watching the smoke from my cigar rise. I was trying to look at anything *other* than Liezle in her bikini.

"I have a phobia of them. I don't remember what happened, but my mother said I got caught in one as a child somehow. I have never set foot on one since I can remember. There's something about how those steps disappear beneath the metal teeth…"

"But you are assigned the *Triumph*, with a two-level dining room. There are no stairs, only escalators!"

"I know. Give me another gin."

"I have some good news and some bad news," Srinivas said to me. "The good news is that your vacation is scheduled for about the same time as your girlfriend's, and your plan for a work break after your training is all O.K.'d. You'll work as a team waiter for a month, a head waiter for one, and then train as assistant maitre d' for two months. After that you go on your work break and come back as full assistant maitre d'."

Good news indeed! In the middle of a contract every employee, if approved, was entitled to a work break. This was an allowed interruption of the contract, of no more than three weeks. Bianca and I scheduled things so that we would both have most of June off for a vacation in Transylvania.

"And the bad news?"

"You and Liezle will not overnight together in Mexico. They decided to keep you here in Miami until you join up in New Orleans. So you get an extra two days off, but you can't take advantage of that sexy Mexican air."

Liezle splashed water at him.

I pretended to sigh heavily. "Does this mean I get back all the bribe money I spent?"

I reflected on how much I would miss these people. There had been thirty of us in the class, and I still remember the horror of the name-learning game we played, that required everyone to repeat the whole list of names. I was always horrible at remembering names, but in Carnival College I learned that had the circle been Bob, John, and Mary I would have been in trouble. But Yhasmina, Kalina, Egle, Medea, and Ravi were exotic to me, and therefore easier. The three Martinas threw us all for a loop, however. We had to learn their last names: Fucikova, Mrzljak, and one we all abandoned and just said Z. I hardly knew these people, yet knew I would miss them dearly.

I also pondered the nationalities and tried to categorize them. I had already learned that the easiest way to deal with the five dozen new nationalities was to stereotype faster, and then abandon those generalities equally fast. I was no longer frightened of racial typecasting, something that would have horrified me back home. Here I was just coping, and I knew to drop the labels as soon as I knew the names. When one is just trying to survive, one is less apologetic and more open-minded.

In my short experience I had learned that Filipinos were extremely hard working and incapable of not smiling. The Indonesians were about the same, though not so eager to please. Croatians were probably the tallest Caucasians on earth. The Hungarians had the most difficult language barrier of the Europeans, yet were very talkative and my favorites. Their appearances were generally less appealing than their neighbors, the Czechs and Slovakians, who supplied more supermodels than any other nationality. I saw many, but met few, Bulgarians. I noticed that the women were either gorgeous or unsightly, with little in between.

My recollections had all turned toward the women and my level of attraction to them. Was this all I learned in the last month, that I was more interested in women than ever? I could obsess all I wanted, but I would never cheat. I was the proverbial Boy Scout who abhorred lying, and could never find pleasure while doing so. But, really, could my copious amounts of potential guilt compete with *Carnival Conquest's* crew of over one thousand, half of them European women whom I was particularly interested in?

What on earth did my future hold?

PART II

Waiter
(Promotion)

Where's the ribald, where?

—DANTE ALIGHIERI, *Inferno*

1 *My First, and Only, Clingy Lingerie Model*

LIKE EVERY OTHER DAY IN THE PAST FOUR WEEKS, I woke up exhausted. My alarm went off at 4 A.M. Liezle had asked me to call her when I woke up, just in case her buzzer was not enough to wake her. Indeed it was not, nor was the phone. Her roommate woke up and angrily answered. Today was the day we traveled from Miami to our new home port of New Orleans.

On the flight, Liezle never ceased squeezing the blood from my arm. Even after we landed in Dallas and walked to our connecting flight, she never released her grip. I enjoyed it in the beginning, but I quickly began to feel smothered.

"Why are you so scared? You flew into Miami all right."

"Because," Liezle whispered fiercely as she held me tighter, "I traveled with a friend over the Atlantic. This is my first flight alone."

"What am I, chopped liver? You're not alone," I replied. "At least you are squeezing me awake. Say, why are you whispering?"

"I have never been so far into the United States. Do you think the CIA knows I'm here?"

"Who knows? It should be exciting being hunted by the CIA. Don't you watch movies? No, really, we are quite harmless here. We're not going into any ganglands and the hidden CIA prisons are all in other countries so we can maintain our plausible deniability."

"Huh?"

"Forget it. But don't worry, we don't eat foreigners anymore, it's in poor taste."

"Like your jokes? Look, that lady over there is following us."

"Oh, please. Will you stop it?"

Yet the woman did, indeed, appear to follow us. She was an extremely attractive and fit woman of perhaps fifty years of age. She wore a smart black suit and her hair was pulled into a severely tight bundle atop her head. Liezle dug her fingers deeper into my flesh as we were tailed across the entire airport. I had to grudgingly admit to myself that the woman did look somehow "official."

"Ouch! Will you relax? I'm delicate, don't you know. Look, she's coming over here. Good, let's see what's up."

"No!" Liezle pleaded. "Why can't she just leave me alone?"

"Maybe it's *me* she wants," I replied sourly. "It happens sometimes. Well, not really, but it should."

"No, she's looking at me. Do you think she is a gay?"

I was startled. "I don't know, why?"

"America is full of gays."

"So?"

Liezle cut her reply short with a squeak as the woman directly approached us. She offered her hand to Liezle, and I had to gently nudge her to respond politely.

"Hello," she said briskly. "I am Courtney Harrelson. What's your name, dear?"

"Liezle."

Courtney's thin lips curled into a smile. "Of course: a European girl. Liezle, you're gorgeous. Do you live in America?"

"No, I am visiting."

"Too bad. Well here's my card. I am a model scout. If you ever want to audition as a model, let me know."

"Model?"

"Yes, we provide models for all the major suppliers of lingerie and bathing suits. There would be a spot for you. Definitely."

With that, Courtney sharply strode away.

"Well how about that," I said. "What am I, chopped liver?"

"Why do you keep saying that? You like liver?"

"It means I am being overlooked. I got more action from that big security lady who patted me down twice. But you, my dear, should be flattered. Bravo."

Liezle looked at me with eyes four times larger than before.

"Well, don't let the model scouts bother you. They keep trying to catch me, of course, but I'm too quick for them."

I gazed up at the massive *Conquest* in wonder. It was very impressive with crisp, smart lines and geometry and clean, fresh white paint. A huge banner unfurled along the side some fifty feet long read "The Fun Ships." This was the largest cruise ship in the world, and it dwarfed the Riverside shopping mall along New Orleans's Mississippi bank. It was three football fields long and rose to a towering thirteen decks, not including the three decks below the waterline where the real action happened.

"It's so big," Liezle breathed in awe.

"It's nice inside, too," I commented, resisting the urge for a tasteless dirty joke regarding size. "Far nicer looking than *Fantasy*. The whole ship has an impressionist painter theme. The main dining room is the Monet, and the main lounge is the Degas."

I pushed Liezle to hurry onboard, because I was anxious to see my girlfriend. Though I hadn't seen her in three months, I knew I would not have a whole lot of time to see her today:

home port was always a crushingly busy day. Bianca had made arrangements for us to share a cabin, so at least I would see her before we went to sleep!

The I-95 of *Conquest* was surprisingly different from that of *Fantasy*. The height was significantly lower, and the width was also much reduced. Add this cramped feeling to the extra 200 feet of length and it had a very claustrophobic effect. Though *Conquest* was such an immense ship, it was also densely packed: the cabins were smaller, the halls narrower, and the ceilings lower. The ship was a full 110,000 tons of displaced water weight.

"What is the route again?" Liezle asked.

"It's a seven-day cruise," I answered as we sought the purser's office. "The first two days are sea days, then Grand Cayman, where we tender in. We dock in Jamaica and then Cozumel, followed by another day at sea. Ah, here's the purser's office."

The purser was an extremely important man. There were always several crew pursers on a ship of such size, and they handled all the business matters for the crew. They organized cabin assignments, supplied room keys, and arranged for tax matters. They were also responsible for all the crew's passports. The purser took our photos and created our room keys, which doubled as our ID cards to leave the ship. He was a handsome and surprisingly young fellow from the Philippines. Actually, because Asians age so well, he could have been forty-five for all I knew.

"You are in cabin A650," he said to me, "with your girlfriend."

"Yay!"

"And you," he informed Liezle, "are on B deck with another girl signing on today. Both of you can drop your stuff in the cabin and meet with the safety officer at 1 P.M. You can buy your uniforms from the supply chief after that, who is Clarence today. You can't miss him, he's nine feet tall and black. He's in the supply office, past the marshalling area."

Finished with the preliminaries, we found ourselves in the I-95 again. I peeked into the crew mess and the crew bar, but could not find Bianca. She was most likely working at this hour anyway. The early guests arrived by noon and usually went straight for the Lido deck for the huge buffet and pool on the top deck. I figured I would find her there. When I had my uniform I would go check, but I was not allowed in the guest areas out of uniform.

Toting our luggage through the narrow halls below decks, we passed dozens of men and women signing on. With a ship as enormous as *Conquest*, several dozen changes occurred weekly. The halls felt cramped but were fairly clean below decks, designed with smart lines and no visible pipes and wires and conduits and the all-around ugly items that were so pervasive in *Fantasy*. The walls were instead smoothly paneled. The lighting was a sickly yellow color giving everything a very sanitized and unnatural feel.

I found my cabin easily and threw my luggage on the floor. I had seen the cabins before on *Conquest*, but had forgotten just how small they were. Somehow Carnival managed to fit two bunks, a desk, a chair, two wardrobes, and a sink into the same amount of space as my closet back home. The thirteen-inch TV literally covered the top of the desk in its entirety, and Bianca's two suitcases were shoved in the hollow beneath where the chair was supposed to go. I had no idea what I would do with my suitcase. I knew I would be sleeping nightly with my carry-on luggage. The amount of floor space was literally less than six feet. I could not do a push-up.

A nearby door to the shared toilet and shower boasted a small red light to indicate occupancy. Two couples' cabins shared the facilities, and, to my great delight, they were mercifully clean. Unfortunately, standing in front of the sink blocked access to both the wardrobes *and* the bathroom. I looked about the cabin but could identify nothing personal from Bianca's belongings, no pictures or memorabilia to hint that I was close to finally seeing her after three months. Then I noted her underwear filling my bunk. If I had wanted a tease, I sure got one!

After dropping off my luggage, Liezle and I spent quite some time finding her cabin on the lower deck. Though both of us were beginning as team waiters, I was staying with a head waitress and therefore on the A deck. It was not an actual rule, but generally the lower the rank, the lower the cabin.

We were arguing about which direction to go when I saw someone slowly descending the metal steps toward us. The gait was slow and almost melodramatic. Even before I saw the face I knew who it was as I watched the fingernails trail along the railing. She strode down the steps with tremendous aplomb and a mischievous smirk on her lips.

Bianca! I had finally reached Bianca! Like all Romanians, she had black hair and a dark beauty about her. Her figure was not tall but statuesque. Her face was round and white, with very expressive lips. Her real beauty lay in her grace, for she carried herself well and was simply alluring to all. One of the smartest women I had ever known, Bianca also had a joie de vivre that was unparalleled. She was a social creature loved by all, but none more than I.

2 *Pancake Darwinism*

BIANCA AND I HUGGED SO TIGHTLY WE REFUSED TO release even for a kiss.

And then she was gone.

Bianca had to run back to her station on the Lido deck. She had snuck off to greet me, but couldn't risk being caught away from her station for too long. Such things as life and emotion were completely secondary to bussing tables, even if there were only fifty guests onboard, over three hundred clean tables, and forty bored waiters.

Indeed, I did not see Bianca again that day. Several hours passed as Liezle and I went through the safety training and orientation programs. We found our life rafts, proved that we knew how to manually operate a watertight door, and that we understood garbage separation. Then we were tasked with getting our uniforms.

Standard procedure was to collect equipment from the supply room. Crew paid for the items, standard being two pairs of pants, two formal shirts, three informal shirts, one vest, one formal jacket, two aprons, and a wine opener. Shoes were available, though most of the women chose to purchase their own. Since few of the crew members could afford such a large quantity of clothing, it was deducted from their first paycheck.

Finding the supply room was difficult, but even more so was finding the supply officer. Clarence, from Trinidad, was perhaps not nine feet tall as the purser said, but was surely seven and skinny as a rail, which made him look even taller. He refused to supply us because our paperwork was not signed by Dan, the senior maitre d'.

So we ran up to deck four to find Dan, who said he didn't need to sign anything.

So we ran down to the supply office, but Clarence was now in the supply room.

So we ran down to the supply room, but Clarence needed the stamp in his office.

So we ran up to his office to get his stamp.

So we ran, finally, to the supply room, ready to receive.

Of course, these separate locations ranged over the entire ship. It took us two hours to get our uniforms.

"Here," Clarence said to me. "We are out of your collar size for the tuxedo shirts, but this will work."

"Clarence, this is an 18-inch neck."

"It's close."

"Close? Even Mike Tyson doesn't have an 18-inch neck!"

"Come back in a few weeks. I'll have one then."

"Do I have to buy that one, too?"

He just smiled.

I was assigned to work midnight buffet. This was universally considered best because it was the *only job* that offered eight hours between shifts (except before home port). I suspected this nice assignment was courtesy of Dan. Only team waiters were allowed to work midnight buffet, so Bianca worked breakfast in the dining room. This meant that I was only able to see Bianca in the two hours between lunch and dinner, which was the time universally allocated for naps. Such naps could not be removed, because after months of hard labor and only four hours of sleep a night, a body required more rest.

We lived together, but saw each other awake less than fifteen minutes a day.

Setting up my station for the first dinner was very stressful. I did not know where anything was in the Renoir dining room, and was horrified to see our pantry was only an oval tray on a folding stand, with the silverware rack beneath it. My head waiter, William, was a middle-aged Filipino who rarely spoke. He was busy polishing and protecting his silver and had no time for me. The danger of pinching was extreme on *Conquest*.

With no warning, a Filipino head waiter grabbed the microphone and began coughing horrendously into it. It was a deep, thick cough that was sickening to listen to.

"Shut up!" someone cried. "Keep your germs to yourself!"

"Antonio! Die quiet, will you?"

But Antonio hacked and wheezed until he nearly passed out. Every corner of the dining room reverberated as the remarkable speakers brought the sound to us all. Some seventy waiters cringed and reflexively covered their mouths. It was so absurd and carried on for so very long that none of us could keep from laughing. I shook my head in wonder: how could ships be so harsh with discipline over trivial things and yet allow a five-minute coughing fest at 120 decibels?

Finally Antonio stopped and, between his panting, said, "Thank you everyone, this is my gift to you all."

Almost immediately my presence became notorious. On the very first day, as I prepared my station, the maitre d' of the Renoir dining room called a meeting. I was unaware that such orders were obeyed with military efficiency. I was casually walking down from the balcony when I observed several dozen waiters already clustered in the center of the dining room.

Maitre d' Reginald looked up at me with a unique blend of annoyance and amusement. I think he was a chronically irritated man, but always hopeful of an opportunity to be funny. He was a very wide German with a shiny shaved head, tiny rimless glasses and a tiny edgeless mustache. He looked distressingly like Heinrich Himmler.

"Would you prefer to remain on high, or would you like to join us in the middle?"

"Absolutely!" I replied boisterously. "I wouldn't have it any other way!"

For some reason the whole room exploded in laughter, and suddenly I was very self conscious. I sheepishly sat at the nearest table.

"*Absolutely* you are welcome to join us," he rebutted with his aggressive voice. "*Absolutely*, you must be the American. What's up with your collar, anyway? Did you lose a hundred pounds or something?"

For the next week I never heard the end of "absolutely" this or "absolutely" that. I discovered very quickly that in the Renoir, only Reginald made the jokes. The crew was allowed to repeat them, but only so long as the glory remained with the boss.

I closely observed the assistant maitre d's, knowing I would be performing the same duty soon. Both assistants and the two hostesses were mocked incessantly behind their backs, but the ship's two maitre d's, Reginald and Dan, were beyond ridicule. There was an unspoken fear of their authority.

Many of the crew was surprised at my casual familiarity with the officers, though none knew of my destiny as management. I speculated on this endlessly but never truly reconciled if this ease was a cultural difference or a Brian quirk. I had heard many times that the American mode of hierarchy was different than elsewhere in the world in that managers could be friendly without losing authority. Most of the Europeans in particular, I noticed, were incapable of camaraderie with their superiors. There were notable exceptions, however, such as Bianca's friends, who were very close with Dan.

During the first night out of port the *Conquest* sailed for almost nine hours along the Mississippi River before reaching the Gulf of Mexico, after which time I noticed the rocking of the waves from the Gulf. I also noticed *Conquest* was a louder ship than *Fantasy*. The crew was not louder, but the machinery of the ship itself was. Indeed, the main dining room in the very rear of the ship shook so roughly from the engine's power that plates and silver hopped off the tables nightly.

On that very first night the inevitable happened: my first embarrassing mistake.

As a team waiter, my job was to fulfill the written orders of my head waiter. This required fifteen to thirty minutes of waiting in the food lines during the crushing heat of dinner. The kitchens of *Conquest* were exceptionally efficient and produced food of amazing quality and variety. Numerous plates of each entrée were available for pickup in the hot window. The waiters went down the line like a buffet and simply grabbed what they needed as the chefs frantically tried to keep pace.

As accomplished as the chefs were, the demands of the guests were simply overwhelming. Any guest who ordered two entrees simultaneously, and there were many, could easily wipe out the entire supply of an entrée. This brought the line to a halt and forced several hundred other guests to wait.

What the guests could not possibly know was that only certain periods during the seating were allocated for certain courses. The first half-hour produced nothing but appetizers on the line. Then they switched everything over to entrees as the waiters worked the salad course. When a guest came in late and the line was no longer prepped for appetizers, the wait was agonizing and the timing was ruined for the entire night.

I handled the gathering of entrees only moderately well. Dinners were not the pell-mell bedlam of breakfast, but they were not exactly smooth, either. Rather it was organized chaos. I began to fear the time when I would encounter the Pancake Darwinism of the day shifts. During breakfast and lunch only the bullies received their food, or the thieves. During dinner the lines were calmer only by comparison.

On that first night I had struggled to find where all the different entrees were located. It was a challenge the first few times. I loaded my large oval tray with fifteen orders of the jumbo shrimp entrée, in three stacks of five. I rushed down the interminably long hallway from the kitchen to the dining room, running as fast as I could with the fully loaded tray on my shoulder. The hallway, lined with metal walls and ceiling, was about one hundred feet long. It was terribly difficult to bring food all the way from the kitchen to the far corners of the dining room before it went cold.

I rushed up the escalator and...WHAM!

My tray rocked wildly, and I wriggled reflexively to right it. Three entrees fell off the top and dropped with a deafening clatter. The sound reverberated off the metal walls to efficiently echo to the far reaches of the kitchen. Everything went cascading down to the bottom, but the moving steps dutifully brought the whole mess right back up. The ceramic shards and soiled shrimps tumbled end over end ceaselessly at the top, with each cycle breaking everything into smaller pieces.

I had struck the ceiling!

But the heat was on: there was no time for clean-up. I rushed back into the kitchen and gathered replacements before the guests grew angry. Half the dining room had heard the crash, and my section gave me a great round of applause when they discovered it was me. Of course this had to happen at first seating, and of course every waiter in the entire dining room had to pass over the revolving mess, which cycled mindlessly for nearly seven hours.

At the end of the evening Reginald made the announcement for those few who did not already know of my accident: "Ladies and gentlemen of the Renoir dining room, I present to you our *absolutely* American waiter!"

I was actually relieved after the accident. A mistake is inevitable, but it is also human nature to dread the baptism by fire. In many ways I was fortunate to get it over with on the first dinner of the first night.

I saw Liezle more than Bianca in those first few days. How ironic, since they were both assigned to the Monet dining room and worked the same schedule. Liezle heard of my accident immediately and was more nervous than ever, knowing her own baptism would soon come. She was terrified it would be as loudly broadcast as mine had been.

Every time Liezle and I spoke, I noticed a Romanian hovered nearby. Only later did I begin to understand the relevance of that observation.

3 *The   Crew   Bar*

CHECK-IN FOR THE MIDNIGHT BUFFET WAS USUALLY 11:30 P.M. Because of the timing of the second seating in the Renoir, I had only a few minutes between shifts. Supervisors understood the scheduling and allowed us to occasionally be late. If I did have free time, I went to the crew bar for a drink. I hated the crew bar, but it was my only opportunity to see Bianca.

Typically Bianca finished her day after 11 P.M. This was her only time for doing laundry or using the internet, though she had to return at 5:30 A.M. to work room service or, occasionally, happily sleep in until 6:15 for the breakfast shift. So even had she gone straight to bed, she would *still* have been denied the necessary sleep. Of course, after such stressful dinners most waiters were high strung and could not possibly sleep. After a few months without a day off, pounding drinks became the preferred way to facilitate the necessary relaxation as fast as possible.

The crew bar at night was insanely loud and lethally smoky. *Conquest's* bar was smaller than that on *Fantasy*, yet serviced an extra 200 people. Every seat was taken, every corner of every counter, and even every available lap! Mixed race couples were the norm, groups of all-male Filipinos jabbering in Tagalog, or perhaps a small cluster of Italian engineers sitting like zombies along the wall. Couples worked each other over in depth to the thumping of the beats that rattled the ice in the drinks.

The Romanian mafia all clumped together in the center of the room, Bianca among them. They did everything together: they served, cleaned, smoked, ate, and slept as one unit. Certainly after dinner they met for a drink without fail, be it in the crew bar or in the halls below decks. Because Bianca worked in the Monet dining room her shift ended half an hour before mine. They were usually on their third drink by the time I arrived.

Perhaps ten Romanians were present, the women mostly sitting on the men for lack of space. Bianca's adorable roommate Viorica, nearly passed out, slumped beside her. Bianca was in the middle of a hot debate with Flaviu, her best friend. He was a bulldog of a man, wickedly intelligent, highly belligerent, and in all ways macho. They argued in their native tongue and chain-smoked cigarettes, much as I saw them do back home in Romania. Bianca was the only woman strong enough to actually argue with the man, and in this case even had the moral high ground as they discussed his girlfriend. Flaviu usually had one squeeze per contract to keep him warm while his wife and kids were at home. This had been continuing for years, but only on *Conquest* was he in danger of falling in love.

I watched Viorica drop her head between her knees for a few moments. She was cute as a button and had the most amusing on/off relationship with Bianca's team waiter, Adrien. Currently they were off, so she had been hitting the wine hard. When she finally rose back up she immediately wiped her mouth with a napkin, even as she reached for another glass of red wine. She had vomited on the carpet. In the dark and the smoke and the noise, I was sure no one else had noticed.

I sat on the edge of Bianca's chair for a few minutes, but I was only able to observe, not participate. I had spent several weeks in Romania with Bianca already, and had learned how powerful observation became when language was a barrier. Of her family, only Bianca spoke English, but I had found the experience delightful. Her parents and I connected on a very real level and learned much about breaking barriers.

But on the ship, things were always different.

Of all the nationalities I interacted with, only the Romanians refused to speak English when I joined them. It annoyed and confused me that they denied me so. Perhaps they assumed I knew more Romanian than I did. They had worked together for a long time as a team, which was highly unusual on the ships. They had an established ritual and it was the only activity that kept them sane. My presence was intrusive, and I felt like a complete alien.

To my surprise, Liezle entered the crew bar, looking for me. I had intermittently seen her briefly here and there, but was curious to know how she was adapting. I could tell from the look on her face it was not well. I whispered to Bianca that I was leaving to chat with Liezle for a few minutes before my shift. She hardly noticed me leave as she yelled at Flaviu for playing with people's hearts.

Then, to my surprise, I overheard another comment about me disapprovingly in Romanian, "He's going to that bitch again."

I was shocked, and only too happy to leave them to their little non-inclusive group. I suddenly realized that if you judge a man by the company he keeps, then I did not like Bianca. Since the crew bar literally made me sick with the amount of smoke and noise, I resolved to never bother with it again. I couldn't talk to Bianca anyway and she refused to give up her only relaxation for the entire day. How could I in good conscience ask her to give it up? Yet how in good conscience could she not give it up for the few minutes I had free?

The internet café was next door and designated smoke- and noise-free. Compared to the crew bar it was blindingly lit and held a dozen terminals. Liezle and I sat in a corner and caught up. She was desperate for a familiar face. There were not so many Slovakians on *Conquest* as on *Fantasy*, and she was feeling overwhelmed. The trays that team waiters were required to carry were very heavy for her, and she was both exhausted and lonely. I gave her a pat on the hand and a word of encouragement, but I had to check in on the Lido deck.

I had been onboard for two weeks when we had a visitor during check-in for midnight buffet. Hipolito, a Filipino head waiter, was in charge of organizing the thirty team waiters. It was a small operation and his side job was to run things. All head waiters had a side job, whether it was to collect the tongs after each shift or mop the escalators. Everyone wanted the midnight supervisor side job, but Hipolito was far too efficient to allow anyone to take it from him. Therefore he was shocked when a maitre d' suddenly entered the crowded break room.

"Where's Brian?" Reginald demanded sharply.

"Here," I called, standing up from the mass of waiters.

He stabbed at the doorway with a meaty finger. "Come with me."

Everyone dropped into silence, and I suddenly became nervous. His tone was not kindly, but then it never was. I hadn't done anything wrong, but I was suddenly worried. Did I do something I didn't know was wrong? I awkwardly worked my way out of the crowd and met him in the hall.

"I was going over some lyrics for new songs," he began tersely.

I waited in pain, sensing this was the beginning of a discovery that he wasn't pleased with. He took his time and my mind raced for an answer. Both maitre d's on the *Conquest* sang during the dinners to entertain the guests. This was initiated by Dan, who did a staggeringly perfect rendition of Frank

Sinatra. Indeed, he was discovered singing in a drunken stupor in an Irish pub by a former agent of Old Blue Eyes himself. The man had been so impressed that he urged him to make a career of his singing!

Dan's singing was so overwhelmingly popular that Reginald insisted on doing the same. Though he was decidedly mediocre, the guests loved him all the more for his apparent lack of talent. I suddenly feared that he was going to chastise me for my constant singing. I was actually pretty good, and I knew he liked to be the center of attention. He was already outclassed by Dan. Was he going to take his frustrations out on me? I waited for the blow.

"What is this word?" he blurted, pronouncing something like "shawl," but I could tell it was not that. I looked over at his lyric sheet and smiled in relief.

"Shall? No wonder you don't know it. That's an old-fashioned word, like something from Shakespeare or older. It means 'will.' Such as, 'He shall sing Elvis.'"

Suddenly Reginald placed a hand to his breast and dramatically began singing a classic love song from the King: "Wise men say…only fools rush in…"

Irresistibly I joined in, "But I can't help…falling in love…with…you…"

After several minutes we finished the song and a huge applause sounded from within the break room.

From that moment I was "in" with Reginald. Everyone was scared of him because his temper was vicious. He was so completely outclassed by Dan that he had a vendetta with everyone. But Reginald and I shared a type of camaraderie that was new to me on the ships: we were both from first-world nations. While Germany and the United States were different in many ways, they were equally successful nations. During my time with Carnival I noticed most of the few first-worlders sought me out. I understood their desires. We were all longing for someone who could understand where we came from, even if just a little.

I got off work early and was free just after 2 A.M. Already feeling dirty and irritable, I found myself in the crew bar. They usually stopped serving at 2 A.M. to conform with U.S. norms, though we were in international waters and they could serve if they so chose. Most people ordered a six-pack of beer for last call and continued drinking until they passed out. Therefore a drink was always available if you worked the crowd. I intended to do so.

I am an extremely patient man, but I was annoyed with Bianca. I had worked very hard to join her on the ships, and she had fought very hard to gain me the opportunity. Yet now that we were together we never saw each other, and when we did it was filled with tension. She had warned me that she was different on the ships, and I began to understand how right she was.

We were *all* different on ships. No one could understand the life unless they lived it. The closest comparison was being off at war, though such an analogy is certainly unfair to the veterans of the world. We were not risking our lives, but our freedom was completely absorbed by the huge organization we lived within, and its goals. For the tremendous burden of keeping us alive, the company deserved to ask more of us, and it most certainly did. Ships were, quite literally, sweatshops building entertainment.

A voice suddenly interrupted my thoughts. "Ah, Bianca's man."

At the end of the bar, completely lost in a haze of smoke that curled beneath a lamp, was a chef. His uniform was streaked with stains and wrinkled. He was very thin and gangly in appearance, with thick black glasses and curly, oily black hair. He was not an attractive man by any definition.

He handed me a bottle of Corona.

"You are really stupid, you know," he said.

"As long as you provide the beer, you can call me anything

you like," I replied. "...except cheap."

"I'm Etienne," he said as a cigarette jiggled from his thick lips.

I had heard of him. He was one of the rare Frenchmen onboard. Bianca loved to talk to him because she loved speaking his language so much. I had never met anyone who knew French who didn't say it was the most pleasurable language on earth to speak. I knew Bianca would talk to Etienne at any opportunity, though she claims they had little enough to say. I also know he was quite taken with her. At this point I was ready to let him have her.

"Nice to meet you. Perhaps you would care to explain why I am so stupid. Usually people give me the option of being crazy, too."

"I know you are crazy," he replied. "Crazy for Bianca. We all are. I would do crazy things for that woman, too, but not something so stupid as you. You could make $120,000 a year in the United States and take Bianca with you, but you are here. That's stupid."

So much for the first-worlder camaraderie, I thought. I was already in a bad mood, and as excited as I was to meet a man from France, I had no desire to argue. My humor was forced as I said acidly, "Yeah, well, I do miss driving my Ferrari."

"Everyone in America makes money. I lived in your country, and I know. I used to work in Las Vegas and I made $100,000 a year."

"Oh, very convincing," I sarcastically replied. "So you also gave it all up for a woman, eh? A lot of that going around these days."

"No," he replied seriously. "Women are not worth it. But I could get a job like that again in an instant. I know your country, I lived there for almost five years. You're stupid."

"Etienne," I snapped, "Cut the 'stupid' crap, all right? I lived there for thirty years, so quit feeding me your bullshit."

"You don't think it's easy to get a job that pays more than here?"

"I never said that," I retorted. "But you could be the worst chef on earth and still get a job anywhere in America. You're French. Just saying 'we have a French chef' will bring in customers, so any greasy spoon would hire you."

"I would never give that up to follow a woman here. It's stupid."

I stood up sharply and kicked the barstool away from me. "This conversation is over."

I wanted to argue with him, but I couldn't. He was right.

4 *My Heart Will Go On*

IKE IN A BIG CITY, THERE ARE RARELY MANY STARS to be seen on a ship at night. Cruise ships emit so much light pollution that you see nothing but black. To aft, port, and starboard I saw nothing but impenetrable black, yet far to the north was the orange glow of oil refineries illuminating the swamps of Louisiana. We were nearing the mouth of the Mississippi River and numerous beacons of red and green popped through the surface of the sea.

"What happens if I fall overboard?" A man had asked me earlier. It was such a common question that my answer had become habit.

"The ship will stop and a boat will pick you up."

But this was only half true. I gazed into the wake of the ship and watched the brown water churn. The waves looked very small from deck ten. If the 100-foot fall did not kill the passenger, he would disappear in the gargantuan swells. Safety training was very clear in the case of an overboard: throw a life-ring first, *then* call the bridge. People assume the life-ring is simply a flotation device, but it is much more. A person's head will disappear from sight within seconds from the deck of a ship this size, assuming the engines don't chop him into chum. We were trained that after calling the bridge to grab someone, anyone, to physically point at the swimmer and not stop until he's found. If not he'll be lost in less than one minute.

But at night? If no one sees you fall?

Goodbye.

Someone had, in fact, gone overboard that cruise. Rumors of how and why among the crew and guests were rampant. Some said it was a suicide, others said honeymooners had argued and there was a push. Yet only one fact was certain: the man was never found until he washed up on the Gulf Coast several days later.

Such events always brought up stories of past deaths recalled by crew members. It was not unheard of for suicides to take a cruise and spend all their savings for a wild, last romp in life: the intention being to jump overboard on the final night.

I focused on a floating piece of flotsam and watched it disappear into the night. It was lost to the blackness within fifteen seconds.

I was still working midnight buffet, though I had been working onboard *Conquest* for over a month. My tour as a team waiter had come to an end a week prior, and I had awaited my breakfast shift with dread. Pancake Darwinism truly offended me, and it was never more raw and revealed than in the mornings. Waiters squabbled over hash browns like hyenas fighting for the scraps stolen from a lion's kill.

Yet such was not my fate. Dan had chosen to keep me on midnight buffet to learn from Hipolito. I had been transferred to the Monet dining room so that Dan could watch over me, though he was careful to keep my station on the upstairs balcony and Bianca's downstairs. So despite working the same dining room, Bianca and I still were unable to see much of each other. She was vastly more human in the dining room than out of it, and our little snippets of time together were enjoyable. The socializing during the never-ending folding of napkins and swapping of menus was the highlight of my day.

As a sign of affection, Bianca began delivering me breakfast in the cabin, knowing how the midnight buffet people always missed breakfast. Two eggs Benedict and a pile of sausage greeted me every morning, even if she couldn't.

On my way to a late check-in of the midnight buffet, I slowly sensed something was wrong. The ketchup bottles began sliding to port. So very high up in the ship any turn too sharp would be amplified, so I was used to this behavior.

But *Conquest* kept listing farther...and farther....

Silverware bundles tumbled off the tables, then the plates. The ship keeled harder and harder. I rushed back to the break room and barked orders at everyone.

"You five in the dish room now! Hold up the stacks of plates! The glasses are in racks, leave 'em! Everyone else get on the floor and grab the centerpieces! Let's go!"

But it was already too late. A loud crash indicated an entire stack of plates was ruined, and then another. Team waiters rushed to snatch up ketchup bottles as they fell to the floor. Suddenly Hipolito appeared and shouted for two people to get behind the buffet to save the displays.

And *Conquest* continued listing.

Simultaneously two dozen ketchup bottles exploded on the tiles. I could hear plates by the hundreds smashing in the dish room before the waiters secured them. I nearly tripped over a pitcher crushed open on the floor. The cream streaked fifty feet across the Lido deck in seconds. Suddenly I had to hold onto something to avoid falling myself.

Then the ship abruptly righted, but far too quickly for us. My team squawked like seagulls as *Conquest* now listed sharply to starboard. This time everyone abandoned protecting property and instead secured themselves. I gripped the buffet tightly. The cream still fascinated me as it slid two feet sideways during the stabilizing, then suddenly shot back in the direction it had come from. Watching the fluid move so violently made me realize there was something much greater to worry about.

There was a waiter working on the pool deck.

I rushed over the slanting floor to the stern with great difficulty. Here was the pizza station, the grill, and the pool. The pool was completely empty, all the water having rushed out and devastated the deck before draining en masse down to deck nine below. Pool deck tables were not secured, so the flood had caught an Indonesian team waiter.

"Ketut!" I shouted, "Get out of there! Jesus, are you all right?"

A dozen dripping tables were washed into the corner as if a tsunami had struck. Sitting on top, soaked to the skin, was a smiling Ketut. I helped him out of the tangle of tables, most on their sides and their legs worked together like the roots of a mangrove.

"Me kaput!" he joked. "Hey, look out!"

I was struck in the back of the head by a falling display. A four-foot sculpture of a cornucopia fell at my feet. Surprised but uninjured, I watched the pieces of Styrofoam slide harmlessly starboard.

Conquest finally stabilized. Even as things leveled, Hipolito and I rushed through the Lido to see that everyone was unhurt and to survey the damage. At a glance I saw no less than fifty bottles of ketchup smashed on the tiles and shards of glass still spinning everywhere. Hipolito reviewed the damage in the dish room while I took inventory of all the team waiters. Fortunately no one was hurt. Ketut was the hero soaked in saltwater from the pool.

Soon guests appeared in their life jackets. They milled around the Lido deck in confusion, not really knowing what to do but prepared to do something. The General Emergency Alarm had never sounded, which was the call to don life jackets and head to the Lido. But the guests were shaken and paranoid. I could only imagine what they had endured in their enclosed cabins, though I knew that the Lido experienced the most damage. A list near the fulcrum, in this case the waterline, was not nearly as devastating as 100 feet higher!

Comically late, a pack of wild children rushed screaming through the Lido. They numbered easily two dozen and ranged from ages ten to fifteen. Completely overcome by panic, none wore life jackets and all were soaking wet. They surged up the stairs to the mezzanine, shrieking hysterically.

It never occurred to me to soothe their fears. I was just glad they hadn't stepped in the ketchup and tracked it all over my dining room. But I knew my responsibilities, so I hurried to calm them. I was intercepted by Reginald, in his pajamas, storming toward them.

"Quiet!" he barked as they disappeared upstairs. They disregarded him until he puffed up to double his size. His bald head fairly glowed pink with anger.

"Shut the hell up, you *goddamn* idiots!" he thundered with fire and brimstone. "*Jesus Christ*!"

The entire troupe of kids silenced instantly in shock. They stared at him with huge eyes, stunned that he actually swore at them. I started laughing. I couldn't help it.

"What are you laughing at?" he asked me with a grin. He was obviously proud of himself.

"I'll tell you what's funny," I replied. "The irony of it all. We get twenty kids panicking, but not one these twenty gorgeous European waitresses jumped into my arms for protection."

5 *The Infamous Filipino Elvis Massacre*

THE NEXT MORNING, I AWOKE TO DISCOVER *CONQUEST* not in New Orleans, but Gulfport, Mississippi. I walked onto the open deck and stared at the small port facilities and the brown water. It was not a striking place, though I saw a number of very attractive antebellum mansions far down the coast.

The melting snow of winter had forced the Mississippi River to rise. *Conquest*, being some thirteen stories tall, could no longer fit beneath the power lines that stretched over the river. These were not minor lines, but carried the electricity for several states.

The city of New Orleans had been informed of this potential trouble over a year earlier and had promised to raise them in order to secure itself as home port of the world's biggest cruise ship. They promised much, but delivered nothing. Now the captain had been forced to dock in relatively nearby Gulfport. I cringed at the thought of all the millions of dollars New Orleans lost in revenue from this oversight: 7,000 guests a week (half signing on and half signing off) were no longer renting taxis, staying in hotels, eating in restaurants, buying souvenirs, and paying taxes. There were also dozens of truck loads of supplies no longer passing through the city.

Carnival was required to bus people directly to and from the airport, some twenty miles outside of New Orleans. *Conquest* had arrived in Gulfport sometime after 3 A.M., yet by early morning there were 300 buses waiting to take all 3,500 passengers directly to the airport. To see the buses lined up for a mile was a staggering sight.

I also learned that a barge leaving Mississippi had not been aware of the huge cruise ship churning toward Gulfport, and had forced *Conquest* to evade in the last moment to avoid a midnight collision. After all the drama on Lido, I was shocked to discover that because our cabin was below the waterline, Bianca had never even awakened!

I loved working with Hipolito as a midnight buffet supervisor. The other head waiter side jobs usually involved a lot of grunt work, but this was merely responsibility for a smooth-running operation. There were no unprecedented problems to solve, barring perhaps a near collision with a barge. I was more of an organizer and morale officer than anything else.

"So," Hipolito instructed one night, "if some *bamboclat* is *boleta*, fix him like a banana. We don't need Rambo, but they can't be *mamagayo*, either. If you treat them like *basura*, they give it back like rice."

I paused to regard the man for a moment.

"Hipolito," I finally said with great sincerity, "that may have been English, but I have absolutely no idea what you just said."

"I always put the pretty ladies on the dessert station," he continued. "Guests love it. I only want women sweeter than sugar."

"*Now* we are speaking the same language!"

Hipolito showed me many of his secrets. He tried his best to put the right people in the right place. While such a strategy sounded obvious to me, it was woefully rare in the real world of political correctness. Politics were usually the name of the game on the ships, international or otherwise. Many women enjoyed benefits by sleeping with management, for example, and certain nationalities were favored.

Hipolito also took advantage of the mafia system. He kept nationalities together instead of forcing them apart as management recommended. In the small environment of the midnight buffet, where there were only thirty employees, things rarely got out of hand. If someone was lazy he would assign them to the hot, busy aft pool deck. There they would have to clean up after the hamburger and pizza lines: overwhelmingly the busiest spots on the ship.

Because Hipolito was Filipino, he preferred the mafia of his paisanos. He assigned them the most important jobs when they occurred. Otherwise he let them work together where they wanted. If anyone made a reasonable request of him, he would grant it if they were good employees. All of his "tricks" as he described them, were just common sense and easily manageable when dealing with only a few dozen employees.

I, too, began to rely on the Filipino mafia. They were my favorites to work with at all times. I rarely, if ever, saw a Filipino who was not smiling and joking even when doing the most menial or difficult of tasks. I soon became a favorite because I empowered them with my trust, much as Hipolito had.

I was even invited to an all-Filipino birthday party below decks. I had been accepted as an honorary Filipino because of my work ethic and my constant need to sing. But after that party, I was the champion of Filipinos forever.

"Brian, find a seat!" Victorio said as he welcomed me to his cabin. He was a solid, middle-aged man who looked like he had led a hard life. Beneath his tired eyes was a large birthmark and more lines than a cracked windshield.

Victorio's tiny cabin on B deck overflowed with Filipino men (there were few, if any, Filipino women on the ship). Both bunks held two or three men and the floor was packed with coolers all surrounding the birthday boy. The bathroom door was open to reveal an equally packed cabin past the bathroom. Hipolito sat on the covered toilet.

"Victorio," I said, shaking his hand, "Happy Birthday! Since I only found out half an hour ago and it's already 2 A.M., I didn't have time to get you anything. You'll have a bottle of Black Label tomorrow."

"Bah!" he scoffed good-naturedly. "We got it covered. I'm just glad you came."

He revealed two bottles of Johnny Walker Blue Label scotch, two Black Labels, three bottles of Chivas Regal, and two coolers filled with Coronas. He predicted that by 5 A.M. they would all be empty.

"You know, Victorio," I said taking a plastic cup of scotch, "you are the only Filipino I've met who actually looks his age. I appreciate your patriotism, though. I swear to Cat your birthmark is the exact shape of Lake Michigan."

Soon I was downing scotch and eating traditional Filipino foods, or what few they could create on an American ship, anyway. My favorite were strips of cold beef marinated in lime juice and an exotic blend of seasonings. I had to force myself to stop before I greedily ate the whole thing. All were generous hosts, however, and all insisted I eat my fill. I could tell they were pleased I liked it.

I was surprised to learn that in the Philippines it was the birthday boy who bought the drinks for all his friends. This was a holdover from their Spanish colonial days. Indeed, much of Europe celebrated birthdays in this manner.

Drinks were downed and refilled quickly. Every available spot was allocated for drinks, and we all went around the cabins telling stories. Like every other crew member I had ever met, each was interested to hear how I had followed a woman to this place. They took a vote and unanimously decided I was crazy, not stupid. By the end of the party, none of us could tell the difference.

At about 3:30 A.M. the party was really rocking. Well, as much as was possible with no women present, anyway. A head waiter named Jeffrey suddenly pushed everyone aside and pulled out a machine that I had taken for a video game console. In fact it was a karaoke machine, complete with microphone and two large speakers. The speakers were so large, in fact, that Victorio slept with one in his bunk.

"Holy Cat, Jeffrey! You can't play that thing now, it's 3:30 A.M.!"

"Where you from?" he replied with his huge grin.

"No singing, please. I'm having all the fun I can handle with these unlimited cheese puffs and Chivas."

"Here," he said handing me the microphone. Karaoke was a great joy for the Filipinos, with a particular passion for rock ballads. Should anyone invoke Bon Jovi, they placed a hand over their hearts. Jeffrey was a phenomenal singer who would periodically pause in the dining room to sing for his guests. His crystalline voice would cut through the restaurant chatter every time, and all guests nearby would listen. His cover of Michael Bolton was barely distinguishable from the real thing. And Jon Secada? They must have been twins.

"No, no, no," I deferred. "You are the singer."

"Come on, I hear you singing Billy Joel in the Hallway to Nowhere every night."

He had a point. The insanely long hallway from the kitchen to the dining rooms was nicknamed the Hallway to Nowhere because even after several minutes you felt like you hadn't made any progress. To keep my spirits high I always sang as I raced down its length. I don't know why, but my two habitual songs were *New York State of Mind* and *O Solo Mio*.

"Who wants to hear Brian sing?" he yelled. The response was a roar of approval.

"I heard you singing Elvis with Reginald once," Jeffrey continued. "Let's see how you do solo."

"All right," I acquiesced. "If we're going to do this, let's do it right. Bring me some Filipino music."

"We've got it, but I thought you liked singing like Elvis."

"Oh, I'll sing it like Elvis."

"You *are* drunk!" Jeffrey beamed to another roar of approval.

Jeffrey tested the microphone and I suddenly grew very self-conscious. It was loud enough to hear on the Lido! On the television a picture of a tropical beach surged, while the lyrics of the song passed by annoyingly fast, for one who could not read Tagalog, anyway. I had secretly hoped their native language would use characters other than the Roman alphabet that English used, so I could get out of it. No such luck.

Within moments I was using my best Elvis voice to sing a sappy love ballad to twenty drunken Filipino men, and the entire B deck of *Carnival Conquest*.

"*Tinapon ng lalaki ang bola sa pader*...something like that. I may not know the words, but I know my fried banana sandwich...thank ya, thank ya vury much.... Say, Jeffrey, what does that mean in your language, anyway?"

"You just tried to say 'the boy threw the ball at the wall.'"

"How romantic. So much for being a hunka hunka burnin' love."

Suddenly there was a pounding on the door. Jeffrey snapped off the power as Victorio answered the door. An insanely muscled security officer stood on the other side. He was Asian, but significantly larger than any I had seen before. He must have weighed more than my 200 pounds and was even an inch taller than me. He did not look happy.

"What the hell is this?" he demanded, looking past Victorio at me angrily. "It's 3:30 a.m. and you're singing karaoke!"

I looked at Victorio for defense, but everyone was watching me instead. "I, well..."

"Victorio said you'd wait till I got off at 4:00!"

When Bianca woke for her room service shift at 5:15, we were still singing.

6 *Great Whites*

"THE GREAT WHITE MUST MOVE OR DIE," ARIC SAID as he scanned the women sunbathing on the beach. His manner was indeed predatory. He kept his hand in his pocket the whole time, which I pretended not to notice.

"Pray tell," I grunted as I searched the straw for the last remnants of my local cocktail. We sat beneath palm trees that flanked the Groovy Grouper, my favorite bar in Montego Bay, Jamaica. The white sand here was incredibly fine and clung to my skin with a tenacity I had never before seen in sand. It was so brilliantly white that I thought perhaps the Jamaicans bleached it at night.

"My girlfriend signed off two weeks ago," he lamented. "And I have not had any action since then. None!"

"Mine leaves in one, so don't talk to me about it."

"My roommate had more action than me!" Aric lamented.

"*Your* roommate is the only fat Indonesian on earth! Sex with Bagus? Surely you jest."

I had learned only recently that everyone from the Indonesian island of Bali had a name that began with I (pronounced "ee"). All names were based upon what order you were born in and what caste you belonged to. There was Made and Wayan and others, but they ran out at Ketut. After a Ketut, they were all Ketuts, only nicknames told them apart. The rules applied to girls, too: their prefix was Ni. It was explained to me by I Made, who even drew a chart for the different castes. When I asked him about the frequent Indonesian name of Ida Bagus, he replied it was a higher caste and beholden to a whole new set of rules. We agreed to leave it at generalizations before my brain melted.

"If I don't move on, I will die," Aric continued as he continued to fumble in his pocket. My newest acquaintance onboard the *Conquest,* Aric was a small Belgian man with curly blond hair and baby blue eyes. His features were what the ladies would call cute. I enjoyed his company primarily because his English was so complete that I could let my vocabulary flow freely. Usually on ships I took pains to stick to simple words, understanding that for most of the crew English was their third language. I liked Aric, but if he continued to play with himself in public I was going to leave him.

"Oh, Brian," he cried, "Look at that one! I'm in love."

"Calm down. By comparison you make me look like a prude, and that's very uncomfortable."

"I haven't had a lunch off in three weeks, so I cannot afford to waste this opportunity."

"Well, there is a beach full of beauties sweating in the sun. Go get 'em, tiger."

"I go! Oh, no, wait a minute…"

He pulled from his pocket a bundle of condoms. Apparently he had been fondling them instead of, well, something else.

"Whew, for a minute I thought I didn't bring enough."

"Make me proud."

The beach was full of tropical luxury; brown skin on white sand was the specialty of the Groovy Grouper. Because crew members had free entry to the private beach, it was occupied almost exclusively by gorgeous European women. Yet the view did not end there by any means. Far across the restless bay loomed the *Conquest*, beyond which rose blue, mist-shrouded mountains. Montego Bay was a sprawling city surrounded by steamy lowlands that hugged the beaches around its namesake body of water. I was not impressed with Mo Bay as a city, but the area was a tropical paradise.

I puffed on my cigar and watched with concern as Aric downed another Red Stripe. On the table were five empty Red Stripe bottles and Aric's pile of condoms.

"You aren't going to get too drunk, are you? Red Stripe is strong beer."

"What, are you my mother?"

"I just don't want you to lose track of the time. We both work at two-thirty."

"Where you from? Oh my God! Look at that! Look at that! I am in love!"

"Which one this time? Oh, no, you don't mean..."

"Aha! The fat American!" Liezle greeted as she strode up with two of her paisanos.

"Aha! The fat Slovak!" I returned. "Melichka...?"

She shook her head with an affected sigh. "You still can't say 'thin' in Czech, can you? Stick to 'fat' in English. It suits you better."

Aric wasted no time in drooling over the new arrivals, and I certainly could not blame him. All three ladies were exceptionally attractive and wearing string bikinis. My favorite thing about European ladies was that they all wore thongs, as if it never even occurred to them that there was an alternative. I did nothing to correct such misconceptions.

"Ladies! Please join us."

They pulled up chairs, pointedly ignoring Aric's gesture for one to sit on his lap. They also pointedly ignored his pile of condoms, which he made no effort to hide.

"I was just going to the bar," I said. "May I bring you anything?"

A chorus of requests for fruity, blended girly drinks ensued, and it took me nearly fifteen minutes and thirty dollars to gather them all. I did not mind, other than being separated for so long from such beauty, because just being there was a delight. The heat was intense, but there was something magical about the salt in the air. The mountains far beyond the bay were washed with rain, and even *Conquest* was shadowed in purple hues. But at the Grouper it was sunny and splendid.

The five of us made the predictable small talk that young people do, especially when alcohol was mixed with such salacious men as ourselves. Aric went too far in his lustful advances, in my humble opinion. I consider myself a decidedly naughty man, but he was more a wannabe libertine. I regarded his statements with the same amusement in which normal people probably regarded me, which was usually going too far but somehow finding it non-offensive and even amusing. The ladies mercilessly toyed with him, revving him up and then ignoring him. It was almost painful to watch.

But real pain came when I realized what time it was.

"Aric!" I snapped suddenly as I glanced at his watch. "What time is it?"

"Uh...two."

"Two? We have to be at work at two-thirty!"

"Not me," he slurred. "I switched with someone. I'm working at three."

"Well thanks for telling me! Cat damn it: it takes thirty minutes to get to the ship!"

"Calm down," he sloppily soothed. "With such beauty as this present, how can you have harsh words?"

I stood up and plunked my cigar into his drink. "Ladies, I beg of you. Don't give this man an inch. He's not worth it!"

"What's an inch?"

"O.K., don't give him any centimeters," I corrected. "He doesn't deserve it! Now, let me borrow one of your bodies for a minute."

Three pairs of pretty eyes stared at me in shock. Aric whistled quietly with admiration.

"I simply meant that a Jamaican taxi driver will cross five lanes of traffic for bikinis like yours, and I am in dire straits."

"Dire whats?"

"Take the boat ferry," Liezle suggested. "See the big man on the beach with orange shorts? That's his boat. For five dollars he will take you right up to *Conquest*."

"I love you!" I blurted as I ran across the blazing-hot sand. Liezle's friends whooped at my words, but I was already running away.

Within moments I was waiting impatiently in a speedboat owned by a perfectly gorgeous Jamaican man. With a body half as defined as his I would have been a model! Despite this, his toenails arrested my attention. They were the most bizarre mix of broken, fragmentary, or simply missing nails I had ever witnessed. His right big toe looked like a yin-yang symbol: half was pink flesh, the other was thick nail. It was completely healed, however. I could only presume he had spent too many years walking barefoot over scalding hot sand.

Time slipped by with alarming speed, though he hardly noticed. I anxiously watched him haul on the anchor repeatedly, but he did not seem able to lift it.

"Hey, can we get going? I'm going to be late."

"Island time, mon," he said casually, abandoning the anchor yet again. "The island is goin' nowhere, mon."

"And neither are we! I have to get to work or I'm in big trouble. I'll pay you double if you get me there in fifteen minutes. Here, I'll get the damn anchor!"

I hauled on the anchor, which was only marginally difficult to move, and we were off. I assumed the man was high on marijuana (he definitely was, actually), and credited his ineffectiveness to that. Yet over the years I met many, many similarly buff Jamaican men who could not lift half as much as I. To my disgust, after ten years of humping weights religiously I still looked pathetic beside them! Genetically they were simply blessed with beauty.

Finally moving, we passed Jimmy Buffet's Margaritaville so

fast my sunglasses nearly blew off. I resolved to visit Margari-taville next. It was built upon a bluff with a waterslide dropping into the bay. They also had numerous floating tram-polines and climbing mountains. My favorite was a "bridge" between two trampolines. It was an inflatable tube perhaps a yard in diameter. With it wet and the revelers drunk, I saw no one make the crossing, but many tried.

Finally at 2:25 P.M. I rushed into my cabin. Miraculously I showered, shaved, dressed, and ran up eleven flights of stairs in six minutes. Literally. I was extremely proud of myself, but within another month such quick fixes would become the norm. When four hours of uninterrupted sleep is hard to come by, every single minute counted in a way most Americans could never understand. Indeed, I commonly set my alarm for five minutes before duty in the morning. I was never late.

Once a week my schedule evolved into twelve straight hours without even a single break. Jamaican afternoons I worked Lido from 2:30 until 5:30, then went straight into the dining room for dinner, followed by midnight buffet. I pride myself on my work ethic, but after say, ten hours, I usually feel a fifteen-minute break is justified. Yet all this was a small price to pay for a few hours free at that magical beach. Of course, my free time never coincided with Bianca's.

That evening not a single guest came in for dinner on my first seating. I was shocked! Guests have many choices for din-ing; they can enjoy room service, the Lido buffet, or perhaps the Supper Club. If the ship stayed late enough they could even dine ashore.

A quiet night in the dining room may sound like welcome relief, but in fact all these options proved dangerous for the waiters. Some 95 percent of their money came from tips, though the cruise lines don't want guests to know that. The cruise line courteously recommends the appropriate amount of gratuity, but neglects to mention it is the only money the waiters ever see. If the guests never ate in the dining room, or simply preferred room service, for example, they would withhold the tips. That meant no money for the waiter. The simple reality was that every now and then *every* waiter had his share of bad luck and slaved a full week for mere pennies.

With an unprecedented first seating off, I decided to have a drink in the crew bar because I knew it would be quiet. I ordered a beer and glanced through the nearly empty room. To my surprise, whom did I see there? Why the Great White himself, Aric, of course!

I approached Aric slowly, sensing something was wrong. Sitting in the darkest corner, he stared at something cupped in his hands. His face was entirely slack, but for the furrow across his brow. He was like a stunned child staring at his dead pet mouse, trying desperately to comprehend mortality.

"Uh, Aric?"

He said nothing.

"You're creeping me out, man. What'cha got there?"

I leaned in and saw he held his three unopened packages of condoms.

"No luck today, eh?"

"W-why?" he asked me pitifully. He looked at me with eyes pooling with confusion, now more like a dog who had been kicked and didn't understand why.

"We can't win every time."

"I was there," he droned with a faraway look in his eyes. "The land of beauty. It would make a mere mortal man cry, Brian. Cry! Do you understand?"

"Sure do."

"A...a *sea* of tanned skin," he suddenly animated melodramatically. "I dove in!"

"You sure did."

"I tried to dive in," he amended lamely, arms falling again to the table to the unused equipment. "The Great White..."

Only then did I notice what he was drinking. I had assumed he was drinking a large cola, but the odor of alcohol suddenly pierced the acrid smell of old smoke that hung in the crew bar.

"What are you drinking?"

"Double vodka and cokes. I didn't like the first, but now they are going down fast."

"Aric! What the hell are you doing? You have to work midnight buffet! Are you already drunk?"

"Don't worry," he slurred. "I will be there, boss."

"Aric, you know I'm not the only supervisor. I can't hide this from Hipolito! You'd better be there."

"I *was* there," he wailed. "The Great White swam to the land of beauty..."

"Yes, the land of beauty. How about I get you some coffee?"

He ignored me and caressed his condoms, lost in his own world.

Aric did arrive for midnight buffet. He was passed out in the break room when I arrived. I hurriedly checked in the other team waiters and then dealt with him. A few people lingered, hoping for some drama.

I slapped Aric awake and asked harshly, "Can you make it back to your cabin?"

"No, I'm not in my cabin," he whimpered.

"Aric, if you can make it back to your cabin I'll cover for you this one time. Are you able?"

"The Great White must move or die. I move."

"Yes. Swim to your cabin. There is a hot Slovak in there."

"Great...White...."

I wanted to follow him, but I was unable to leave the buffet. Late stays in port always meant busy midnight buffets because people skip dinner and play in port as long as they can. When they finally return, they devour the midnight buffet greedily.

Forty-five minutes later I found Aric passed out in the hallway below the break room. He lay on the metal deck with his head beside a thick metal door to the guest area. Had anyone come through that heavy door, Aric's head would have been hurting from far worse than a mere hangover. Because he was so droopy, six security guards were required to haul him away.

The phone ringing woke me up.

"Yes?"

"Are you ready?" a lady asked with a sexy accent. I blinked a moment and tried to clear my sleep-filled head. This wasn't still a dream...?

"Uh, ready?"

"Cabin change."

"What do you mean?"

"You not ready yet? We only have hour before check-in! What the hell you been doing?"

"I've been sleeping!" I retorted, suddenly very much awake. "I work midnight buffet. I only went to sleep three hours ago. What are you talking about?"

"Go to purser and get your new key," she snapped. "We have one hour to swap *cabinas*. Go!"

She hung up. Confused but awake, I trudged up to the purser's office and discovered that Bianca and I were, indeed, scheduled for a cabin change. Because we had been sharing a bathroom with two ladies for a whole month, which was not allowed, we were required to move. But Bianca was leaving in merely one more cruise, and I would be changing cabins anyway. Why would they upend our lives at this point?

I returned to the cabin to see two very attractive and very angry Czech women waiting outside my door. They immediately commenced their verbal abuse, barging into the cabin with me and throwing their suitcases on the bunks. Within a few minutes I was packed, but I had to gather Bianca's things.

They both stood in the cabin with their arms crossed beneath their breasts, staring at me with daggers for eyes. "This goddamn *cabina* is smaller!"

Bianca had lived in the cabin for several months before I arrived, and was dug in. Her two huge green suitcases, which she lovingly called her "frogs," were not actually large enough to hold all of her belongings. I shoved what I could in them and just hauled armloads of her clothing to the new cabin, all while under the sharp tongues of those women. My annoyance flared into anger, but I kept it in check.

"This place is mess! You *basura*! Why not your woman pack for you? Why not you check purser's board? *Bamboclat*, we have only half hour left!"

I had to reach beneath the bed for some of Bianca's shoes, disturbing a family of dust bunnies in the process. Having no broom, I had to scrounge up some paper towels to sweep them up. The witches just hovered over me and continued their verbal jabs. Finally I told them to either shut up or help out.

On my way out the door, one of the women threw a quarter at me.

"Hey, *babaloo*. Your tip," she snarled.

Finally Bianca returned to the cabin after her room service shift. Before she even said hello the two Czechs verbally blasted into her. Yet by the time Bianca arrived I had removed *everything* except her bathing scrungy-thing in the shower. The abuse was hurled at us both as we crossed the hall, and Bianca fired it right back. It was an ugly European bitch-session on deck A that morning.

Still swearing as only a sailor can, Bianca finally slammed our cabin door. She continued to spew venom at the injustice of it all as she dug through her disarrayed belongings. I stared at her, waiting for some sort of acknowledgment. I had not actually seen her awake in nearly two weeks.

"I'm leaving in a week, the blood clots!" she muttered to herself. "One week! Why they give me such a hard time?"

I quietly locked the door and walked up in front of her. She gazed at me as if surprised I was even there. I firmly pressed my finger to her lips. Her eyes went wide with surprise as I spoke to her with smoldering calm.

"You will not complain. I have moved everything of yours, your frogs, all your clothes and all your shoes and all the other crap you had beneath the bed. I got only three hours of sleep and did all of this while you were gone. I spent an hour under the constant abuse of those two bitchy Czech women. You did nothing. You will not complain about it. I have not seen you in two weeks, and I will not listen to you bitch about something that you weren't even here for. Am I clear?"

She nodded, staring at me with huge eyes, speechless. This was the first cross word I had ever had with her. My frustration with our situation had been brewing for some time, and this eased the pressure.

But with only one week left, it was soon to completely erupt.

7 *Dining on Ashes*

I WATCHED ROBERTINO WITH INCREDULITY AS WE WAITED between sittings in the pantry of the Monet dining room. He had hidden no less than three entrees in the corner service area. Before my very eyes he devoured three courses of lamb in less than two minutes.

"Robertino, you eat like an American," his assistant Rasa said with disgust.

"Play nice," I chided.

The three of us constantly teased each other. Our stations bordered each other in the upstairs corner, and we shared our limited supplies and pantry space communally. My team waitress Svetlana was a sweet girl from the countryside of Lithuania. She was the very image of a shy, innocent peasant girl in her apron and two thick, blonde braids. Svetlana rarely spoke, and was clearly overwhelmed by ship life. My self-assigned duty had been to make her laugh since I became her head waiter. I had yet to succeed.

But our neighbors were the truly interesting ones. Robertino was short for a Croatian, being only a few inches above six feet. His shoulders were immense and thick from the weight of war. He had a sharply pointed nose and chin, and the laugh lines that defined them twitched when he smiled. His eyes were sunken and purple, though that was common enough among waiters.

Though he was quick with a laugh and very kind, I sensed Robertino was an exceptionally dangerous man. Over several weeks I had coaxed out of him his role in the Croatian war. He had been a sniper. He had stopped counting how many men he had killed after the first ten because it was pointless. His stories helped me understand his occasional lapses into inexplicable rage.

Rasa, his team waitress, was the perfect partner for him. Her features and personality were beautiful, bold, and strong. She wore long, naturally platinum hair usually wrapped into a European-style bun. Rasa had a voluptuous figure that turned every head in the room. Women were jealous of her and men were in awe of her. She had a wide smile with absolutely perfect teeth.

"So, Brian," Robertino continued as he gulped more food. "You're American. How many guns do you have?"

"I beg your pardon? I don't like guns."

"Sure you do. All Americans have a gun."

"Why do you say that?"

"Everyone knows it. You all shoot each other every day. I would be safer in Afghanistan than in L.A. There are more guns in American suburbs than in all Croatia during the war."

"Well, I don't know about that. Not all Americans have a gun."

"That is lie," he pressed. "You really don't have gun? You've never fired one?"

"Well, yeah, I've fired one. Dad used to go hunting for pheasant and stuff. He's got a shotgun and some old .22s."

Rasa suddenly butted in. "I thought you said you don't have any guns."

"I—I guess we do. Yeah, O.K. I guess we have five guns."

"*Five*?" Svetlana asked incredulously. "You have *five* guns and didn't think you had *any*? How many guns do you need to own before you can say you like them? The United States really is as dangerous as they say."

"Now hold it. Two are antique black powder rifles that probably can't be fired with modern powder anyway. The .22s are just little guns, you know, for shooting bottles and fun stuff like that. But Dad's shotgun is nice."

"You sure know a lot about guns."

"I don't know anything about guns!" I protested.

"You are such a liar," Rasa pressed. "You say you don't know anything, but you know the powder is different and you shoot things for fun."

"I am *not* a liar," I defended. "None of them have been fired in ten years!"

"You also say you are faithful to your girlfriend," Rasa slyly added, her eyes flashing. "Are you lying about that, too?"

"Whatever," Robertino dismissed. "Guns are great. I remember after the war I was driving my car and this Italian bastard hit me from behind. The whole back crushed, and he yelled at *me*! I grabbed my pistol from under seat, cocked it, and got out of car. One minute later I drive new Peugeot."

"You've got to be joking!"

"Bah," he scoffed. "It was war. You Americans love war, but none have seen it. Lucky you. Really, what he do if I take his car? You think he wants to mess with me?"

Definitely not, I thought.

Robertino wolfed down the last of his third plate of food and disposed of the evidence. I always marveled at the variety and audacity of the meals that were pinched by the waiters. The reality of ship life was that waiters always missed eating dinner because they had to be in the dining room protecting their station from theft. But after serving the guests, and as soon as the management was not looking, every waiter produced a stolen entrée. Such behavior was largely overlooked by management. The blind eye only became focused upon those who otherwise deserved a reprimand but no other excuse could be found, or those who pinched items that were running low. Management was courteously very clear about which entrees were taboo on which nights.

"I don't bitch about Americans like others," Robertino said. "All these Europeans, they would eat same if they could. Look at me! Americans are fat because they can be."

"Not all Americans are fat," Rasa retorted, eyeing me up and down in much the same way Robertino regarded his lamb.

"Say, you want?" Robertino asked me. "You never eat. How you so strong without eating? Second seating, I get you lamb."

"No, that's all right."

"Beef! Americans only eat beef, no?"

"No, really, I can't. I will be management soon, and I have to behave. But it does look delicious."

"If you think that is delicious," Rasa said, looking me straight in the eye, "You should try the Baltic dessert."

Silence reigned and we all stared at each other awkwardly. Suddenly Robertino slapped me roughly on the back with a guffaw. "Ai yai yai! You Americans have everything! You have girlfriend on board, and now *this* woman? If it were me, I would go straight to *cabina* now! To hell with second seating!"

In fact, Rasa was not the only attractive woman making propositions. To my infinite appreciation, it had become a nightly occurrence. I constantly reminded my swelling ego that it was merely from ladies seeking green cards.

While working midnight buffet that night I was accosted by two dazzling but absurdly young guests. They were slender and dressed in jeans somehow shredded to reveal just the right hints of their curves. They both wore halter tops that provided ample evidence that they weren't *that* young. Their faces were completely powdered-over to cover the dread of youth: acne.

"Hello," the brunette asked, nudging the blonde with her elbow. "We have a question for you."

I walked over to them and waited for the question. A tongue-tied pause commenced, but was finally broken by Brunette, who was disappointed Blonde had not spoken.

"Where are you from?"

"I'm from Reno. Divorce capital of the world!"

"But you have an accent!"

I chuckled. "Yeah, I developed it on the ships. I guess I picked up bits and pieces of all the accents here. I roll my *r*'s when around Europeans, for example, and enunciate differently around the Asians. I can't help it. So, how about you girls?"

"We just moved to Tampa. We are going to the University of Tampa starting summer."

"I see. This is a graduation cruise, then?"

"Yes. It's just us, you know," she blurted. "Not our families or anything. We're eighteen!"

Brunette left another opening for Blonde, but she was too shy to take the bait. Eventually Brunette continued, "What brought you to the cruise ship?"

"I followed my girlfriend."

"Oh," said Brunette. Blonde looked down with obvious disappointment. "That answers our question, then."

I smiled kindly at them. They were adorable. Brunette nudged Blonde one last time, and she finally spoke up. "You are welcome to join us for a party in our cabin later."

"Thank you, ladies, but I work until almost 3 A.M."

"Oh, that's no problem!" Blonde tentatively reached for my hand. Obligingly I gave it to her and she wrote a cabin number on my palm. Then they fled.

Half an hour later an eye-catching black woman in her thirties approached me from the pool. While still dripping wet in her one-piece and with no towel, she asked to borrow my pen. Confused, I handed it to her. She immediately grabbed my left hand.

"You are *so* cute," she said with a wink. She wrote her cabin number above the other one already on my palm. "If you want someone with more experience than those two girls, drop on by."

That night I lay back in the lounge chair and blew my cigar smoke at the stars. The hour was 3 A.M., and I was finally able to relax. It was a hot, humid night, but the sea breeze was refreshing. The crash of the bow through the waves was loud yet soothing, much like the surf crashing against a shore. The night was mostly dark and moonless. There was no one else on the open deck because everyone wanted to rest up for the port day tomorrow. I was alone for the first time in a long, long while.

I had felt the need to reflect. With such a hectic life, it was extremely difficult to find the time to do so. Most free time was allocated to sleeping or frenzied entertainment. For the first time since I had joined the ships, I pondered the question I had parried for so long: Was I crazy or just stupid?

I had been beset by women all day. Rasa's advances were becoming more frequent and more aggressive, not to mention other team waitresses. I had an open invitation for action from a very sexy Hungarian hostess, and I couldn't even consider all the guests' summons. I was living with my girlfriend who I had chased halfway across the planet. But it was Liezle who had identified my ironic problem.

I was lonely.

Liezle had seen it because she was in the same situation. Her "boyfriend" on *Conquest* had turned out to be very nice and very funny...and very flat in bed. So she, too, was not getting the physical comfort she needed. The ship environment was so incredibly cold that the need for contact was very real, sexual or otherwise. Since sex was so much easier to come by than true affection, it was the preferred quick fix. But I didn't want a band-aid, I wanted a cure.

I felt farther away from Bianca than ever before. She had

the appearance of being a wild and free party animal, but in fact she was deeply traditional. She accepted little romance in the horrid, artificial conditions of a ship. I could hardly blame her. Finding the mood in a tiny bunk you shared with your luggage was difficult at best, and when you had only fifteen minutes, what's the point? Had we not already experienced such a torrid, fanatical love affair across three continents, I would have thought I had completely misunderstood my relationship with this woman.

What was I doing wrong? Every way I looked at it, I could only fault her. But life was a two-way street. I must be over-looking something. I tried to look at our situation from the outside, but I just couldn't figure it out. The environment was so harsh here, and I desperately wanted to bring some warmth into it. Bianca obviously needed it as much as I did, but why wouldn't she allow it?

Surely she wasn't upset at my relationship with Liezle. She *had* to know me too well to think we were having an affair. No, I feared it was the opposite, that I was too honest. Per-haps Bianca understood better the coarse machismo of the men in her society. Her best friend, Flaviu, came to my mind. He thought I was a gay-loving wimp, while I thought he was a petty Neanderthal. Bianca was used to men being bullies, cheating on their women and fighting the world. Was she con-fused, or even turned off, by a man who was comfortable with his existence?

She had once commented that I was naïve because I never had to fight so hard for things like the others on board. My citizenship took care of me, they all kept saying. I lived in a land of milk and honey, where everyone was rich and you only had to worry because everyone had a gun. It was true that I had never risked starvation because my nation lacked food or opportunity. Yet I had my story, too. In just the last six months my partner had shattered our company and forced it into bankruptcy, my wife had left me, I was broke, jobless, and *then* my bank took my car to pay for my ex-wife's bad debts!

Frustrated, I got up and paced the open deck. The lights of the Mexican coast glowed low on the horizon from the city of Playa del Carmen. I thought it strange how intensely orange the lights of Playa were, while just ten miles away on Isla de Cozumel they were white. But I discarded such trifling thoughts for the heavy words of Oscar Wilde: "Men marry because they are tired, women because they are curious. Both are disappointed."

Is that what happened here? Was I simply tired of dealing with women problems I was familiar with, and seeking something foreign in the hope it was better? Was she just curious about life with a man who considered women equal and not really serious about our relationship?

Certainly we were both disappointed.

The hot Mexican sun baked me, but I was steaming for another reason entirely. I had fought with Bianca for this last port day alone together, but she had denied me. She insisted on lunch with all of her paisanos at everyone's favorite restaurant, La Ceiba. They had all laughed at jokes in Romanian over lunch, none of which I could translate. My only company was the octopus ceviche.

After lunch the group split asunder, and I had barely managed to carry Bianca off for a little personal time. We lay in the sun but said little. Now that she was alone with me she was quiet, as if she had used up her allotted laughter over lunch.

"Do you still want me to go to Romania in June?" I asked her. We had made arrangements long ago to coincide our time off together. But I had spoken with her so little lately that I didn't know if I really wanted to go or not. How ironic! The only thing on this sweatshop ship I didn't enjoy was being with her! I had felt far more love and affection from our e-mails when we were apart. I actually wished to be transferred to another ship so the e-mails could continue!

She did not immediately answer. She was saved the trouble when Flaviu and his girlfriend arrived. Suddenly all smiles, she invited them to join us. Within moments they were all jabbering in Romanian and laughing. I abruptly rose and packed my beach bag.

"You're leaving?" Bianca asked, surprised.

"Yes," I snapped. "I'm tired. I'll see you later."

Finally sensing my annoyance, Bianca hastily gathered her towel and struggled to keep pace with me as I stormed back to *Conquest*. We said nothing as security scanned our bags and patted us down. Once in the cabin, Bianca asked me what the matter was.

"What the hell do you think?" I demanded, finally venting my frustrations. "I never see you. I don't know why I am here. I get more attention from everyone else onboard. I know enough Romanian to understand how your friends all refer to Liezle as 'that bitch' because they think she is moving in on your turf. And why the hell not? I see her more than I see you, and we live together!"

"What does that mean? You haven't…?"

"No I haven't, though perhaps I should have! I see you only a few minutes a day, and I won't even bring up how pissed off I get in the crew bar. You never laugh anymore around me, but then your Romanian friends come and you are all happiness. I mean, what the hell was this afternoon? This is our *last* port of our *last* week. I won't see you for over a month, and you want to hang out with Flaviu and his girlfriend-for-a-day. People always ask me if I'm crazy or stupid for being on the ships, and the answer is obviously stupid!"

The phone suddenly rang. Bianca fairly leapt on it. It was a paisano of hers.

Cut off and exasperated, I jumped into the shower. When I got out, Bianca was napping in her bunk, as if she had no care in the world.

That night at dinner my team waiter was sick and there was no last-minute replacement. Considering the sheer pandemonium of the average dinner with a team of two, I was completely behind all night. Because *Conquest* remained in Cozumel late, my first seating was only half full and I muddled through mostly unscathed. But second seating was packed, and I was hopelessly crushed beneath the weight of the orders. By the time I finished dinner, I was too angry at fate to be tired.

I only had a few minutes before I had to work midnight buffet, and I cruised by Bianca's station to see if she would care to chat. She was decidedly neutral about it, and I departed in a huff.

At the midnight buffet I fumed. I tried my best to put on the happy face for the guests and my team, but Liezle saw right through it. She asked me if there was anything she could do.

"Yeah," I said suddenly. "Tell Hipolito that I'll be back in half an hour."

I rushed down the ten flights of stairs to the I-95 and happened to catch Bianca as she and a friend were heading into the crew bar. I grabbed her arm and told her we needed to talk. I began pulling her toward our cabin and she asked roughly, "Where are we going?"

"I want to talk alone. No interruptions this time."

"Well, let's get a corner in the bar so I can smoke."

"Fine. Bring a full pack."

Settling into the dark, I interrogated her point-blank.

"What is going on in your mind? I don't want to make any assumptions about anything, and I don't want to be disappointed this June in Romania. Was this all a bad mistake? Do you really think it could possibly be the way it was before you ignored me here on *Conquest*?"

"Yes," she answered shortly, "in Romania."

"In Romania," I repeated.

"Not here. I felt my grumpiness beginning just before you arrived. I was worried this would happen with us."

"Oh, that's nice. Thanks for the warning," I said, mocking her. "'Honey, change your life entirely and work like a slave, and maybe there's a small chance I won't turn into an ice queen.' I really am stupid."

"I'm sorry," she whispered. "I know I'm different on the ships. It's the ships! I turn off all emotion here. It's how I survive. I hate the ships and the life so much, and happiness just doesn't belong here. I even yelled at Viorica this morning because she's in love with Adrien and they are so happy and bubbly. And you! You are always happy! *Always*! I hate that!"

I stared at her for a moment, incredulous. "*You* are mad at *me?* Because I am happy? What the hell is that?"

"You are always so patient and understanding with me, and you never lose your sense of humor. How can you never let anything make you mad?"

"Who says I don't?"

"Come to Romania. It's all planned already, let me make it up to you there. Let's rekindle the magic! It was so amazing how we met, our trip to Egypt, please don't let this be the end. Though I...I wouldn't blame you."

I sighed. "I don't want it to be the end, either, but this is absurd."

"Come to Romania and let's forget these ten weeks ever happened. It will be your thirtieth birthday. I'll take you to the Black Sea."

I looked at her, torn. She was saying exactly what I wanted to hear, but was I just being foolish? I did want to go to Romania, I did want to find what he had before. Was it possible? I knew there was only one way to find out.

"Deal."

8 *The Slings and Arrows of Outrageous Assumption*

AT THE END OF A SUCCESSFUL EIGHT-MONTH CONTRACT of working seven days a week without a single day off, there was no "thank you" or "job well done." Instead Carnival forced employees to work breakfast or lunch right up until the minute their bus left the terminal.

Breakfasts in home ports were always the most trying as guests lost all pretense of civility in their effort to squeeze every last penny out of their vacation. Between these up-to-the-last servings, getting luggage to security, moving out of the cabin, having it checked by the supervisor, and immigration procedures, Bianca's and my goodbye was exceptionally short.

I moved to a new cabin that happily offered an extra four square inches of floor space. My new roommate Omar came from the same situation as me, his Romanian girlfriend had also signed off. Unlike me, however, he didn't let that bother him. Omar was an insanely handsome black Moroccan. He never spent a single night in our cabin, but instead found a different companion each night. I was indeed jealous, for he was a quad-lingual, world-class diver with six-pack abs. Next to him I looked like a bleached sack of potatoes.

Surprisingly enough, the biggest change for me was not the new roommate or the lack of a girlfriend, but leaving midnight buffet. I was assigned to work the dining room for breakfast and lunch every day, and I simply knew I would hate it. None of my foreign companions could understand my deep aversion to it. I hated all things about it, from the open seating, to the overwhelming individuality of the orders, to the Pancake Darwinism. Some deep chord in my soul was offended at having to serve breakfast; though ironically my ego had no qualms with sorting garbage and doing dishes. I was simply "too good" to sling hash. I knew somewhere in my gut that if I were ever to break on the ships, it would be because of breakfast or lunch. I since learned that my gut was never wrong.

Open seating on ships was very different from on land, and was thrust upon the guests, whether they liked it or not. Every seat was systematically filled in order, regardless of who sat in it. The host began at the first chair of the first table and then snaked around to fill every seat before moving on to the next table. There were no exceptions; reservations were not allowed nor were private tables. Half the guests hated it and half loved it.

Such a division applied to the waiters as well. Some at the end of the dining room never had guests at all. If any guests did get seated, they came at the very last moment and stayed well into a waiter's nap time. But for the first few sections, waiters got walloped with a full section instantly.

The worst of luck was being assigned the first station on my first breakfast. All head waiters were assigned dining room breakfast and lunch, while the team waiters all worked the Lido buffets. Sections varied daily, though head waiters usually worked with the same companion. The partnerships were another of management's ways to fix waiters causing dramas. A problematic waiter would find himself partnered with the laziest *mamagayo* available.

My partner was mercifully a friend of Bianca's named Regina. Had it not been for the Romanian mafia, I would doubtless have jumped overboard. Regina was a typical Romanian woman, being petite with black hair, extremely slender, and pretty. She was from the Black Sea coast.

"This happens fast," Regina instructed. "You need to be ready. You might as well fill their water glasses before they arrive. People are impatient for breakfast, so here's how it works:

"When they sit, I take their orders. You don't know the menu anyway. You serve coffee, juice; give bread, rolls, croissants, and Danish. If they order milk you run for it. If they order *rasclat* hot tea you run for it. If they order *bamboclat* pineapple juice, or tomato, or prune, you run for it. If they *basura* and order bagel you run for it...*and* wait for it to be double-toasted. It will take you twenty minutes to get everything everyone wants, but I will have their orders in five."

"Lovely."

"The mafia will help you. No two Rambos in the world can handle sixteen Americans for breakfast. Most easy people go buffet. All *basura* guests onboard come to dining room to give us hard time. It is American rule taught in schools or something."

"Lovely."

"Oh, and don't clean any table until I say. If you reset tables too fast, they seat them twice and *mamagayos* in the back don't serve anyone. With luck we have a forty-five minute break between breakfast and lunch, but only sometimes. So in morning prepare for two back-to-back shifts. Today I go kitchen for hot food because it's hard time."

"I love you."

"Wait in line, Romeo. Then again, now that Bianca is gone, let's go."

Despite Regina's warning, I was stunned at the flood of hungry humanity that rushed in. Romanians buzzed around our section like bees, but even with an additional half-dozen helpers we were completely overwhelmed by the demands. Every guest insisted on a level of personal attention that was simply impossible to provide. They demanded only the muffins I ran out of, or spontaneously tried pineapple juice only if I had orange juice ready. If I was lucky to actually have the cold cereal they requested on hand, invariably they asked for soy milk. It was a disaster.

The Romanians worked together like a dream. They had been doing such tasks seven days a week for months. My appreciation of their clique went up a notch, and I was incredibly grateful to have been included in their mafia.

The next morning I discovered the true depths of Pancake Darwinism. Because I was the first waiter, I should have had a minute of peace to request my order from the chefs. However, within thirty seconds the others had already caught up.

"Hi, chef," I began. "I need, uh, six orders of eggs over-easy, two with pancakes, one with bacon, one with pancakes *and* bacon, two with sausage and bacon, and one with pancakes, sausage, bacon, *and* hash browns. I need two orders of eggs over-hard with pancakes and sausage, and…"

"Hey, new boy, out of my way," interrupted another waiter. He bellowed, "SIX OVER-HARD, PANCAKES, BACON, BROWNS! Let's go!"

"Filipino," an Indian waiter chided. "Leave the guy alone. Chef, ignore him *and* the American. Help a paisano. Give me four scrambled, two with browns, four with…."

"*Rasclat*, get your hands off my pancakes!"

"*Absolutely*!"

"Those are my hash browns, you bastard! I also need four scrambled, two with bacon, one with sausage, and one with browns."

"F**k you! Chef, are those my hash browns?"

"Kiss my ass, Euro-boy. Colonize elsewhere!"

"Hey, why are you giving him *my* eggs?" I asked. "America never colonized anybody."

"No, but you bomb everybody. Pinch my oil but not my eggs. What *bamboclat* pinched my over-easies? Chef, lay those eggs faster!"

"Do I look like a chicken to you? You know any black chickens, motherf**ker?"

"Get your f**king jelly off my tray, *basura*!"

"How do you say chicken in your white-monkey language?"

"F*** you!"

"No, f**k you!"

"F**k you both. Where are my sausages? No, not the f**king links, the f**king patties, blood clot!"

At that point everyone dropped civility and the language turned truly ugly.

Sounds of passion bombarded me while my friend Calypso searched through her cluttered desk for a wine opener. If it were truly hiding among the dozens of bottles of perfume, conditioners, lotions, and lubricants, I would have plenty of time to watch the show in the nearby bunks. Both bunks in her cabin were curtained and obviously occupied. Arms and legs pressed against the nylon to create a bizarre image, like tormented souls clawing out from some primordial torture.

"Will you hurry up?" I chided. "You're a team waitress. You should always have a wine opener."

"Shut up," she snipped. "You are a head waiter and you don't have one."

"Yeah, well that's because I'm a bad person. You're not."

"We just met. How do you know?"

"Well, the bathroom stall said you were good."

She chuckled and turned to give me one of her massive smiles. "Voilá! The wine opener!" Calypso was a short woman with dirty-blond hair, a mass of freckles, and a huge mouth with big, perfect teeth. The moans from the lower bunk pulled my attention back to the show. The curtains shimmied in their own dance.

"Say, if your roommate is in one bunk and you are here, who's in the other bunk?"

"I don't know," she said. "It could be anyone."

"Do you always let strangers have sex in your cabin?"

"Let's find out, shall we?"

Before I could stop her, she reached over to the top bunk and stuck her head between the curtains. "Who's in here? Oh, Saskia, hello. I don't know you, sir, but have fun."

Suddenly it was my turn to chuckle. *That* took guts! "So was that your bunk or your roommate's?"

"Oh, that was Rhonetta's. I don't let strangers shag in my bed. Rhonetta knows that when she throws a party she gets my bunk."

"How thoughtful."

"Yes," she said with a big smile. After a moment she eyed me shrewdly. "Shall we?"

"Shall we what?"

"Hit the sack!"

"Absolutely!"

We stepped out of her very-occupied cabin and into the quiet hallway. Calypso's cabin was in a very unusual location on deck A. It was in a cul-de-sac that ended in a wide emergency staircase to the open deck. Because it was a dead-end there was no foot traffic and was therefore extremely private after hours. Certainly more private than her cabin!

With my new schedule, I frequently found myself free after dinner for a much-needed drink, but was loath to spend the time in the crew bar. Calypso was formerly one of my team waitresses from midnight buffet who had also switched schedules. We found we shared the distaste for the bar but a desire for a drink.

We both enjoyed a level of conversation that was difficult to find onboard due to a lack of native English speakers. Even the Great White Aric had a pale conversation compared to Calypso. She, being white South African, was also a native English speaker and well read. With Bianca gone, Calypso was probably the smartest woman onboard.

"Say," I asked her. "Why are you named after a Greek

Goddess? You're from Africa. That can't be real. What, is your real name Beulah or something?"

Calypso stared at me in surprise. "I have been onboard four months, and you are the first American who has actually read *The Odyssey*. My father is from Greece. Since most names in the West have Greek origins, he had to look hard to find something uniquely Greek. Who would have thought I would end up in the Caribbean, where Calypso has a whole different meaning?"

"Interesting."

"So, you are going to Romania, Lothario?"

"Yeah, we'll give it one last hurrah."

"Or perhaps a new beginning. That's cool. Don't judge her too harshly, ships are hard. None of us are our usual selves. On land I look just like Nicole Kidman."

We uncorked our white wine and poured it into red wine glasses. Whites were difficult to pinch because they were in higher demand from the guests. We sat upon the stairs and listened to the waves strike the hull outside. Usually A deck was silent to sounds from outside, but the cul-de-sac was close to the bow where the deck tapered in to bring in the sound.

"So, are you going to shag anyone until then? You have a month of free reign."

"No, I don't think so."

"Sounds to me like you're free to do so."

"Oh, I am, I guess. We parted badly enough to implement a 'don't ask, don't tell' policy. But I don't want to. Well, maybe Rasa. No, I'm still crazy for my woman. It didn't work, but I want to try again. I love the ladies, don't get me wrong, but I still am nuts about that one. I mean, I followed her from North America to Europe to Africa within one month of meeting her!"

"Lucky girl. Cheers!"

Calypso and Rhonetta were both wannabe hippies, revealed by their tie-dyed clothing, beads, flowers, and style of eyeglasses. Though I did not practice free love, I did relish free thinking, so we got along fabulously. Calypso and I became best friends on board, and managed to meet most mornings for a coffee. She referred to me as her "coffee mate."

The social aspects of ship life were sometimes painfully similar to that of high school. We suffered the slings and arrows of outrageous assumption because if we spoke to each other, we were "obviously" sleeping together. While such childish rumors ordinarily did not concern me, I was unnerved by the Romanians watching me through narrowed eyes. Who knew what bizarre lies they were sending to Bianca?

The first crew party on *Conquest* that I was able to attend occurred one week after Bianca left. Because I had always worked midnight buffet, the party usually wound down by the time I got off work. Carnival was diligent about providing recreation for its crew, whether licentious or benign. They had more crew bingo and ping pong tables than any other cruise line I subsequently worked with, and certainly more parties. As a rule they had at least one all-out bash a month, usually two.

On *Conquest*, management closed off the pool deck for a party once a month, keeping the pizza stand and grill open. The previous month, everyone on the dance floor had spontaneously jumped into the pool at 2 A.M., causing a terrible mess throughout the entire Lido deck. We had worked extra late to clean up and had missed even the after-parties.

This crew party, however, was at Alfred's. This was a large, beautiful guest lounge that boasted a well-stocked bar with premium liquors (which the crew bar did not) and a labyrinth of booths, loveseats, and dark corners. It was extremely loud and only moderately smoky. It was also packed with reveling crew members of all types.

Carnival hired more women than probably any other cruise line, most of whom were European. This became relevant during the crew parties, where all roads pointed to the Europeans. The men from East Asia and the Caribbean tended to dress down at parties, but the Indians and the Europeans were very flashy. The ladies dressed to kill, and the sexual heat in the room was powerful indeed.

The sound system was excellent and the selection of music was culturally varied, uniformly thumping and painfully loud. The dance music from all the different cultures fascinated me, and I discovered firsthand that music truly transcended all borders. I smiled when I recognized Romanian pop songs.

As I stood in a corner and screamed a conversation with Robertino, Rasa slid through the crowd toward us. She wore tight jeans and a spandex red top with crazy patterns of holes designed to optimize her magnificent cleavage. Her platinum hair was loose and fell around her shoulders. In a word, she looked unbelievably, extraordinarily, and astoundingly sexy. She had a bottle of white wine and two glasses and looked suggestively at me.

If I wanted to remain celibate, I was in trouble.

If I *didn't* want to remain celibate, I was *really* in trouble!

"Hi Brian," she said into my ear. My skin tingled where her breath touched my neck. "Open deck?"

The open deck was an important area for the crew, being the only real access to nature allowed. We lived in an area of artificial air below the waterline where the constant air conditioning fairly ruined our sinuses. I fought to breathe in some natural air for at least ten minutes every few days, whereas Bianca's solution, like most crew, had been to smoke an extra cigarette.

The metal deck was also used for sunbathing. Two dozen reclining lounge chairs were available and quietly fought for, though usually only the white crew were interested in a tan. Generally every race wanted what it didn't have. Whites wanted darker skin and respected tans, while the blacks and browns wanted to be lighter and therefore avoided the sun. Invariably everyone fell asleep within minutes of lying down. Those without a wristwatch gently woke neighbors to ask them to set their alarms for them.

Of course, the entire open deck was directly beneath the bridge. The lustful Italian officers dutifully kept their vigilance on the waters *and* the women. I don't know how many pairs of binoculars were on the bridge, but I spotted several spying the thong bikinis below. On more than one occasion my lady friends were informed by a low-ranking officer that the chief officer or even the captain "noticed them around the ship" and sought a private social encounter. While Bianca had laughed at such an advance, Liezle's cheeks burned red when she was accosted in such a manner.

But the real function of the open deck was not for sun, bikinis, or even simply fresh air. It was for anonymity. If a couple did not care for sexual contact in a crowded cabin, it was not uncommon to seek the darkness of the open deck.

Rasa and I left Alfred's and navigated our way through deck four to the backstage of the main lounge, then finally through the management's cabin area. One more hall later and we saw a massive weatherproof door ajar. Beyond it was nothing but darkness. My eyes slowly adjusted to the starlight and I saw the expanse of the open deck was littered with scattered clumps of affectionate couples. Murmurs in half a dozen languages cut through the night.

"Too late," I said to Rasa finally. "I think it's a full house."

"We can take this to your cabin."

"The night is gorgeous! Look, we could sit on that bin over there."

"Or we could take this to *my* cabin."

"Next time, darlin', O.K.?"

"I'll remember you said that."

We sat on the bins that held extra life jackets. Over the next half hour we enjoyed the aggressive tug of the wind and listened to the waves crashing far below. The sounds of romance reminded us that we were not alone. I ignored the many opportunities she allowed for me to make a move. I inwardly pondered why I had joined her, knowing full well what she intended. It was unimaginable for me, or probably any heterosexual male, to resist such an invitation.

Realistically, Bianca had probably already heard from a dozen Romanians that I was "sleeping" with Calypso. Why *not* sleep with Rasa? If I was to serve the sentence, I should at least have done the crime. But I decided that it was not what I wanted.

"Oh," she said after we heard a particularly loud groan. "Did you hear that?"

"How could I not?"

"Sounded nice, didn't it? Care to join the orchestra?"

"You're killing me, Rasa."

"Say, let's go to my *cabina*. I need to grab something."

"Grab it for me, too, will you?"

I winced as soon as I said it, knowing it was too flirtatious.

"That's it!" she cried, and leaned over to kiss me. Half laughing at my own foolishness, I struggled to free myself.

"Look, Rasa, wait! I have a girlfriend!"

"What, the one you never saw? She's not here. I am. What's your problem, anyway? It's obvious you are lonely."

"Yeah, but...I don't know. I'm nuts for this girl, what we had."

"*Had* being the key word. Jesus, Brian. Forget it. Let's just drink."

We drank the wine and finally relaxed, laughing over silly jokes and still flirting harmlessly. As time moved on, the dark shapes began to disperse and we moved onto the reclining chairs. The caress of the sea breeze and the gentle rush of the waves was extremely relaxing, and with the alcohol swimming through our bodies, we both fell asleep sometime after 4 A.M.

"Have a nice sleep?" A voice cut through my haze of dreams. I woke with a start and was shocked to see sunlight all around me. Heat blasted me and I was completely disoriented.

"Wha—?"

On the reclining chair beside me, Rasa stretched like a cat in a patch of sunlight. Empty wine bottles gently rolled back and forth on the metal deck between us, and we both reeked of smoke and alcohol. Half a dozen Indonesians stared with amusement, each grinning like the Cheshire cat. They wore their life jackets and hugged the walls in an effort to evade the hot sun.

"Boat drill!" the man boomed with enthusiasm.

"Boat drill? Wha— what time is it?"

"It's 7 A.M.!" an Indian cook answered, approaching. He was the raft leader for section. "You both have about four minutes to get your life jackets and get to your muster stations."

Sharing an embarrassed smile with Rasa, who was positively mute at this early hour, we both pulled our sleep-thickened bodies up and ran to our cabins. I was actually pleased, however. If there had not been a boat drill, we would have both missed our breakfast shifts in thirty minutes.

9 *Stripping in the Dining Room*

AN HAD ARRANGED FOR ME TO MEET THE FOOD and beverage manager. This man was powerful indeed, because he was responsible for the entire operations of the kitchens and all the dining rooms and lounges, not to forget the heavy burden of dealing with the tons of food daily left unconsumed.

While cruise ships enjoy teasing the public about the overwhelming amount of food they consume, the reality was that most food was thrown into the sea. Americans in particular demand their buffets to be fully stocked at every moment. Each guest must feel as if first in line, even if the buffet closes in two minutes. Therefore at the end of every shift a full buffet is discarded.

I thought my meeting with the F&B manager went well. We discussed my schedule upon returning in three weeks from my break to Romania. I was to be assigned to the Renoir dining room as an assistant maitre d' in the evenings. He felt it was a logical place to utilize my skills as a congenial American host. For breakfast and lunch I was to run the Lido deck, which would expand upon my limited buffet supervision.

So finally the last week of my training as a waiter arrived. I fairly floated through life, happy as could be. I had discovered much about the world and a little about myself in those three months. Certainly I had learned how to make a home, perhaps even thrive, in a very foreign environment.

In seven short days I was to travel to Romania. Had things remained with Bianca as they were on the ship, I would have cancelled it. However, as soon as Bianca left the ship I noticed a resurgence of the vibrant woman I had first met, the one who lured me through three continents in three months. Her long e-mails and short phone calls were what I had longed for in person while on the ship. Even if I was making a mistake, I was excited about a few weeks in Transylvania and to celebrate my thirtieth birthday on the Black Sea coast.

My final week's first seating in the dining room was surprisingly light, for which I was grateful. I did not care if I made less money due to the lack of paying guests, preferring to focus on the lack of stress. But my jaw dropped when I saw the second seating: twenty co-eds who had just graduated from college. They were all twenty-two years old, brainy, and absolutely gorgeous. These women wanted to party and indulge in every aspect of the Fun Ships they could. Such maximization invariably included lethal flirting with their waiter.

Yes, I was in heaven.

At the end of the first night, while the dining room emptied of guests, my ladies remained longer than most. They observed that I was different from the other waiters. I assumed it was simply because I was the lone American, but they revealed it was something else.

"Why are you so happy?" blurted Jessica, the long-haired, long-legged goddess. She had a delicate smattering of freckles on her cheeks over alluring, perky lips.

"Because I'm going on vacation at the end of this cruise!"

"Anywhere exotic?"

"How's Transylvania for exotic?"

"Really? Why?"

"Uh, no reason, really."

"Normal people don't go to Transylvania for no reason. Are you some horror geek loser?"

"What? No! Well, kind of..."

"So what's her name?" asked Sheila, the tanned, petite beauty with bobbed black hair. She wore a tight orange top that was very distracting.

"Bianca," I admitted. "She's worthy enough that I won't even notice any of you for the rest of the cruise. Back, you vile temptresses of evil delight!"

"That's sweet," said Lisa as she pulled me down to sit on the booth beside her. She had a girl-next-door freshness about her, with auburn hair and rosy cheeks. Suddenly all the women slid closer and I was in danger of drowning in beauty. The questions came in a flurry: How did you meet her? Oh, she isn't here now? So you are free for a harmless drink or three? Can you show us your cabin?

"I have work, ladies," I stammered, fighting my way to my feet. I scanned the dining room for signs of management, but only saw other waiters shooting jealous glances my way.

"Why don't you dance like the others?" Sheila asked.

In the dining rooms of many cruise ships, not just Carnival, the waiters performed nightly for the guests. The lights dropped to signal the waiters to don silly hats and wigs and *babaloo* sleeves (ridiculous red jackets). The music kicked in and all were required to dance and sing pop songs for their section. Such diversion was overwhelmingly popular with the guests, but I detested doing it. I took great pride in entertaining my guests, but I refused to dance like a court jester for their amusement. I was ridiculed for lacking a sense of humor, though more accurately I lacked a sense of humility. However, I had one ace up my sleeve.

"I'm in management training. They don't want me looking like an idiot in front of those who I will be in charge of."

"That's a convenient lie."

"No, it's true. You can't imagine how happy I was."

"But *we* want you to dance for us," they pleaded.

"Only if you dance for me," I retorted.

The gauntlet thrown, the ladies rose and suddenly I was surrounded by spinning, whirling, and gyrating bodies. I looked on helplessly, realizing I was going to be outdone by these women.

"Come on! Join us!"

"No way."

"You promised!"

"Fine!" I yelled. "I won't do the dinner dances, but I'll do one better. On the last day I'll do a striptease."

Their applause made me realize just how stupid a mistake I had just made.

My final week progressed quickly. What little free time I had was used in making preparations for the trip. I had to pack and to say my goodbyes, which included a final romp at the Groovy Grouper with Calypso. We were both so tired we fell asleep beneath the palm trees. There are few things on the earth more satisfying than waking up from an afternoon nap and the first thing you see are gently swaying palm fronds above you.

On the final port day, I wandered alone. I had seen all of my friends and had spent the entire week saying goodbye. I wanted time to reflect before I flew to Europe. I was excited but also nervous that I was yet again foolishly chasing a dream. I wandered the streets of Cozumel with my cigar and felt the sun sink into my skin. I wore nothing but shorts and sandals. I daresay I looked funny with an extra cigar in my pants pocket, but fortunately it was a huge eight-inch Churchill. Never before had I been confident enough to wander in public so bare, but after months on the ships I was bronzed and trim and muscular like never before. Though an avid athlete for years, I had never before made that final step from fit to fantastic.

A cluster of bars along the waterfront near the international pier was my favorite place to hang out. Fat Tuesday's, the ubiquitous chain of frozen-cocktail bars, was every crew member's favorite because it was so close to the ship. I could hammer double shots of tequila and still be onboard within five minutes. The building was large and open, with a thatched roof and no walls to allow in the sea breeze. Tables pushed out from the shade and into the glorious Caribbean sun.

Beside Fat Tuesday's was another establishment that MTV had commandeered for an episode on wild dance parties in Mexico. The floor was sand and the seats at the bar were actually wooden swings for two. Apparently the graduates had all seen the show, for they were working hard to reenact it.

"Brian!" they shouted above the music, surging into the street to pull me in. I was pulled into a crowd of bikini-clad vixens drinking and dancing with wild abandon. Slushy tequila drinks spilled as they danced, pouring over their hot bodies. I was surrounded by sticky and sweaty and drunk babes. What more could a man ask for? Soon I was equally high and dancing like an idiot with them, all to the pumping house music as the sun blasted the beach around us. I endured a painful number of jokes about the cigar in my pants. Secretly I was hoping to have my shorts stolen again.

We drank, cheered, took photos, and danced the afternoon away. The convergence of the sun, the people, the desires, the music, the very energy of the universe all chose to focus on that one spot for that one afternoon. It was a spontaneous, memorable event that I will never forget.

By check-in time for dinner, I was thoroughly trashed. I had spoken in advance with my first-seating guests and all had assured me they would dine in Cozumel. Therefore my libations of the afternoon were undertaken with that knowledge pickled somewhere in the back of my mind. So instead of properly setting up my station, I had expounded in a highly literate, highly inebriated manner on my feelings about ship life and the world in general. I wandered from station to station like a sideshow performer and solved the world's problems. All the other waiters hovered nearby to listen in, though that was easy enough with my booming voice.

Waiters are required to remain in the dining room for thirty minutes, whether or not they have any guests. Just as I was about to leave for a much-needed nap, the hostess sat a table of six people in my section. I stared at them in a stupor for several minutes before Svetlana nudged me to go talk to them.

I stumbled through apologies to my surprise guests, trying vainly to appear sober. I didn't recognize any of them. I explained delicately that we were not prepared for them, and it would be a few minutes while I stole some water pitchers, stole some ice, stole some bread baskets, stole the bread that goes in them, stole some butter, stole some menus and discovered what, if any, specials there were.

Frustrated and stressed to get these *boleta* guests out of my station in time, I was shocked to see the hostess set another group of six, and then *another!* Within five minutes my station was maxed out, and both Svetlana and I were stretched to our limits. With such a large group coming in so very late, and my poor preparation, we were hopelessly behind and still struggling with dinner entrees when the call was made that all first-seating guests had to leave to make way for second-seating guests. The situation was only tolerable because the diners were, astoundingly, more inebriated than their waiter. Poor Svetlana was the only sober individual of us all.

I had hoped that the graduates would also skip dinner due to their exertions of the day, and perhaps try the buffet. No such luck. Even as I struggled to clear the previous section's mess, twenty grinning babes came bouncing in.

The final night of my stay as a waiter finally came. I was high as a kite, and finally understood the unparalleled joy others exhibited at such a time. While I had only been on ships for a total of four months, compared to a usual contract of eight to ten months, I was moving into an exciting new phase. The feeling of complete freedom in anticipation of my vacation was intoxicating.

As always, serving the graduates was not work, but a true pleasure. They were patient for all things barring their wine service, which I was only too happy to provide. We laughed and flirted shamelessly. All week they had been trying to kiss me in the dining room. First one group would push me toward Jessica at one end of my section, then another group would apprehend me and thrust me upon Lisa, and so it would go. The kiss became a game for us all, a silly little prize that both sides refused to relinquish.

The night drew to a close, and I regretted leaving my ladies. Other guests filed out of the dining room, but the graduates remained to finish their wine. I was in no hurry to push them out, even though I had a farewell party planned for later that night. The neighboring stations emptied, and soon we were an island of gaiety in the corner of the Monet dining room.

"It's the last night," Jessica called, even as she blushed. "Where's our strip tease?"

Suddenly they all cheered, chanting, "Strip! Strip! Strip!"

"I can't," I replied lamely, fishing for an excuse, "I would have to do it on a stage, and we just don't have one here. And the music is missing."

"Regina!" Lisa called to my neighboring waitress. She had been setting her station for the next morning, but one table had apparently been forgotten and was still empty. Only *then* did I realize it had not been forgotten at all. Upon command she yanked the tablecloth free to reveal an ideal stage.

"But there's still no music," I observed gratefully. Smirking, Regina rushed over to the maitre d' stand and conversed with a hostess. Suddenly "I'm Too Sexy" began playing over the dining room speakers at tremendous volume.

I had been set up. But this was the end of my last seating

ever as a waiter, and I was going on vacation in just twelve short hours. Why not?

"Ladies," I said, grinning. "Anything worth doing is worth *over*doing."

I leapt onto the table and began my little dance, whipping off my bowtie and flinging it around my head. With the most awkward moves ever witnessed, I removed my vest and began unbuttoning my shirt.

Cheers roared from the graduates as they surrounded me.

Applause echoed from waiters in all corners of the dining room.

Chanting to the beat rose from everywhere, and I saw the hostesses leering at me.

Then Dan entered the room.

I stopped in mid-swing, stunned into inaction. But the ladies were not satisfied. They rushed from their seats and yanked me from the table. Dozens of hands ripped at my shirt. The buttons popped out and flew in all directions. My shirt was half ripped off before I knew what happened. I had heard that women got far wilder than men at strip clubs, but this was ridiculous! I felt my belt slipped out of the loops and had to grip my pants before they were yanked down. I began bellowing, not unlike an elephant seal in heat, and thrashed and fought against the overwhelming superiority of dozens of red-tipped fingernails. Here I was living my fantasy since puberty, yet I was fighting it like mad!

After a few minutes the ladies finally relented, and I sat on the booth beside Lisa, panting. Just when I thought I was safe, she regarded me with a sly smile. I grew nervous again.

"May I see your chest again?"

"No, my dear, you may not. My boss is here now, and I think there are still other guests, too!"

"How about a kiss on the cheek?" she asked kindly, "As a reward for not taking advantage of you in this moment of weakness."

"Well, that seems harmless—"

Immediately she gripped my ears and pulled me into the booth, legs flailing in the air. She planted the longest, most aggressive kiss on my lips I had ever dreamed of. Hoots and hollers rose from the group even as my lungs screamed for air. My head was spinning and I saw visions of streaking stars and supernovae spiral overhead. Then Lisa released me. I sagged in the booth like a wet noodle, panting, stunned, but not at all displeased.

Jessica pushed toward me and handed me some photos.

"I took these yesterday," she said, a smile playing on her pretty lips. "These are for you."

I looked at several images of us all dancing and frolicking in Cozumel. The snapshots were taken by an obviously drunken camera operator, and the exposure was all whacked from the intense Caribbean sun. Yet the pictures captured a moment that I had thought could never be visited again.

"I developed them on the ship because I thought you might want them."

"Indeed I do!" I replied, truly touched. "That is amazingly kind of you."

"Are they worth a kiss?"

"Anything worth doing is worth overdoing."

PART III

Assistant Maitre d'
(Demotion)

*There is nothing so desperately
monotonous as the sea, and I no longer
wonder at the cruelty of pirates.*

—JAMES RUSSELL LOWELL

1 *Bogo*

OVING TO THE OFFICERS' CABINS SHOULD HAVE been an exciting advancement for me, but my new home on deck four, forward was anything but rousing. Upon first arriving I noted our private bathroom door was open and steam rolled into the tiny cabin. Obviously my new roommate, Randall Bogo, was in the shower, because his music blasted loud enough to be heard over the water. My feelings of unease began to spiral already as I took in more and more details of the surroundings.

First, and of great importance to me, was the distressing lack of alcohol in the cabin. Everything was in disarray, with numerous notes and leaflets covered in Hindi writing and a staggering surplus of CDs with little crosses drawn on them. Wincing under the onslaught of the music, I tried to place my luggage on the upper bunk, but it would not fit. No, not because the bunk was smaller than any others, but because it fairly overflowed with books. That, at least, was a good sign in my opinion.

I focused on the deafening lyrics which battered me, applying the skills I obtained on *Fantasy*. After a month enduring the Jamaicans' noise, I had learned to appreciate music in all its forms. I could now safely listen to hip hop lyrics, for example, knowing they were simply fantasizing about having lots of money or being successful with the ladies. Yet this music proved much more unnerving to me. I had gone from, "Yo, yo, we Rockefellers. Got me a stack of benjamins three miles high, the bitches want to bang me for my bucks," to "Let your light shine through me, oh Lord, my shepherd."

With sudden alarm, I looked to the pile of books filling my bunk to capacity.

Bibles.

I was rooming with a Reborn Christian!

To think, I had just spent three weeks living in the medieval Transylvanian township where Dracula himself was born in 1431. I resolved not to share that little tidbit with this Bogo.

Bianca and I had enjoyed three glorious, relaxing weeks touring much of Romania and the Black Sea coast. The vacation had been everything I had hoped and far more. As if descending from that heaven wasn't hard enough, the trip back to *Conquest* had been hell, with connecting flights from Bucharest to Frankfurt to Chicago to New Orleans, only to take a taxi for the hour drive to Gulfport and be on duty within a few hours of signing on. Needless to say, I was exhausted. I was scheduled to work all afternoon, evening, and then midnight buffet! If anything stopped me from sleeping tonight, it was surely an acknowledgement of no justice on this earth and I resolved to jump overboard to end the pain.

Just as I was leaving, my roommate came out from the bathroom, dripping and steaming and *naked*. First Alexandro in Miami, then Ben on *Fantasy*...and now Bogo on *Conquest*. Why was it that all of my roommates with Carnival were naked, except Bianca?!

Bogo was a light-skinned Indian, with a graying Persian-style mustache and shaved head. He had a strange series of indentations on the back of his skull, not unlike someone pressing their fingers into a wet ball of clay. How he shaved in those grooves I had no clue. The purple circles beneath his eyes were horrific, but his smile was benevolent.

"Hello!" he screamed above the music, shaking my hand. "I'm Bogo."

"Brian," I hollered in reply. "Nice to meet you. I would stay and chat, but I have to be on Lido deck already."

"Of course, no rest for the wicked."

He lingered on the final word, eyeing me up and down suspiciously. Only reluctantly did he lower the volume of his music. "Let me clear the top bunk for you."

He reached over to clear the excess Bibles from my bunk. He removed a dozen that were piled atop my sheets, and dipped into my private drawer to remove another six. "You can keep them, if you want," he added enthusiastically. "It's always good to have a few extras." I braced for the awkwardness that was sure to come.

"Oh, no, thanks. I don't need one."

"Already have some, eh? It never hurts to have a few extras," he repeated. "These are the King James."

"I'm good, thanks."

He regarded me skeptically. "You *are* Christian, aren't you? You're white."

"Nope," I replied noncommittally.

"Oh, I would love to hear about your faith," he beamed. "When you get off work tonight we can talk about it!"

I edged toward the door, not wanting to mention that I was an atheist. After acknowledging my absence of faith nearly a decade before, I had learned that nothing begged "sell me your faith" more than claiming to have none. Most people assumed it simply meant you couldn't decide which denomination to choose, so they raved about their own. Claiming to be a Satanist was literally less of an ordeal because most people immediately gave up on you.

"I'd love to, Bogo, but I supervise the midnight buffet. I'm working the next twelve hours straight."

"Not to worry! I have chronic insomnia. I assure you, I will be up far later than you every night. That's my favorite time to talk because there are no distractions. We'll talk tonight."

The last time I had been on the Lido deck had been three weeks ago, but I felt as if I had never left. Because it was noon on embarkation day, the dining area was not yet full. The early sign-ons were already picking their way through the buffet, but the majority of the 3,500 guests had yet to arrive. It was a hot day in Mississippi, and I sped through the aft pool deck quickly, seeking the relief of the air-conditioning. I was still wearing my waiter's black polyester, which was stifling hot. I was due to pick up my short-sleeve white officer's uniform this afternoon, after meeting the food and beverage manager to finalize my promotion arrangements.

"Sir! Oh, sir!" a grating voice called out. I was beckoned by the mother of a family who filled a large booth beside the window. The owner of the voice was a very plump woman of an indeterminate age somewhere between thirty and fifty. Four children squirmed beneath the table like worms, occasionally surfacing but mostly rooting about in the darkness beneath. The husband, a beaten-looking man with a horrendous comb-over, stared through the window at the snaking line of guests waiting to embark.

"I want to talk to you," the woman snapped. "I have a tremendous problem with you."

"With me, ma'am?"

"With Carnival," she spat. Before my very eyes her face scrunched into annoyance. "I can't believe you allow your staff to use such awful language."

I leaned in, concerned. "I'm sorry to hear this. I will handle it immediately."

"As well you should, if you are worth anything," she curtly replied. "That whole group over there. They have used *the word* a dozen times already. I have children here!"

I followed her accusing finger toward a group of Romanian head waiters. I knew all of them because they were friends of Bianca's. They clustered together around a bus station, obviously bored and tired, conversing quietly in their native tongue.

"I don't understand. What word have you heard, may I ask?"

Her face wrinkled deeply in disgust. "The *F-word!* Constantly, right here in front of my well mannered and well rounded children!"

"But they are speaking Romanian," I replied, confused.

"There!" she suddenly shrieked. "I just heard it again! I demand you do something. I demand a free cruise for my family! I will not pay to come here and be subjected to such uncouth, horrendous behavior from some dirty foreigners. They are surely French."

I listened in, and suddenly chuckled. The woman gasped in shock, offended even deeper.

"No, no, it's O.K., ma'am," I soothed. "In Romanian, their word for '*I do*' or '*I make*' sounds just like our F-word. He just said '*I'll make the coffee.*'"

"That is an absurd lie!" she shrieked. "I can't believe you are defending those horrible foreigners. They should be deported at once! America is only for Americans!"

I looked helplessly as she continued resentfully beneath her breath, "...come to *my* country with their foul tongues...go back to the shacks they were born in..."

"Please, ma'am," I begged, torn between my own indignation and wanting to placate her. "I *assure* you that they are not swearing. They should be speaking English in the guest areas, however, and I will talk to them immediately."

"So you are calling me a liar?"

"Of course not! It's actually a common concern because it's integral in their language."

"So now you're calling me common? Oh! Oh! I *demand* to see who's in charge!"

"Ma'am, I am in charge. I assure you, this is all a simple misunderstanding."

Spluttering with rage, she dismissed me with a regal wave. "Simple! I'll show you simple, you horrible little man, when they simply *eject* you back to whatever undeveloped rat-hole you come from!"

"I'm from Iowa."

"Not hardly. You may leave now. Oh, the purser will hear about this!"

Suddenly I wasn't sure if I wanted to be promoted or not!

Eventually that day Bogo took over on the Lido deck and allowed me to visit the food and beverage manager's office. I was numb with fatigue and the waiting outside Omar's office made it even worse. Omar was a Turkish man who was very friendly and very competent, having been with the company for over a decade. Yet instead of Omar's usual boom I heard a thin, tired voice speak, apparently on the phone. The smartly correct English carried an accent that revealed Scandinavian background.

The environmental officer suddenly rushed past me and into the office. He barked some orders, muttered something in Italian, then stormed back down the hallway. The phone demanded repeated calls and answers even as I wavered closer to falling asleep.

Finally I was called in. Behind a huge stack of papers and files on the desk sat an emaciated, hunched man. His uniform was wrinkled and he looked simply overwhelmed. The purple bags beneath his eyes humbled my own fatigue and made Bogo look fresh.

"Brian," he greeted indifferently. His voice was just like his frame: slight and weak, exuding exhaustion and poor health. "I'm Gunnar."

"Nice to meet you."

"Yes," he said with lack of interest, pushing a file out of the way. The phone rang yet again, and he answered it. He listened for a few minutes, acknowledged the call, and then set the phone down tiredly.

"Yesterday some airplane flying over the gulf noticed a trail of oil behind us," he muttered, more complaining to himself than explaining to me. "Instead of calling us and helping avert an environmental problem, he preferred to be on TV and contacted the American media. By the time we were contacted by the U.S. Coast Guard...*hours* later...they had video of us leaking what the news instantly labeled pollution."

"Leaking? That sounds bad."

"It could have been engine oil, but was probably just vegetable oil from the fryers in the kitchen. I need to visually account for all of it, the fresh, the used, the reserve. We have dozens of safeguards, I cannot believe it. Just what I need, a fine of hundreds of thousands of dollars from the U.S. government, on my first ship as F&B!"

"Do you want me to come back later?"

He shook his head and let out a profound sigh. "So, you are also American."

"Yes, sir."

"And you want to be an assistant maitre d'," he stated. After a long moment he added, "I don't understand why an American would want to work here."

"Well, my girlfriend works here, and I have lots of experience in the dining room. I wanted to see some of the world, too."

He regarded me skeptically.

"It just doesn't make any sense. There are no Americans here, except the entertainers, of course."

"So I have discovered! It's a challenge all right, but I like it."

"Well, you're not going to be an AMD."

"I beg your pardon?"

"Why should I allow it?"

"Well, it was cleared by Omar as well as both maitre d's. Ask Dan. Ask Reginald."

"They aren't here anymore."

"I've only been gone for three weeks, and both MDs and the F&B all switched? Wow. No worries, though, I was hired by Mladen and put on the fast track. I've worked every level of restaurant in the last four months, from dishwasher to busboy to even working in the kitchen for a time."

"Mladen who?"

"From Miami."

"*The* Mladen? I doubt it. No, you'll stay as a waiter. No Americans have ever survived the dining room, and you don't look special."

"I've already lasted half my contract and done all the dirty work," I replied, now wide awake. "Look, I understand your reservations, but I'm not going anywhere. If I wanted to quit, I would have when I was doing dishes, not when I'm about to become management. Besides, if I wanted out, why would I have returned to the ship today?"

"Maybe Omar said it was O.K., but it's *my* name on your file now if I promote you. I won't put it there. You will fail."

I didn't know what to say. I was not as surprised as I was sick of this constant argument. What did I have to do to prove myself to these people? Was this some sort of final test of my resolve?

"Look, I understand your position," I said, relenting. "I have three months left in my contract. Why don't we make it a probationary period as AMD? If you have tangible reasons to deny me then, I'll leave with no questions asked. That seems fair to me."

"No, I don't want to give you the whites."

"But you don't even know me! Don't you trust the opinions of all three managers that were here before you?"

He didn't reply.

"Gunnar, this is unacceptable. I have gone through every hurdle to get here, maybe even more than most."

"I doubt that. It took me over ten years to become an assistant bar manager."

"But did you have over a decade of experience in fine dining, serving Americans?"

He stared at me mutely for a few moments. I met his gaze but made an effort not to be as adversarial as I was inclined to be. Finally he let loose a long, heavy sigh.

"O.K., I'll give you the whites, but not the formals. You'll be an AMD *trainee* during the days and during midnight buffet, but in the evening I want you as a waiter. You'll pick up a section tonight. You won't get the AMD salary, but be paid like a waiter."

"What! The dining room is what it's all about, that's why I was hired! Why would you deny me that and force me on the midnight buffet? I already supervised that for months!"

"That's as good as it's going to get. I have things to do. Leave now."

Utterly exhausted, I leaned on the rail of the Lido deck and watched the waves far below fade into the black of night. Even though my vacation had been paradise, I had to admit that I missed the waves of the ocean. I could smell the salt of the sea, but also the humid, cloying scent of the Gulf Coast. We were barely outside the mighty range of the Mississippi Delta, and below me the waters were murky brown. The buoys made a line of red and green in the dark, creating a path in the otherwise trackless waters.

I pondered how long it had been since I had last slept. In the afternoon two days ago I had left Sighisoara, the charming Transylvanian town where Bianca lived, and driven the four hours to nearby Brasov. In that city we had waited for a few hours and at midnight drove the next five hours to Bucharest. *Then* I took a flight to Frankfurt, which lasted nearly three hours, *then* onto the transatlantic flight to Chicago. I sat next to several children who either played violently or cried loudly the entire eleven hours, denying me even a nap. *Then* I flew the five hours south to New Orleans, *then* hopped on a taxi for the hour-plus drive to Gulfport. *Then* onboard I had been assigned to work from noon until three in the morning without a break.

I had not slept a wink in over seven thousand miles and fifty hours.

What kept me going was not anger toward Gunnar, to my surprise, but the afterglow of my vacation. Though Bianca and I had argued tremendously while on *Conquest* together, in Romania we had captured all the magic of our first encounter, times ten. My head was still spinning with the pure elation of the trip. It made all the slings and arrows of my outrageous situation simply vanish. I could still feel her touch, see her smile, and hear her laugh.

I would not see Bianca again for some months, while we worked out the next phase of our plan to be together. She was on vacation for a while longer, after which she would be sent to the shipyards of Montfalcone, Italy, to prepare the next *Conquest* class vessel. She was part of a privileged team of head waiters who followed Dan, who always opened the new ships. For me, as a new low-level manager, there was no chance at all of being assigned to the newest ship. They only allowed me on *Conquest* because Dan was doing Bianca a favor and I was merely a trainee for half of my contract. Now I was to be a trainee for my *entire* contract. With her memory so fresh in my otherwise drained mind, I knew Bianca was worth it.

Tired, bedazzled, and bedeviled, I stumbled through the remainder of the shift. Finally I shuffled to my cabin. My eyes burned, my head pounded, and my muscles had long since stopped screaming and now merely whimpered.

Too tired to do anything, even undress, I pulled my heavy body up onto the bunk in the dark. Ecstasy was closing my eyes, soothing the itch, watching the redness melt lovingly into cool blackness. I drifted gratefully into slumber...until a voice sharply cut through.

"Would you like me to lead you in a prayer?"

2 *E n e m y   M i n e*

RUNNING TO THE RENOIR DINING ROOM FROM MY cabin, I cursed and sweat and swore. Check-in was at 5:30, but it was already 5:40. Punctuality was a huge issue on the ships and I hated being late, but the real fear was that my section would already have been rifled through for all my silverware and saucers.

I had told my new team waitress, Camilla, to guard our stuff because I knew I would be late. Lido supervisors worked until 5:30 and usually had half an hour before they returned there to begin the dinner shift. Because of my unique situation, I was forced to run down to deck four, forward, change my uniform and gather my tools of the trade, then rush all the way to deck three, aft. It was a miracle I took only ten minutes.

Camilla was waiting for me with a sour look on her face. Though Romanian, Camilla somehow had natural blond hair and wore it long over her shoulders. She had pretty brown eyes with sparkles of green in them, but an otherwise very unattractive face with an overly large and flat nose. Her figure was athletic and appealing, though an extra donut or two would probably have done her some good. Her English was flawless and she comfortably used a great deal of large vocabulary. Though quick with a joke and an enthusiastic conversationalist, she was nonetheless an overall negative person.

Camilla and I worked in a small section near the front entrance of the Renoir dining room. The new maitre d', a Frenchman named Ferrand, had assured me it was a good section despite all evidence to the contrary. Because it was close to the entrance it was guaranteed to be filled every cruise, which meant maximum money potential. He was aware of my situation and was sympathetic...on the surface, at least.

We enjoyed a nicely sized pantry, but it was a small station. With a maximum of only eighteen guests, it was nearly as small as a section could be, but that suited me fine. The majority of waiters wanted the full twenty-four guests because every dollar counted when you took the money home overseas. For me the backbreaking stress and labor of a maxed-out section was not worth the extra hundred dollars a week. Besides, I knew it was all temporary and I wanted less hassle so I could perform better.

Camilla watched the guests file into the dining room, relaxed because she knew our first-seating guests were not going to show up. Our guests had a reservation in the supper club tonight. We watched with wry amusement as our pantry-mates rushed like mad to accommodate their guests.

Tekin, a burly Turk head waiter, shared the pantry with us. He was big in all ways: his physique was large, including his bald head, huge lips, and even bigger teeth with a slight gap between each. It made him look like an ogre. His voice fit the image, too, being louder than it should be and very deep. Though he drank too much, smoked too much, and gambled too much, I felt he obsessed over women just the right amount. Despite his repulsiveness, I found his lust for life enjoyable.

But his team waitress was another story entirely. As if my life was not complicated enough, Tekin's assistant was none other than the sexy Rasa from Lithuania.

From my relaxed vantage in the pantry, it all looked like chaos. To the guests, however, all seemed smooth. Both Tekin and Rasa were Rambo, and they were lightning-fast. Rasa was so distractingly beautiful that most of the guests never noticed Tekin cut every corner and break every rule to get them in and out faster. Honestly, most Americans preferred speed to finesse in the dining room anyway. Management insisted on the later, but the waiters knew their priorities.

"Oh, how I hate the cow animals," lamented Camilla as she surveyed the obese line-up of guests in Tekin's section. We had overheard them all order two entrées each, some three. So this was to be the subject of her daily gripe.

"I wouldn't let the Indians hear you say that with such disdain."

"No, silly, the Americans. They are all cow animals. I can't stand them. They are all really huge and nice and easy to please, just like cows. Give them lots of food and they are compliant and stupid."

"You think?" I replied with amused patience.

"*Evident!* Have you noticed how they eat at the buffets? The first thing they do when arriving onboard is to go to the Lido. Their English is horrendous, asking 'Where da food at?'"

"O.K., that's true," I acknowledged, eyeing the very large family that squeezed behind the tables with difficulty. "But you must realize the cruise lines push the unlimited food as a major selling point, and it's quite good. Remember, too, that we are in the south, and they have the highest percentage of overweight people in America. Even over the Midwest."

"Oh, come on. Two out of three Americans are overweight, everyone knows that. There are more obese people in the States than the rest of the world combined."

"That may be an exaggeration, but probably not. Certainly it's a stereotype. It's kind of like saying all Romanians are gypsies. Still, I guess I never noticed."

"Surely you jest!" Camilla demanded. "Tell me you weren't shocked the first time you met the Americans."

"Well, I was really little at the time," I commented dryly.

"What do you mean?" she asked, confused.

I reviewed her frown and realized that something I had thought obvious was not clear. "Uh, Camilla, you *do* know I'm American, do you not?"

Her jaw dropped and her eyes opened wide.

"I thought you were German!"

"I'm from Iowa, baby doll."

"But, but you look good!"

"You should see me naked."

"Oh my God! So you were a potato farmer?"

We watched in surprise as a new host began seating guests in our section. Camilla gave me a concerned glance. Having known our first seating would be empty, we had not prepared properly. With growing dismay we saw all eighteen seats fill up with incredibly large people.

"Holy Cat! Camilla, get some water, quick!"

"Who the hell are these people?"

"I don't know, but that guy sat them in our section. Who the hell is he?"

"That's Leo, the new assistant maitre d'."

"So, we are going to run our tails off for these people, and we won't even get paid for it? They are someone else's guests! What's he doing seating them here?"

"Who cares," she cried as she ran off, "if he looks like that? Did you see his ass?"

Happily our pantry was one of the few to contain running water, but it was out of ice. Meanwhile I eagerly sought Tekin's stash of menus, because mine were not yet ready. If I didn't get the orders from these very late guests soon, we were in serious danger of running overtime and not being ready for our paying, second-seating guests.

"Rasa!" I called, running up to her. "Where are your menus?"

"Why?" she asked with fake innocence, fluttering her eyes. Stuck in the pantry with her alone for a mere thirty seconds and she was already working it!

"No games, woman!"

"What will you give me for them?"

"Anything, anything!"

She grinned in victory. "I'll remember you said this."

Suddenly Tekin came around the corner and saw me holding his menus. He wrenched them from me and boomed in his deep bass, "Hey, why you pinch?"

"Rasa said I could borrow them."

"*My* menus, Yankee boy, not hers!"

A still smirking Rasa excused herself from the pantry with a whisper, "I'll collect from you later."

"What will you give me for them?" Tekin demanded, towering over me. Tekin made my lean 200 pounds look small. If all Turks were his size, it was no wonder they dominated the Mediterranean for centuries.

"I don't have time for this, Tekin."

"I know!" he gloated, laughing with a perfectly sinister, "Bwaa-ha-ha!"

For some reason Tekin would always spit when he spoke. He had very clear, proper English with only a delicate accent. He had no lisp or any other form of speech impediment, yet every single word showered me with white foam and spittle. When he drank it was even worse.

"For an extra smoke break on Lido, and you can take them," he offered, handing me the faux-leather folders. As I grabbed for them he pulled back and said, "*Two* smoke breaks."

"Turkish dog," I called, snatching them from him with a rueful smile.

"Supply and demand," he replied with a wolfish grin. "I love capitalism!"

Just as I exited the pantry a hostess named Catalina intercepted me. She was the first overweight Romanian I had met, and tried to distract attention from her large behind by dying her hair fiery red.

"Brian, you have some guests who missed their dinners in the Monet Room."

"I noticed."

"Be nice, they are related to some big dog in Carnival. Leo knew you are American, so he thought they might like to meet their only paisano. I hear they eat two or three entrees each, so you better hurry."

"Great. Hey, who is this Leo guy, anyway?"

"Oh, he's a new trainee for assistant maitre d'."

Despite the pressure of time, I paused. "I beg your pardon? *He* is training in the dining room while I'm a waiter? Why, he's just a kid!"

Catalina shrugged, but her eyes glinted with the excitement of intrigue. "He just transferred from the bar department, that's all I know. Except that he's so hot."

"The *bar*?" I asked with growing annoyance. "He doesn't even have any restaurant experience, and he's in the dining room before me? What is that?"

"Get to work," she ordered, gloating.

Just after our exhausting second seating, I followed Camilla through the door beside our pantry to a small private dining room just off of the Renoir. The Cassatt Room was unused and lit only by the light spearing in through the glass door to the hall. The tables were pushed into the center of the room, while the chairs filled the dark corners. Knowing it was impossible to see us from the hall, we both eased into the upholstered chairs with a sigh.

"You know," Camilla commented after a while, "you are a lot better of a waiter than my last head waiter, Romeo. He was a lot faster, but your ass is better."

"Well, at least I've got something going for me. You worked with Romeo Smochine? I met him in Brasov, Romania. He's a friend of my girlfriend."

"Yes, he was my first head waiter. He doesn't talk much, though."

I sank deeper into the chair with a tired groan, muttering, "*Romeo, Romeo, wherefore art thou Romeo? Deny thy father and refuse thy name, or if thou wilt not, then something or other.*"

Camilla reacted with surprise. "An American who knows Shakespeare? I don't believe it!"

"Oh, get off it."

"All roses smell the same," she intoned dramatically.

"Almost," I replied.

"Almost? You mean all roses smell *almost* the same?"

"No, the line is '*a rose by any other name smells just as sweet.*'"

"What are you talking about? Typical American, thinking you know more than everyone else."

"Camilla," I defended, "It's *my* language, not yours."

"Your *only* one," she jibed. "I might as well give you that."

"O.K., Shakespearette, how many languages have you mastered?"

"Four. Romanian, French, Magyar, and English. My Spanish isn't bad, either, and I'm learning some Tagalog."

"Yeah? Well I know how to say '*the boy threw the ball at the wall*' in Tagalog. So there."

"Don't try to impress me," she replied sourly. "Just shut up, show me your butt, and we'll get along fine."

"Well, your English sucks," I retorted, "I guess your ass isn't so bad, though."

She took a deep breath, preparing for war, but I cut her off with a laugh. I was finally cheering a little. "Actually you have amazing English, and you seem well read, indeed."

"Thank you. I love Shakespeare. A collection of his plays was one of my earliest books read as a child."

"As a child? What, are you some sort of genius? Who can read that as a child? I was in junior high when I started, and it took us weeks to slog through it."

"Why? Are all Americans as stupid as you?"

"Thanks for that," I said sourly. "The language is so different. I mean, it's 500-year-old English. You can't read it without a guide."

"Didn't seem tough to me."

"How could it not? I mean…wait a minute! It was translated into simple Romanian, wasn't it?"

"Of course."

From beneath a napkin Camilla wearily produced a covered entree. She sat down at a table and started eating the vegetarian dish of the evening, a fine-looking tower of roasted vegetables rising from a mound of citrus-accented couscous.

"Oh, the new vegetarian tower. How is it?"

"Not bad! Try some."

"I'm tempted, but I had better not. I have to be a good boy."

"Oh, it's just a sample," she scoffed. "Everyone asked us what it tasted like tonight and you couldn't answer. Now you can."

Shrugging, I picked up a fork. "True enough. I guess a taste would be all right, since you already stole it."

I reached over her shoulder and speared a grilled red pepper when some inner warning bade me stop. I looked up and saw Gunnar watching us through the window of the door. I froze like a deer caught in headlights, simply dumbfounded at the horrendous timing. I had never seen a food and beverage manager scouting out the dining room before.

Gunnar entered the room and stood before me. I sheepishly set down my fork, and waited for the attack.

"I thought so," Gunnar finally said condescendingly.

"Now, Gunnar, wait a minute—"

"Stealing food *already*. I knew you wouldn't be a good role model, and here you are on the very first cruise."

"Oh, come on, Gunnar," I defended robustly. "I was just going to sample this new menu item. I had a dozen guests ask me what it's like, and I couldn't answer. How can I take care of my guests this way?"

"So you stole it? If you want to try something, talk to the maitre d'."

"You know as well as I do that no one allows the waiters to

sample anything, not the maitre d' and certainly not the chef."

"Is that so?"

"Yes it is. Look, I have never stolen anything, despite a thousand opportunities. Ask anyone. I have been a saint."

"So following the rules is to be applauded as something special?"

Maitre d' Ferrand entered, with Catalina hovering behind and gloating. She was almost giddy with joy.

"Ferrand," Gunnar asked, "if Brian wanted to sample a menu item, would you grant him permission?"

"Of course," he answered with obvious obeisance. "Anytime."

"I've seen enough," Gunnar said with arrogant dismissal.

"Gunnar…"

But he spun on his heel and departed the room. Ferrand gave me a sympathetic look and shrugged. "Bad timing, eh? If I were you, I would be extra careful. I think your life will be difficult for a while."

"Oh, I'll keep an eye on him," Catalina oozed, shooting me another vile look.

Ferrand seemed surprised to find her right on his heel. He gave her a look of disgust at her obsequiousness and departed, remarking, "Whatever."

I tried desperately to remain cheery as I pulled off my sweaty waiter's uniform. One of the fringe benefits to being an officer was the complimentary laundry service. Every ship had the "Chinese laundry," invariably run by Indonesians, far down in the bowels of the ship. On *Conquest* it was on B deck below the waterline and was so hot and steamy the Indonesians probably felt right at home. Nearly every head waiter I knew paid for their services. When I first used it upon returning they had tried to charge me because I had a waiter's uniform. When they discovered I was American they were so confused they simply didn't argue.

I was sorely offended that I was required to toil as a waiter while this Leo fellow just waltzed in and got what he wanted. I was not unaware that some businesses prefer new management without experience in order to better mold them in their image, but this was ridiculous. He was a young bartender who had never even been a busboy. Both of us were from first-world nations, so why was he the golden boy? Maybe his ass really was that much better than mine.

And Gunnar! While it could be that he was just doing his job by making the rounds, I doubted it. None of my friends had seen him in the Renoir before, and the consensus seemed to be that he was checking on me.

I was almost more dumbfounded than angry at this horrendous timing...almost. After months of great pains to be a model employee, one little slip up and I was branded a nuisance to him forever. His holier-than-thou attitude irked me as well. While I grant that I have an exceptionally large ego, it was never used to denigrate others.

Frustration and pressure built up in me. I had been great for so long, but I am human, too. I realized, suddenly, that I was dealing with the same crap that everyone else did regarding this paisano business. Many were jealous that Americans and English moved up so fast through the ranks. Well, I was being held back for that very same reason. Any petty thing to make their own candle seem brighter. Maybe I was deluding myself, but I had been warned this would happen. I resolved to be very careful with how I handled things.

Quietly I listened to some music to inspire me, trying frantically not to become outraged. Bogo entered our cabin, his eyes shot with red streaks and the purple beneath them deep, like an eggplant. He pulled off his officer's whites with the same fatigue and disgust as I had my own soiled uniform.

"Brian, what is this horrendous music?"

"Don't like hard rock, eh? Sorry, I'll turn it off."

"Yes, let me play you some inspiring music. Why, listen to these words this man is saying, 'Bring me down, bring me down.'

This is not music. Music should be uplifting and joyful."

"Oh, it's called 'The Down Town,' and he's saying that though everyone around him keeps trying to bring him down, he won't let it. It's a positive song about self-reliance."

"I don't think so. I sense you are a negative person, Brian."

I stopped and stared at him incredulously. "Me? Negative? Huh. Well, I am in a bad mood today, true enough. I just discovered a new AMD trainee is working the dining room and I'm not. I have ten years of restaurant experience, including management, and he just transferred from being a *bartender*."

"Oh, you mean Leo," Bogo said. "Yes, you'll be training him next cruise."

"I beg your pardon?"

"Well, I can't work every shift on Lido. When I'm not there you will be the one teaching him."

"They won't let me be a full trainee, yet I'm supposed to train *him*? Holy Cat! What is that?"

Bogo shook his head as he turned off my music and started up his Christian soft rock. "So negative! What did you say your religion was, again?"

My mind reeling, I certainly didn't want to have this conversation with Bogo right now. "I was raised Roman Catholic," I answered honestly.

"Oh, wonderful! We can read the scripture together when you get back from work!"

"Maybe next time, Bogo. I am fairly confident that when I return from midnight buffet I am going to get rip-roaring drunk."

"Wait a moment," Bogo replied, his bald forehead wrinkling. "Did you just say 'Holy...Cat'?"

3 *The Other Sexy Bitch*

I WAS PLEASED TO BE ASSIGNED MIDNIGHT BUFFET SUPER-vision, though I would have preferred to be in my prime element, the dining room. I was naturally a morning person, but I found the peace of the small hours a wonderful balance for the hectic remainder of the ship life day...assuming no collisions with oil tankers. With Hipolito still present as a supervisor, I had nothing at all to do. Unfortunately it also meant there was little opportunity to show my stuff to the powers that be.

I strode past the empty tables and reviewed the orderliness of things. It was nearly 3 A.M., and most of the tables had been cleared and prepared for the breakfast buffet in just a few short hours. In anticipation of the rush, I had assigned several extra team waiters to rolling silverware bundles. They sat in the break room before huge tubs of cleaned silverware and mountains of pressed napkins. All wore homemade masks to keep the dust from the cloth out of their lungs. Five heads bobbed in unison to Tagalog love ballads. The remainder of the team waiters stood idly in their stations, merely waiting for their time to elapse.

The back pool area was the only outlet for food at this late hour. The pizza station ran twenty-four hours a day, controlled by the gentle yet iron-grip of Rajesh, the Pizza Phenomenon. He was a slight, brown-skinned Indian with a thick mustache tickling the underside of his nose. His smile was faster and more generous than even his pizza-dispensing, if that were possible. I had witnessed him laughing and joking unperturbed before a line of hungry, drunken guests fifty deep.

The roof to the back pool was closed, giving the whole area a warm, steamy feeling. The unpleasant scent of the chefs cleaning the burger grill wafted past my nose, but was cut by chlorine. I was beckoned by a petite African American woman of middle age. Her hair was bundled up tightly, but a few loose strands jutted out in a disarrayed halo, reminding me of the Statue of Liberty. She laughed alongside two college-age white ladies, all sharing a bottle of wine. As soon as I approached, the two younger women clammed up tight, struggling to contain their mirth.

"Oh, could you come here for a moment, young man? You can answer a question for me," she said as she rearranged her bathrobe.

"Yes, ma'am?"

She opened her robe to reveal no clothing beneath it. I leaned back, startled, as she cupped a breast and presented it to me.

"Now," she said, looking me dead in the eye, "Does this look like the breast of a forty-year-old woman?"

I tried not to look, but there was no helping it. The two coeds snorted with laughter, and I was sorely tempted to really run with the situation.

"Not hardly," I replied graciously. "I refuse to believe it. Now kindly reserve such a treat for another place and time. We are in a public area, as you may have noticed."

"Oh, I noticed," she said, pulling her robe wide open. "If you like one, then perhaps you'll like two even better."

I leaned back on my heels, sure that Gunnar had set me up.

"Play nice," I ordered.

"Oh, I'll play any way you want."

The three women all collapsed into laughter, allowing me a strategic retreat. "He didn't blush at all!" cried one of the youths.

"The last time I blushed," I replied, backing up, "I was thirteen and had just discovered what girls were. It was all downhill from there."

"Mmm-mmm!" purred Ms. Bathrobe, "I'll bet *I* can make you blush. Just give me some time, sugar!"

"Of that I have no doubt," I called, just before I ran away.

I stood on the mezzanine overlooking the main buffet line, watching the ebb and flow of food-toting humanity. While it vaguely reminded me of a colony of ants, with everyone coming and going with their load of food, it was not nearly as organized or wholesome.

I had finally met the new assistant maitre d' trainee, Leo. He was an exceptionally handsome South African man with spiky blond hair and a dash of freckles. He stood an inch taller than me and had ramrod straight posture. Leo was quick with a laugh and wonderfully vulgar, so we hit it off instantly. It only took me a few moments to realize that Leo was an ally in my situation with Gunnar.

"It happened again," I said. "More breasts."

"Again?" he repeated with a grin. "That makes, what three times?"

"Yes, or five breasts, if you're counting. The second time she only showed me one."

"That is truly amazing," he said with a thick Afrikaans role of his tongue. His r's rolled like a boulder down a mountainside. The sound was not intimidating, but intriguing. "You are the man!"

"Yeah, mention that to Gunnar. Maybe he'll let me have that officer's stripe I was denied."

"Ugh, that man has problems. Have you seen his posture? His spine is like a question mark. Anyway, I had another today myself. It was a group of four."

Now it was my turn to shake my head in awe. Leo looked so splendid in his clean white uniform that he was repeatedly asked by guests for a picture taken with him.

"Four? Were they the usual? *Middle*-aged?" I needled. Leo was still under the delusion that only college-age women were attractive.

"Yep," he said, "But hey…bitches are bitches. I still get a notch for it."

"Ah, Casanova, how could you *not* sweep them off their feet?"

"I need only drop my pants for that. Still, I would rather have them show me their tits than ask for a picture of me."

"I guess we can't all have what we want. Perhaps someday I'll be worthy of a photo request."

He looked me up and down thoughtfully. "Maybe. You got some big arms. Yeah, you are good-looking."

"No comments on my ass, then?"

"Huh?"

"Forget it. I always thought of myself as a sexy bitch, but as long as I qualify for the lesser…but still nice…good-looking, I'm happy."

Leo loosed another long, deep Afrikaans laugh. "Sexy bitches, yeah, that's what we are. Since you coined the term and are older, you are *the* sexy bitch. I'll be the *other* sexy bitch. I give credit where it's due."

Leo reminded me of an eighteen-year-old, though he was twenty-four. He was obsessed with women and drinking, and everything else was of secondary importance. We immensely enjoyed each other's company, despite being very different men. He only pretended to be devoted to his girlfriend at home. Yet I couldn't blame him for playing with the beauties from all over the world. Sometimes I still wondered why I wasn't!

After a few weeks onboard and socializing with Leo, I found myself immersed in a sea of South Africans who personified *carpe diem*. Even if they were sleeping, they would wake for a party. And with such an incredibly attractive and popular buddy as Leo, it was inevitable to have a following of the ladies. Needless to say, Calypso was completely smitten.

So one night after getting off as early as 2:30 A.M., I dove below the waterline and discovered a number of people hitting the sack. Calypso sat on the deck with her back to the wall, her fingers lazily sliding around the rim of a red wine glass. Her roommate Rhonetta danced next to a music box, while Leo sat upon the stairs that led nowhere, surrounded by empty beer bottles. Beside him, fairly clinging to his leg, was another paisana of theirs, Lorena.

Lorena was a dark-haired gal from Leo's hometown of Pretoria. Aware that she was rather plain in appearance, she compensated by painting a thick black line on her lower eyelids to give herself an exotic look. She was an enigma to herself, one who hadn't quite figured out who she was yet and who she enjoyed being around. She would cling to whatever group, or even male, was nearby.

"Brian!" Calypso called out happily, "Yay! Have some wine."

"I'm so glad you're here. Bogo was starting to talk psalm again."

"I don't know how you handle it."

"He talks until exhaustion takes him, regardless if the lights are out and my curtain is closed."

I slumped onto the floor beside her and took the offered glass. The Doors played quietly and Rhonetta spun before me, narrowly missing my outstretched legs. I watched Lorena slide her hand up Leo's shirt.

"Leo," I said, "when did you last sleep more than, say, three hours?"

"Hmm?" he slurred. His handsome eyes were bloodshot, but mercifully near to closing. He was oblivious to Lorena stroking his chest.

"Say, Brian," Calypso asked, tearing her gaze from the absent affection beside us, "What have you done to upset Catalina?"

"Here we go," I replied, still sour about the encounter two weeks ago with Gunnar and the food. "What did she say?"

"She demanded to know how long we've been sleeping together. She refused to believe we are just friends and obviously had an attitude about you. Is she another friend of Bianca?"

"Not that I am aware of. She seems too petty for Bianca to hang with. She caught me with some food a while back."

"So?"

I shrugged. "Maybe she is just angry that I am 'cheating' on her paisana, regardless of their being friends or not."

"More likely she's mad you aren't shagging her. So why don't you and save yourself a lot of trouble?"

"I'm thinking about it. Say, look at that! Leo has a tattoo."

We both viewed the action going on beside us. Lorena had completely unbuttoned Leo's shirt and was sliding her hands over his trim waist and chest. She highlighted a tiny yin-yang tattoo on Leo's stomach with a Vanna White-like flourish.

"Who would get a tattoo like that?" I wondered aloud.

"I got it to force myself to stay trim," Leo mumbled, his eyes closed and head drooping.

"Oh, he has another," Lorena added. Without hesitation she pulled his right arm from the shirt to reveal a tribal star on his shoulder. It reminded me of a circular saw blade with an exotic, primitive twist.

"Wow," I commented honestly. "I have never wanted a tattoo, or even seen one that I liked before, but that is cool. If I ever got a tattoo, it would be just like that."

"He got it his first week here," Calypso said. "He inherited my Tattoo Goo."

"What's that?"

"When you get a tattoo, you have to keep it lubricated for the first few days. After I got my tattoo, I gave him my Goo."

"Anything you want to show me?"

"You wish," she said with her Cheshire cat smile.

Because we were at the dead end of the hall, it was a surprise to see a small group of people turn the corner. I started when I recognized who was among them, and knocked over my wine glass.

"Rasa!"

"I've been looking for you!" Rasa said curtly, leaning toward me to shove her incredible cleavage in my face. She snatched up my wine glass as I sheepishly fumbled to contain the spreading pool of red. "You still owe me some action."

"Hello!" Leo exclaimed, waking with a start at hearing such words. He watched with envy as Rasa slid down to my side. Apparently he was still unaware of the young woman caressing his chest. Rasa had arrived with Clarence, the incredibly tall assistant maitre d' from Grenada and two team waiters I did not know. The small party swelled to fill the entire cul-de-sac.

I sat between Calypso and Rasa, enjoying it immensely. We were all friends here, and felt no need to hide our rampant flirtations. Calypso and I found amusement in the misconception of our sleeping together, despite the occasional wrinkle with the Romanian mafia. Rasa also was not privy to our platonics and worked ever harder to wrest me away from this apparent new rival.

Within another half hour we had procured several more bottles of wine and the group grew even further to over a dozen. Though cramming the cul-de-sac tightly, leaning against every bulkhead, step, and door, we somehow retained enough space for Rhonetta to continue her lazy dance. She was oblivious to us all until she encountered an outstretched foot and nearly tripped.

Finally a neighbor of Calypso returned from work and had to wade through our laughing, wavering, drunken selves.

Tiptoeing to avoid stepping on hands, legs, ashtrays, and drinks, she barely managed to get into her cabin.

"It's 4 A.M.," she commented as she closed her door. "You guys might want to take it to the open deck."

Inspired by the idea, we gathered our alcohol and prepared to move en masse to the open deck. Leo rose and trudged off without a word, spinning Lorena off like a leaf fallen from a tree. With surprising quiet, eight of us strode up to the open deck. Outside the night was warm, damp, and dark. Usually by 4 A.M. many of the couples had departed, so we mostly had the deck to ourselves. We clustered around the life jacket bin. Lorena brought her guitar and she and Calypso sang songs softly together. I sat beside Rasa in the dark, periodically slapping her groping hands away.

Caribbean air has a magic quality to it so late at night, with the sea breeze tugging at your hair and making your skin almost clammy. Time seemed irrelevant up there, forty feet above the surging waves cut so noisily by *Conquest's* bow. After a while Clarence rose to his full, staggering height and declared it was time to leave. We all looked at our watches in surprise. Sudden awareness of the late hour anchored us to reality, and the same spontaneity that created our little party was the same that pulled it apart. That was a metaphor for ship life.

In a blink the party was down to only three individuals cramming onto the life jacket bin together; Calypso, Lorena, and myself. Calypso, now drunk as a skunk, perched atop my lap. The atmosphere changed into a drained, yet enchanted mood. We enjoyed each other's physical and emotional proximity, enjoying the much-needed human touch in this cold, artificial life we lived. The sky eased from its blackness into a deep blue, and we all dropped into reflective, fatigued silence.

Eventually the ship hit a wave roughly, shaking us from our reverie. "I need to go to bed," Calypso said with a start, realizing that she had fallen asleep. "Brian, can you give me a wake-up call at 5:30? I work at 6:00."

"No worries," I said. "I'll still be awake anyway because I don't work until 11:00 today."

"Lucky boy."

She had no idea how lucky I felt. Though similar social events materialized and vanished regularly for us all on *Conquest* that summer, there was something special about this party. With this night I confirmed what I already knew: life was about people. The need for human touch, for companionship in this otherwise all-work and no-play environment was paramount. Suddenly I did not blame those who came to ships and cheated on their spouses. You did whatever it took to survive, and everyone present knew that it meant nothing more than that.

I knew dozens and dozens of happily married men working the dining rooms who cheated on their wives. Anyone who wanted to could get some action on a ship, even Aric's fat Indonesian roommate, Made. The vast majority of these men were literally 10,000 miles from home and slaving like animals to ensure a better life for their wives and children. They did not want to be here, it was backbreaking work that chewed up your sanity and broke your body, and as a bonus it was desperately impartial and lonely. In this case I definitely thought the end justified the means.

I was able to get the intimacy I needed without sexual intercourse, but for so many people they were too young, naïve, or macho to understand this. Until now I had always considered infidelity a lack of respect for one's spouse, regardless if the society considered women equal or not. While it could be said that I "cheated" on Bianca in mind and spirit, I had never slept with anyone else and had no intention of doing so. So was I any better than the others?

Reflecting on our own internal issues, Lorena and I leaned against each other and watched the sunrise quietly, the only two survivors of the impromptu party.

4 *Tattoo Goo*

BARELY A MONTH AFTER MY THIRTIETH BIRTHDAY, I found myself walking down the streets of the island of Cozumel, Mexico on a mission. I was accompanied by Leo and our mutual friend Nikolo. It was a beautiful, if hot, summer day, so Leo and I wore shorts and tank-tops. Nikolo, however, remained in his usual jeans and heavy t-shirt. We refrained from mentioning his inappropriately hot attire because we knew he wore it in order to better hide his extra pounds. He was the only short and round Croatian I had met. He buzzed his hair more from sloth than any other reason. He was a low-key and solid acquaintance of ours, a good foil to our outrageous behavior.

Our first order of business on this steamy Caribbean Friday was to find a few drinks. Unfortunately we had a fair distance to walk before we could obtain any. The international pier was built three miles south of the main pier, the one directly across from the mainland's nearest city, Playa del Carmen. Mega-ships like *Conquest* needed extra depth and exclusively docked to the south. The main downtown area of Cozumel blossomed around the original pier, so we had a good half hour walk to reach the cluster of bars and restaurants and shops. By then the sexy bitches were thirsty and Nikolo was exhausted.

We found a fantastic balcony bar called Terra Maya, whose entire wall facing the sea was open. Instead of a wall, or even windows, there was a long, S-shaped bar and open air. The sea breeze blew in and ruffled the palm fronds above us, as well as pushed us on our rope-swing seats. We ordered two rounds of frozen margaritas in those ubiquitous touristic yard-long plastic containers, and enjoyed the unparalleled view. Before us floated a perfect, perpendicular view of the Carnival *Paradise*, the world's only non-smoking cruise ship. Leo had transferred from *Paradise* and took no end of photos of it from this fantastic view. Far in the distance we could barely make out the hotels of Playa del Carmen across the straight.

"Well," I eventually said with a slam of my empty margarita container, "I'm sufficiently lubed. Shall we?"

"Damn straight," Leo answered, rising to his full, impressive height.

"Are you really going to do this?" asked Nikolo. "Are you crazy?"

"Finally someone who observes that I am crazy and not merely stupid. Of course I'm going to do this. Leo, you have your arm with you?"

"Got it, boss."

"Then let's do it."

We walked a block away to a small tattoo parlor perched above a series of shops selling cheap serapes and Kahlua. It was a single room with walls covered in photos of tattoos past. One wall held a huge mirror, before which sat the work chair and an exceptionally well-muscled Mexican. His face was very dark and wide, revealing his heritage as Mayan rather than Spanish, and his arms were sheathed in tattoos of jaguars, jade jewelry, and all manner of cultural icons. It was magnificent artwork and worthy of a few minutes gawking.

"That's amazing work," I commented with a hiccup. "Who did it?"

He shrugged, obviously not comprehending English. I gestured to the tattoo and asked "Who?" in poor Spanish, "*¿Quien?*"

"*Mi hermano.*"

"Your brother?"

"*Si, señor,*" he answered. "*¿Qué desea?*"

"Uh," I began in my inebriated state. "See this tattoo?" I pointed to Leo's arm. "*Uh...¿Mira el tattoo aqui?*"

He chuckled at my terrible Spanish, but seemed pleased I was trying.

"*Yo quiero,*" I added, meaning "I want it."

"*¿El mismo?*"

"Yes, *mismo*...this one. *Exactamundo.*"

He nodded and strode over to a cabinet. From inside he retrieved some carbon paper and began tracing the tattoo directly from Leo's arm. Once working, he ignored us completely.

"So you're actually doing the same tattoo as Leo, eh?" Nikolo asked. "I don't think I'm cool enough to do that."

"You are," Leo assured. "One of the few. We'll make a sexy bitch out of you yet."

"I thought about that, too," I said, "I never thought I would ever get a tattoo. So permanent, you know? But over the last month I realized that it is exactly the kind of tattoo I want. I do feel a bit odd, though, like I'm some sort of Leo groupie."

"So many are," Leo said with his usual Afrikaans-tinted thunder. "But you are *the* Sexy Bitch. You'll take it and make it yours."

"Well, this place seems clean. I mean, getting a tattoo in Mexico can potentially be a bad idea. I wish he spoke English."

Leo laughed. "Typical American. You wish *he* spoke English even though you're in *his* country. Only Americans think their language is the only one on earth. So, Mr. Arrogance: you're in Mexico, speak Spanish."

"Fair enough."

The artist finished his pattern and traced it on my arm. He gestured to the mirror and looked at me expectantly. I nodded, we agreed on a price via notes on paper, and he prepared for action. I watched him pull fresh needles from their original plastic containers, and he donned fresh latex gloves. I looked to Leo one last time and shrugged as we shared a grin.

The artist inked the outline of the tribal sun on the ball of my right shoulder, then stepped back to review it. Whether I liked it or not I had to go through with it now. Before continuing, to my surprise, the artist pulled a bottle of tequila from a nearby drawer and downed a slug. Six eyes stared at him in mute horror, and he slowly lowered the bottle as he sensed something awkward. Then all four of us burst out laughing.

To my surprise, the tattoo did not hurt at all. Though the alcohol numbed me, I had been assured by many that tattoos rarely hurt with modern equipment. I insisted that Leo take a few photos of the procedure, half to remember the time because I was going to be too drunk to, and half to reassure my long-suffering mother that the place was clean.

About forty minutes later we were at Señor Frog's, shirtless, and holding a shot of tequila. I was the proud owner of a brand new, glistening, jet-black tattoo. It was hidden beneath large white gauze, taped aggressively to my shoulder. With great ceremony Leo handed me a small purple jar.

"This, my friend," he said over the blasting music with a deep Afrikaans rumble, "is the Tattoo Goo. I inherited this from Calypso when I got my tattoo, and it is now yours. Use it wisely."

The three of us downed the shot in unison.

"Lube it well for a few days. The black will rise into a scab, then fall off. You can stop then."

"Nikolo, you're next," I teased. "Next week it is your turn to inherit the sacred sauce."

He eyed my blood-soaked gauze warily, but said nothing.

Drinking and laughing, we took idiotic photos of each other and were caught up in the party atmosphere. There were hundreds of wildly drunk vacationers, invariably from the States, all dancing, drinking, shouting, vomiting, and everything in between. We had to scream at each other to be heard. After a while a sexy waitress slinked over to the table and caught our attention. Incredibly beautiful, her brown skin was smooth and lined with an alluring veneer of sweat. She wore little more than an Old West-style double holster with bottles of tequila instead of six-guns.

"I must! I must!" cried Leo, nearly falling off his seat to lean closer to her. She smiled up at him with lips red, full, and lined flawlessly with dark brown.

"We just did, like, forty-five shots," I warned over the music of 120 decibels.

Nikolo, not enjoying himself nearly as much as his two wild companions, pulled money from his wallet and handed it to the waitress. He indicated Leo with a nod.

She reached out to caress Leo's cheek and, in a well-practiced maneuver, pulled his head down to her breasts. Without warning she cranked his head around, whipped a bottle from her belt, and poured a long shot into his open mouth. Leo spluttered and hollered as she then rubbed his head on her breasts and shook it like a cement mixer. Then she vanished like a wet dream, leaving him panting and fouled.

Occasionally the music blasted even louder as everyone created a giant mamba line. Swarthy Mexican bartenders stood on chairs over the line, pouring tequila roughly into the gaping mouths of those who passed beneath. We all agreed that as good a party as it was, it paled in comparison to a crew party. After all, this was public and no one could actually have sex on the dance floor. I was fairly confident there were no soiled pants, either.

We lost most sense of reality and started doing double shots at approximately 4 P.M. Nikolo saved us when he observed the time. We paid off our drinks, took a few more embarrassing photos of ourselves, and finally rushed off to find a taxi. Work was within the hour!

5 The Torture of Funship Freddy

DESPITE MY TREMENDOUS EFFORTS TO AVOID BOGO, I still had to live with the man. I was secure in my beliefs and comfortable around his excessively numerous accoutrements of faith, but to avoid a debate I had to tread carefully.

Fortunately Bogo had found something new to obsess over: his infant son. He fairly floated over the decks, insisting on showing everyone he encountered a photo of his first baby boy. I was genuinely happy for him and knew he would be a good father, so I didn't mind his repeated praising of God while I was shaving, sleeping, everything.

Yet even as he rejoiced, Bogo secretly wept. His request for a work break was denied. This was his first such request in over ten years, yet the company gave no reason for its decision. He would have to wait another five months to meet his newborn son.

Secretly I was aghast at the baby photos he plastered on all the walls of our cabin. I had no doubt that the moment of birth was monumental and wonderful, but I was equally sure no one wanted to see photos of it. I couldn't fathom why he didn't show photos of a two-minute baby, carefully cleaned and warmly wrapped in a blanket with Mom. Instead I was barraged with the junior's first terrifying seconds in this world: discolored, slimy, and screaming. Bogo displayed no less than fifteen full-sized glossy photos by his bunk. They scared me so much that I jumped up onto my bunk like a child trying to avoid the monster under the bed.

I was swapping uniforms one evening when Bogo stormed into the cabin in a huff. He was exceptionally angry, his bald head a deep red that offset the purple beneath his eyes in a frightening manner. He stood before the desk for a moment to close his eyes and catch his breath, nearly trembling with rage.

"Bogo, what's wrong?" I had the time to be considerate this week because, by some miracle, my schedule allowed thirty minutes between shifts. Of course, that still made me a full thirty minutes "late" for my dinner shift because waiters had to guard their stations from roving packs of head waiters.

Bogo turned to me with emotions warring over his features. He was obviously trying to control an emotional outburst, but was losing the battle.

"I just don't understand!" he finally blurted. "What did I do to him? Nothing!"

"Who?"

"You know who!" he seethed. "Gunnar! Can you believe the man had the gall to deny me my morning coffee? I work day and night nonstop, seven days a week without complaint. I take a ten minute break with my coffee, an apple, and my book...and that's too much for him!"

All of the AMDs took an occasional break on the mezzanine above the Lido deck. Instead of going into the break room and out of sight, we would grab a quick coffee and still be able to supervise the buffet from above. Unlike regular employees, we never had time for a proper lunch break so we took only snippets of time.

"Because of his *spies*," Bogo continued angrily. "I noticed some unusual employees hanging around the mezzanine. Then suddenly I get called down to Gunnar's office and chastised because of a 'reported misconduct.' He made it absolutely clear that there was to be no eating unless on official break time."

"*Official* break time?" I asked. "We don't get breaks."

"Exactly, and I said so to him. He shrugged his shoulders and said most employees eat between shifts, and we should learn to do the same. But I work all day straight, only taking a few minutes to change my uniform in the evening!"

"Me too! I leave the Lido the very minute I'm supposed to be checking in at Renoir. He can't be serious?"

"I would watch your behind," he warned. "This is because of you."

"Me?"

"Oh, yes. He expected to catch *you* stealing food again."

"That was *once*! I'm like the *only* crew member who's only done it once, Cat damn it!"

Bogo became calmer and more serious. "None of these dramas happened before you came along. He has it out for you, and he is making the rest of us suffer for it. And what is this I hear about a Lido report you gave to the maitre d'?"

"I wrote a four-page report on my recommendations regarding the Lido. Nothing reflects on you, Bogo. It was all policies and layout stuff, things that I thought could be improved. If I am going to be management, I should act like it."

"Did he ask you to write this?"

"No."

"What's wrong with you, man?"

"He implied such things would be expected of me, why wouldn't I?"

"He was just posturing. He doesn't want you to think! He wants sycophants and automatons. He wants stupid people to just do what he says. What, are you trying to make me look bad? I've never written any reports."

"Jesus, I'm just trying to show my worth. There's little enough I can do during midnight buffet, and as a waiter there's nothing I can do."

"Don't take the Lord's name in vain," he chided. "Brian, listen to me: you need to just shut up and stay out of trouble. That's the wise thing to do."

"But—"

"You see, there is a big difference between intelligence and wisdom," Bogo preached. "I want wise employees, not smart ones. I'm not Greek: I can't stand around to discuss politics and philosophy. I have work to do. You, you hang around with intelligent people and you think too much. Act like Leo: shut up, obey, and try not to get caught drunk too often."

"How does that improve anything?"

"That's not our problem. Carnival is making their money, so just do what Gunnar says. He's not going to give you your stripe anyway. I have been working here for ten years and all I have is a single stripe."

"Maybe that's because you simply obey, and don't try to organize and lead. Being a leader is a lot more than just telling people what to do."

Bogo shook his head sadly. "Altruistic nonsense. I know what happened to you. You were promised a full stripe by Dan and Reginald, but it's not going to happen with Gunnar. You could save his child from a burning building and he still wouldn't give it to you. Just stay out of trouble and hope he is transferred soon so someone else will promote you."

Five minutes later I rushed down to the Renoir, mind on my performance. I always took tremendous pains to ensure I was the best I could be. Even my tattoo Friday was organized, planned for a day when my guests went to the supper club. As far as I was aware, my only imperfection was the dreaded Vegetable Tower Tragedy.

I was still sore about Gunnar catching me and making assumptions that fit his preconceptions. Of the literally hundreds of entrees that were stolen *every night* in the dining rooms by waiters, why did he catch me? Perhaps it was because I was not an experienced thief. I recalled how Tekin would sit in the Renoir with two entrees on the chair beside him. He would notice management across the room and not flinch. Once when Ferrand entered the dining room, Tekin merely laid down his fork and waited patiently with a plate *on his lap*. At the last moment Ferrand turned elsewhere and Tekin casually resumed as if nothing were amiss.

So I was a terrible thief and an even worse liar...did that preclude me from management? Somehow I felt Carnival would not like to hear that!

Camilla was dutifully guarding our supplies and folding napkins on a chair in the center of our station. Today's pattern was not the usual spiraling candles, but some funky corncob-looking thing.

"How are you today, my dear?" I asked.

Camilla threw aside her lapful of linens and looked up at me with eyes swollen from tears. Though we were short on time, I saw immediately that we needed a few minutes to talk.

"Uh-oh! What's wrong?"

Fighting back further sobs, she sniffed loudly and rubbed her large nose with almost comical urgency. "You know I went to the doctor yesterday?"

"Of course," I said.

Camilla had been fighting a skin condition for the last three weeks. Small, itchy red dots had appeared all over her body and refused to go away despite her best efforts. She could barely sleep because it felt like she was covered with biting red ants.

In the beginning we had both brainstormed on the cause, but knew it could be anything. The water we showered in was chemically dense, our towels and bed linens were aggressively cleaned with harsh detergents, and even the air itself below decks was sanitized and artificial. The ability to obtain quality lotions was limited to whenever we actually got off the ship in port. Needless to say, the touristic areas of Jamaica were not exactly renowned for skin-exfoliation specialists on every street corner.

"He gave me an ointment that was supposed to help," Camilla continued, "but this morning I woke up in worse pain than ever! The little dots all doubled in size and became even *more* sensitive!"

She showed me hands covered with the evidence. It looked somewhat like a bad case of the chicken pox, but the marks were strangely neater and more uniform. Each blemish insisted on a centimeter of no-dot's land between itself and its neighbor. Mercifully her face was somehow immune.

"They are worse everywhere," she lamented. "So I went to Gunnar for permission to go to a doctor in the States. I can't believe they sent me to that guy in Mexico. He hardly spoke English, for Christ's sake! Are they really so cheap?"

"Well, it's a corporation," I said sympathetically. "They were just going through the cheaper motions first. I'm sure Gunnar can get you into a higher quality doctor in America."

"Are you kidding? You know what he said? He told me to change my sheets every day and toughen up. You know how long that takes; you think I have an extra hour every day to wait in line for pillows and sheets?"

"But they have to get you to a doctor," I insisted. "You can't go around serving food with a condition like that. If the ship doctor doesn't know what it is, he can sign for you to see a dermatologist."

"That's the problem!" she wailed. "I *can't* serve food with this condition. Gunnar hinted very strongly that if they can't figure out what it is, they will send me home."

"What? Surely they have to exhaust their options before firing you!"

"I borrowed money to get here," Camilla continued under her sobs. "How else could I afford to fly halfway around the world? Do you know how hard it is to borrow U.S. $1,000 back home? If I get fired, I won't be able to pay it back forever!"

"Don't worry, Camilla," I soothed, "We'll get it figured out. Seriously, it's not hard to get you to a doctor when we are in home port. Even if we have to pay for it, that beats losing your job and going back home!"

"Y-you could you help me get a doctor in the States?"

"Of course! I—"

"Brian!" a high-pitched, snobbish voice interrupted. Plump, toadying Catalina bounced toward us. "Gunnar wants to talk to you."

I gave her a disagreeable look even as Camilla wiped her tears. "Catalina, can't you see we are in the middle of something?"

"When the boss wants to talk to you," she replied with a haughty tone, "you drop what you are doing and go."

"He wants to see me now, before dinner?"

"Seems like you are wasting time now. You want me to tell him that?"

"Oh, come on! Fine. Camilla, I'll be right back."

I rushed down to Gunnar's office on the I-95. I couldn't imagine what he wanted, and all sorts of negative thoughts flooded my mind. I knew I had done nothing wrong, so why did I feel guilty?

At his desk, Gunnar sat behind a stack of papers that threatened to fall over. He was not a neat man, despite the Scandinavian propensity for it. When he saw me he set his pen down casually, as if there were all the time in the world.

"Hi, Gunnar," I greeted with merely a hint of optimism. I didn't want to seem too artificial, but I wanted to be positive.

"Brian," he said, "I am informing all the lesser officers personally of this, which I guess should probably include you. I will not allow any more food to be eaten during breaks on the Lido."

"O.K.," I said neutrally. "Why is that?"

He looked at me with annoyance. "Because I said so."

I smiled in an effort to ease his mild indignation. "Of course. I was just curious if there was something specific. You know, something to keep my eyes open for. So I won't eat on my

Lido breaks. I'll just eat, well, wait a minute…I won't be able to eat at all!"

Though my conversation earlier with Bogo had implied this would happen, I had not really taken it seriously. But now I realized that Gunnar was actually sincere about denying me food. Sure I could toughen up a bit, maybe skip a meal every day, but this was something else entirely. His look made it obvious that he couldn't care less about the predicament he was placing me in.

"You can eat during meal times like everyone else," he said.

"But I can't," I explained. "My only time off during the whole day is a few fifteen minute breaks while on Lido. I can't get all the way down to the dining room, wait in line, eat, clean my dishes, *and* return up ten decks in only fifteen minutes!"

"So you miss lunch," Gunnar said blandly. "Is that too hard for you?"

"But I miss dinner, too."

"Why is that?"

"You know that hardly any waiters ever make it to dinner during the scheduled mealtime. We have to be in the dining room protecting our supplies."

"Protecting your supplies from what?"

I paused, mouth open and about to speak. This man was in charge of all the dining on board, and he didn't know the first thing about the dining room life!

"Well," I continued carefully, "I get off Lido at 5 P.M. I am to sign on to Renoir at 5:30. I can't shower, change, wait in line for and then eat dinner, and then get to the dining room all on time. That's the weird thing about my, uh, *unique* situation."

"Well, you can still eat breakfast every day. Eat your meal then."

"I work midnight buffet!" I protested. "I get off at 3 A.M. Breakfast stops at 7:30 in the morning! I am to sleep for a few hours, wake up for my *one meal* of the day, and then go back to sleep again? That's not exactly realistic, or fair."

Gunnar waved me away in dismissal. "You'll figure it out.

I'm sure you'll steal something again. You're not a guest, but are here to work. Maybe now you will understand that."

"No, I don't understand anything. How can you condemn me to only one meal a day? That's like a punishment for some crime I didn't commit!"

"I'm sure a good waiter would be in the dining room by now," Gunnar said as he nonchalantly gazed at his watch.

6 *Hunger Pains*

L ATE ONE MORNING BEFORE OUR LUNCH SHIFT ON Lido, I walked with Leo along the I-95. We passed groups of smoking crew members sitting on steps or huddling into corners. Zombies passed us with loads of laundry, bound for the continuously used and eternally trashed washing facilities in the bow. Shrink-wrapped pallet loads of supplies towered over us along the entire length of the hallway, forcing the traffic into narrow lines. Tomorrow we were in home port, and many offloads already crammed the halls, waiting for the forklifts.

We swung into the officers' mess briefly for a beverage. I had an apple and a cup of water, while he poured soft-serve ice cream into his cup before filling it with coffee.

Leo looked into my cup and said with a rueful smile, "Funship Freddy allows water, doesn't he?"

"For the moment, yes," I said.

"You should have heard Bogo during breakfast," Leo said with a rumbling laugh. "He was still complaining that he is not allowed to read his bible on break. I asked him why he can't read in his cabin like everyone else, and he said it was because of his roommate."

"He can't read with me in the cabin?"

"I guess it's too distracting with you sleeping there *alone.* You need to bring some bitches in there and really give him something to complain about."

"I can barely fit into the bunk by myself, let alone with someone else. How is it that people can handle their roommates having sex while in the cabin, but my roomie can't read when I am sleeping? Bogo is a strange beast."

"Speaking of strange beasts, you should have heard my roommate and his girlfriend last night. I felt sorry for the man."

"F&B trainee Ravi? What do you mean?"

"I was trying to get some sleep for a change, and they were at it as long as he could handle it. But Ravi couldn't take anymore. You should have heard him apologizing. It was pathetic."

"Well, not everyone can be a sexual champion. That's what makes you so special."

Leo began badly imitating his roommate Ravi by slouching and pretending to be incredibly tired. His deep, rolling r's sounded ludicrous with the fake, lilting Indian accent, "I do not have any more love for you, baby, I am sorry."

"Ai yai yai, Leo," I chided. "Everyone is watching. Will you keep it down?"

"Ugh, what kind of man is that? I guess he did all right, though, for an old man. They did it twice in half an hour."

"This is really not of interest to me, you know. Can we talk about cheeseburgers instead?"

"Anyway, you might be in for it," Leo continued. "I accidentally let it slip where you were on your last vacation."

"So?"

"Not to Ravi, but Bogo," he pressed. "You were in *Transylvania.* He'll probably toss holy water on you, or at least bless you in your sleep."

"Too bad he can't put a stake through Gunnar's heart. He's the undead predator of man."

"Maybe if you wore garlic it would ward him off."

"Don't mention garlic, I'm hungry enough as it is."

At this hour there was no food available, but sometimes there was fruit in the officers' mess. Ice cream was accessible at all hours, but that was a poor breakfast. It had been nearly a month since Gunnar's crackdown on eating during breaks. I thought he may have just been posturing again, but in the first week I noticed a surprising number of bartenders skulking around the buffets. Of course they had no business being there and were probably spies.

Ironically, head waiters and team waiters were allowed to get a plate of food from the guest buffet on their breaks, assuming there was no line. Yet the Lido officers were denied this. As a regular trainee, Leo had plenty of time for meals and was unaffected by the crackdown, while Bogo had plenty of paisanos in the kitchen who shared their Indian food at any hour, day or night.

All I had was maybe an apple or a tomato once a day during the allowed times. I was literally surviving on the pizza I stole every other day at 3 A.M. That was the only time I felt safe, protected by my honorary membership in the Filipino mafia.

I was already fifteen pounds lighter from my forced diet and my twelve hours a day of continuous walking. Prior to joining the ships I had enjoyed great health as a marathon runner, mountain climber, and practitioner of yoga. I had been six foot one and a robust 200 pounds, but now I was in *truly* remarkable shape. For the first time in my life I had a washboard stomach. At all hours I was brimming with energy and vitality, living the natural high that athletes enjoyed. Yet I was hungry every minute of every day and bitterly resentful of it all.

"By the way, I'm up to eight," Leo mentioned, indicating the number of photo requests he had received so far this cruise. "Whatcha got?"

"Six," I replied. Another advantage of the new super-sexy and super-hungry Brian was the flood of female attention.

"Oh!" he chided, "Getting close, are you? I'm still taller than you'll ever be."

"And I'm older than you'll ever be, if you don't shut up."

We had begun competing in everything. If he could do thirty pushups in a minute, I was honor-bound to defeat him. I never could, but I would best him on pull-ups instead. He could down twice as many beers as I could, but I could hammer shots of tequila with impunity.

One subject I refused to compete over, however, was the women. As he saw more and more opportunity to sleep with more and more gorgeous women, he struggled less to remain faithful. Finally a few days ago he had resolved his inner debate and had taken a drunken Australian into his cabin. Since then it was a different woman every night.

He constantly asked me questions about Bianca, how we met and what our vacations were like together. He was simply in awe that I had found a woman that I felt was too good to cheat on.

"It's a matter of priorities," I explained as we walked. "I feel the same urges as you, but my priority is getting with Bianca. I won't do anything to jeopardize that, whether it means subsisting on one tomato a day or abstaining from sleeping with all the hot, hot bodies around me. More's the pity."

"*Oh*, are they hot," Leo agreed solemnly. "You know, last night I slept with Lorena."

"Oh?"

"You know, she's kinda weird, but it was good." He sounded genuinely surprised.

"That's great."

"You should give it a try. That bitch is hot for you, you know."

"Maybe next time."

Suddenly Leo started laughing so hard he nearly choked. He elbowed me and gestured down the I-95. "Look at Funship Freddy," he chortled.

Thirty feet before us was Gunnar eating from a small bowl of ice cream. He stood sideways to us, revealing the horrendous curvature of his spine. I winced in disgust at his noodly posture. Why, his shoulders drooped so low that he honestly looked hunchbacked! I couldn't believe it didn't hurt to slouch so much.

"He's so gross," Leo laughed, rolling the r like thunder.

"You know, I pity that man," I said honestly. Just then Gunnar called for us to stop.

"Brian," Gunnar said, looking me in the eye. "I want you to stop wearing your necklace. It looks unprofessional and is not allowed, anyway."

I blinked in surprise. I wore a thin string of black beads from Jamaica. I had thought it very unobtrusive, and said as much.

"You've got to be joking!" I protested. "Every Italian officer on board is wearing half a kilo of gold around their necks! Most of them mousse up their chest hair, for cryin' out loud, and I swear I saw the second officer wearing his *astrological* sign!"

"So you're comparing yourself to senior officers already?"

Seeing that he was deadly serious, my humor crashed and I shut my mouth. "O.K., Gunnar, I'll take it off right now."

"Of course you will."

Without a word or even a glance at Leo, Gunnar stalked away with his arms locked tightly behind his back and chin resting on his breastbone. I shared a meaningful look with Leo and we both started laughing. Leo fingered the necklace he was wearing: a thick cord sprouting dozens of thorny beads that made it look like barbed wire on steroids.

As we resumed our walk, I just shook my head in wonder at the overt favoritism. Leo felt like he had won another point in our competition, and began singing boldly his favorite hip hop lyrics to every crew member we passed, *"Ain't got the time for all the bitches on my cock..."*

Conquest silently sailed up the Mississippi River on our way to New Orleans. As was my habit, I haunted the open deck. The moon was full this night, and so brilliant that the silvery glow was enough to read by. Both river banks were lined with swampy forest canopy, wild and untouched. Being up on deck four felt like I was flying because I was higher than the treetops. Without any waves crashing on the hull, we floated in silence that furthered the sense of ghostly flying.

I was mesmerized by the silver highlights of the forest as they morphed into the dark, mysterious green depths of the foliage. The horizon held numerous pockets of lights, many orange, some white, and a few red. These were oil refineries, punctuating the distance so that it never faded into black but was visible for miles and miles.

I smoked my cigar quietly, wearing nothing but the shorts that Diana had stolen during the toga party on *Fantasy*. The cool breeze seemed at odds with the humid night, tickling my skin strangely and with that subtle, magical vigor I usually attributed to the tropics.

The night was ripe for reflection, and I indulged. Was I happy? Was my plan to get with Bianca working? I had just read a long, sweet e-mail from her as she prepared to sign on the newest Carnival ship. I was all but guaranteed to not see her for a long time now. I had asked her to *not* request the newest ship in order for us to work together, but she wanted to follow all her colleagues going there. I recalled bitterly how her friends alone enable her to survive the tribulations of ship life.

Realistically, if Bianca came to *Conquest* now, we would only have a few months together before I signed off, leaving her completely alone. So rather than both of us being lonely, it was only I. Numerous times I had said I would do anything to be with that woman, and I meant it. But I *wasn't* with her, and it appeared I wouldn't be for many months. Before we could do anything else, I had to secure my place with Carnival. Only then could we make a plan.

But was it worth literally starving for?

I tried to justify Gunnar's rules and our strained relationship. Were my feelings of persecution justified? Was he out to get me, or was he simply an ass to everyone? After all, he had denied Camilla access to proper medical treatment and wouldn't let Bogo read his bible on break. Meanwhile Leo repeatedly came to work so drunk that he sometimes literally passed out in the corner...and he was on the fast track for a full stripe.

Maybe I wouldn't see Bianca for a while, but the best things in life were worth fighting for. I simply had to find the joys in my life to offset the trials. And I was happy with my newfound vitality, the snippets of time off in the Caribbean, and the spontaneous crew parties. I was a social creature and while acutely lonely, I was simultaneously overwhelmed with flirtations with women of all races and colors. My ego was caressed even if nothing else was!

The ship began to slide past the density of New Orleans, and I watched with fascination. Rooftops glowed a watery orange where the city lights outshone the moon. We passed dirty warehouses and dark streets dripping with intrigue. Misty globes from gas lamps glistened off wet brick streets and the silvery lines of canals shot into the distance like veins.

Finally we slowed near the famed St. Louis Cathedral. The huge statue of Andrew Jackson was a black outline before the massive, ornate church. To add to the mysterious vibe, dark forms of crew members slumped in the shadows, whispering in strange languages. They were on the phone with families and friends back home, taking advantage of our home port's cellular access.

Tiny figures below scrambled over the dock as *Conquest* sidled up to a riverside shopping mall and convention center. Before us towered the beastly metal bridge of the Crescent City Connection which marked the farthest *Conquest* could travel upriver. Bundles of smashed rope and rubber the size of Volkswagen Beetles held the ship away from the concrete pier. The pressure of such a goliath rubbing against the bumpers to the ebb and flow of the mighty Mississippi created bizarre, smooshed shapes and deafening squeaks.

On our mooring deck able seamen secured the ship. The heavy mooring lines, called hawsers, were far too thick to throw to shore. Instead they were married to lighter ropes that could be hurled over the gap. It was a fast, frantic maneuver for the dock workers to grab the lines before they slid into the river. After they were caught, the lines were hauled back, tugging the hawsers along. Finally the hawsers were wrapped around the huge iron supports anchored deep in the concrete.

Fascinated, I watched the captain supervising from the Bridge deck above. He was required by international law to be present whenever the ship docked. I smiled when I recognized him as the one who had made an advance on Bianca. Most likely he had made overtures to any bikini he observed on the open deck. Like all the other Italian officers, other than the vital chief officer, he was also a nightly resident of the smoke-filled crew bar.

It was fascinating to watch so much action at 4 A.M. Yes, happiness in life was appreciating moments like this, the little things. I believed strongly that life was made up of moments, and living on the ship afforded me a wealth of those!

I stubbed out my cigar. All this inner reflection was fine and dandy, but it was also a load of crap. No matter how I tried to justify my situation, I had dropped from a waist of size thirty-five to thirty-two in one month...all this hassle to be with a woman I would not see again for untold months. The price was too high.

7 *Viral Infections and You*

I SNAPPED OFF THE WATER OF MY SHOWER THE SECOND I realized an announcement was sounding over the PA system. Other than the weekly boat drills, nothing was piped into the officers' cabins unless it was extremely important.

I stood listening, dripping, tense.

"Ladies and gentlemen," a voice continued with grave sincerity, "I will now demonstrate."

A painfully accented Italian voice began singing, "Happy Birthday to me...Happy Birthday to me...Happy Birthday Dear Capitan...Happy Birthday to me."

Captain Banducci continued, "As I mention before, I am obligated to remind everyone that to wash of hands is very *importante*. Wash the hands and remember to sing for *venti secondi*, that is, twenty seconds for soap to destroy germs. Thank you and enjoy your cruise."

Perhaps inevitably, the most dreaded scourge of the seas had stricken *Conquest*: no, not pirates, but the plague. Norovirus, to be precise. I had heard of it in the past because of the news, when they trumpeted how Bianca's ship was *almost* not allowed in port. While in fact cleaner than any public restaurant on land, the media gleefully compared *Conquest* to rats infected with Bubonic Plague.

Like many Americans, I had naively assumed our media was uncensored because it was not government run. When I left the States and its biases behind, I discovered that, perhaps even worse than government censorship was that America's news was run by the *public*. Popularity and thus advertising dollars dictated what was shown. Therefore Americans were mostly ignorant of anything embarrassing we've ever done as a nation, and dangers were escalated into hysteria to appease our morbid fascination.

Outbreaks surprised me because the crew meticulously bleached the very walls and ceilings of the kitchen and service areas daily. As a Lido supervisor, my job was to check the stations and tables by running a finger into corners, searching for grease or even dust. I did this nightly. Restaurants on land had laughable cleanliness standards compared to ships, and that is saying a great deal indeed.

To further ensure that health codes were upheld, ships sailing in American waters were subject to a random USPH inspection. The United States Public Health searches came twice a year, usually granting a few weeks' notice only because they needed customs clearance. During these times the tension level escalated through the roof, and little joy was to be found on the waves.

USPH inspections were arguably effective, but most of us felt they were simply absurd. Older ships carried the brunt of the attack because they lost a vital point simply by merit of not being new. A ship a couple of years old was expected to be as perfect as the day the champagne was broken on the hull...despite having carried tens of thousands of revelers tens of thousands of miles.

"Why are the slicers wrapped in plastic?" I asked Bogo one evening before my first USPH inspection. Despite his working eighty hours a week during breakfast, lunch, and dinner, as senior Lido supervisor Bogo was required to stay up late and ensure the Lido was properly cleaned. The wells beneath his eyes had settled into a permanent purplish black, like rotting eggplant.

"Listen and learn," Bogo instructed tiredly. "It is not possible to keep a piece of equipment clean enough to satisfy the USPH."

"Oh, come on."

"With Lord God as my witness," Bogo said to me with absolute sincerity, "we once had a new slicer that had literally *not been used*, and they said it was 'not maintained to acceptable standards.' So I took these two machines apart and labeled them 'out of order.' Even broken they will be thoroughly inspected, but not so outrageously."

"But won't they think it fishy if there are no working slicers in a kitchen that supplies food for thousands of people every day?"

"They haven't figured that one out," Bogo replied with a grin. "And I'm not about to educate them."

"But isn't cleanliness next to godliness?" I teased.

"I'm from India and you make hygiene jokes? Anything verified clean is wrapped in plastic to prevent some ignoramus from placing a dirty cup in the wrong rack and screwing everyone."

I followed Bogo throughout the Lido and observed just how right he was. In the kitchens literally half the equipment was wrapped in plastic or taken apart with a hand-written sign proclaiming, OUT OF ORDER. I watched chefs soaking, bleaching, scrubbing, and swearing in every direction, all under the sharp tongue of the head chef. Every single service station was inspected exhaustively, with Bogo on his back and running a white glove deep into the corners and grooves. He even held a flashlight between his teeth to inspect all the more closely.

Once a USPH inspection was passed, there was invariably a huge crew party to show Carnival's appreciation for all the extra work. While Carnival was extremely generous for all their crew parties, they spared no expense for a winning USPH score. It was a great reward if you were lucky enough to actually not be working at the time.

Yet despite all this extreme effort at maintaining extraordinary cleanliness, outbreaks of norovirus *did* occur. The reason was simple and unpleasant to hear: the unwashed masses brought it aboard and perpetuated it amongst themselves. Anyone who suffered the flu-like symptoms simply did not wash properly.

During my first norovirus outbreak, I had confidently noted all the hand-sanitizers Carnival provided for the guests, foolishly figuring it would be over soon. Sanitation stations greeted guests on the gangway even before security did, and the head of each and every buffet line was so armed. Every bathroom facility had soap as well as sanitizer. Yet after a few days of observation, I saw that hardly anyone ever used them. People were so lazy, in fact, that the captain felt obligated to humiliate himself by singing Happy Birthday over the intercom.

Cruise ships had a certain ratio of sick calls to passenger count they had to maintain. When too many folks complained of illness, the ship was required to report it to the port authorities, who reported it to the Centers for Disease Control. The percentage of sick warranting a report was actually quite low, but when there were almost five thousand people onboard, even 7 percent *looked* like a heckuva lot of sick people. If too many were ill, the ship was even forbidden to dock. As could easily be imagined, the media pounced on even the *hint* of such a thing with more fanfare than the moon landing.

If an outbreak was feared, literally hundreds of employees' lives were turned upside-down with brutal special cleaning duties. Nomadic packs wandered the hallways, bleaching every doorknob, handrail, and wall a hand could possibly touch, and every button on every elevator, coffee machine, and video game. In the dining rooms we bleached the trays, the menus, the saltshakers, the ketchup bottles, the toothpick holders, the sneeze-guards, the *everything*.

During outbreaks we lived in a floating madhouse of buckets, mops, cloths, and for the lucky few, rubber gloves. The system was formalized, exact, and even had a name: the Three Bucket System. We used different colored buckets for clean water, dirtied water, and bleach solution. Every waiter stayed extra late to double-wash the silverware and polish the glasses twice.

Exacerbating the situation, if an employee called in sick his or her roommate was forced into quarantine with them for two days, whether sick or not. It was extremely common for crew members, already taxed to the point of exhaustion, to claim illness just to get a full night's sleep. Such events artificially inflated the sick count, of course, and made finding replacements that much more difficult.

I was proud that, despite my overwork, lack of proper food and sleep, I never contracted the norovirus. My secret? I washed my hands to the tune of *"I'm Too Sexy."*

I'm too healthy for this ship, too healthy for this ship.
I am healthy, if you know what I mean...
'cause I wash my dirty hands on the plague ship.
On the plague ship, yeah, on the plague ship...
I'm the only one who washes on the plague ship...

"Amigo!" I called to our short, round waiter, *"¡Una mas margarita! Rocas, por favor!"*

I swallowed the remainder of my drink, eagerly searching between the ice cubes for every last drop of the life-giving elixir. It was a scorching afternoon in summer, but I enjoyed the sun on my skin. I needed this day very badly. I had not been able to get off the ship in nearly three weeks because of the USPH extra duties, and I was dying for some relaxation.

I sat with Camilla, who hid beneath the umbrella's shade. She wore a long-sleeve shirt and pants in order to hide her rash, sipping delicately from a bottle of Corona. The waiter soon returned to deliver my drink and remove my empty plate.

"Gracias, señor. Oh, uh, dos macho nachos, por favor."

"*¿Dos mas?*" he asked incredulously, eyeing how thin both Camilla and I were. After I nodded, he strode away muttering, "*Gringo loco...*"

"Jeez, Brian," Camilla chided. "This, after steak and enchiladas? I am starting to believe that you truly are American."

"Hey, I haven't had one single full, relaxed meal in over a month. I deserve this. Besides, you could use a few enchiladas yourself. You weigh, what, 105 pounds?"

"I don't know pounds. I am sophisticated and use a logical, neat, and orderly system. Even an ignorant savage like you may have heard of it: it's called metric. Ugh, imagine measuring distance by the length of some dead guy's foot? Americans are so creepy."

I snorted in response. Fate had arranged for both of us to enjoy a rare, if late, lunch off together. We planned to meet Leo and Nikolo when they returned from downtown, but in the meantime had started with some drinks and much-needed nourishment. As always, we had wisely chosen Fat Tuesday's, the closest bar to the ship, knowing we could be back onboard within minutes. While guests were required to walk through the duty-free shops running the length of the pier and chew up their precious port time, crew members could skip it by showing their IDs.

A couple of middle-aged ladies hovered beside our table, prompting us both to look up. They were easily recognizable as Americans: they wore blue jeans, tennis shoes, and a t-shirt large enough to fit a bear. They also were heavily laden with gifts for friends and family: bottles of Kahlua, vanilla, and tequila. One even wore a mini sombrero.

"You work on the ship, right?" Sombrero asked sweetly as she clutched her purse.

"Yes," I said.

"Oh, we loved the show last night!"

"That's great."

"It was so good. Especially in the second half, you know, the duet in the sparkling outfits."

"That's great," I repeated, slyly giving Camilla a knowing look. "But why are you telling me this?"

Sombrero glanced at her friend in confusion. "Aren't you the lead dancer?"

"Yeah," her friend added. "The tall one with the dark hair and pretty eyes."

"Sorry, ladies. I'm flattered, but that wasn't me. I'm in the restaurants."

"Oh! But, but aren't you American?"

"I am."

"But I've never seen any American in the dining room!"

"The one and only, my dear. Enjoy your day, ladies."

As they departed, Camilla gave me a withering look, which I pointedly ignored. This had happened several times in the last few weeks, and each time I received a great deal of ribbing from my assistant.

"Proud of yourself, aren't you?"

"You know it."

Instead of teasing me further, she said, "Ugh. There's Dylan. Act like you don't see him."

"Who's Dylan?"

"You haven't met him? He's a South African who used to work with Leo. He's in the Renoir as a team waiter, though he claims to have been an assistant maitre d' for Royal Caribbean."

"Really?"

"If you believe him, which I don't. He's the one Leo asked us not to tell about his plans today."

"Oh, that one. The one with the bad breath, he said."

"Exactly."

As soon as Dylan spotted us, however, he came directly over. He was a skinny man with sharp, almost rat-like features. His black hair was obviously dyed and aggressively lacquered into some sort of funky, spiky pompadour-thing.

"Camilla," he greeted hurriedly. "Have you seen Leo?"

"Nope," she answered, trying to hide her grimace as the

foul odor of his breath wafted over us. Even I, a cigar smoker, thought it was atrocious.

"Well, if you see him, tell him I'm looking for him, eh?" Like a number of South Africans I had met, his English was British-tinted rather than Afrikaans.

"Sure."

Without a further word, Dylan shot off into the crowd.

"That was brief," I commented.

"Trust me, it's better that way."

"So," I said, "you never told me how your latest visit to the doctor went."

She shook her head sadly. "This special cleaning is killing me."

"Give me your hands," I ordered. She gave them to me reluctantly, and I tried to hide my disappointment. The red pinpoints had flared into angry sores from the constant immersion in bleach.

"I wear three pair of those cheap-ass plastic gloves they gave us, but they didn't help."

"That's it. Next home port I'll find a dermatologist in New Orleans. All we need is a phone book and we are in business."

"Good. You know, we have a new ship doctor onboard. You know what the *bamboclat* said? He prescribed Thera-flu. It's not like I'm throwing up, for Christ's sake."

"Every one of them prescribes Thera-flu. I think they're ordered to."

"It's just my hands that are that bad, you know," she added with strange emphasis. Something was different in the way she added, "Everything *else* is good enough."

"Good enough for what?"

"I mean," she said with intensity, "that we can still have sex."

"To you women it's all sex, sex, sex. What am I, a piece of meat?" I teased with mock innocence. I even managed to bat my eyelids as I breathily said, "I prefer to...*make love*."

She looked at me expectantly, not amused at my joke. I lamely tried to salvage it by adding, "Romance...candles and such?"

"You're not like Leo," she said earnestly, still holding my hands. "You are a man. He won't even look at me because of my spots. Will you please, *please* have sex with me?"

Sensing we were being watched, I looked up to see the waiter staring incredulously at us, steaming nachos held aloft in two huge oven mitts. He said in English. "So you want check now?"

He warily handed the plates over, eyeing Camilla up and down appreciatively. Finally he gave her a wink.

Pretending that I had not heard her, I tore into the nachos with relish. She did not let me off the hook so easily.

"I'm serious. Will you please sleep with me?"

"What are you talking about?"

"I'm talking about sex. Lots of it. *After* the nachos, if you want."

"Camilla, you know I can't."

"Why not?" she pouted with force. "Oh, don't tell me it's because of your girlfriend, what's-her-name. You haven't seen her forever and you won't again for just as long. Besides, who would know?"

"I would."

"Oh, like you're so honest."

"You know I don't sleep around, why are you pressing me?"

"What about Calypso?"

"What about her?"

"Or Rasa. I heard she got you into her cabin for some action."

"That was an ambush," I protested, recalling a close call of the previous night. *Close* was an understatement! "I was nearly raped. I had to fight for my life to get out of there."

"I think you're a gay," Camilla finally said with defeat. "I can understand you saying no to me, but who would say no to Rasa?"

"Oh, come on, Camilla. Don't cut yourself short."

"You're so damn nice," she chided with resignation. "Just use my skin condition as an excuse. That's easier for me to handle than your damn decency."

"Oh, you know I don't care about your skin condition."

"Well, neither did Dennis."

I paused with a handful of chips inches from my mouth. "I beg your pardon?"

Suddenly Camilla beamed as if she were just named prom queen. "Dennis Wayalan and I shagged last night."

I blinked at her in surprise. "Dennis Wayalan? Are you serious?"

Dennis was a very handsome Indonesian man with light brown skin and a dash of waviness to his hair, indicating some Caucasian inheritance somewhere. He was a pleasant man whom I enjoyed working with. I also enjoyed working with his girlfriend.

"But he has a girlfriend!" I protested.

"So?"

"*On board,*" I emphasized. "I am very open-minded about people 10,000 miles from their wives, but he has a girlfriend right here who needs him!"

"That's her problem," Camilla scoffed.

Her attitude had completely changed before my eyes, and she began babbling excitedly about her experience. She narrated how they were working together on the Lido and started flirting one day, and how she finally approached him. Smugly she explained that he didn't mind the blossoming rash on her hands because they were tied back anyway.

As much as I loved naughty details, I didn't want to hear any of it. I was not at all impressed, and was disturbed by her sudden shift from desperation to gloating. I sensed strongly that something was not right in her deep down. For the moment I knew she just needed someone to listen to her first bit of "good news" in a long time. So I listened, and resolved to keep a close eye on her.

Her story was eventually cut off when Leo and Nikolo joined us. A shirtless Leo staggered a bit as they approached and nearly fell into a seat, while Nikolo soberly nodded hello.

"I'm pissed!" Leo blurted, apparently pleased with himself.

"Why? What's wrong?"

"He means piss drunk," Nikolo explained. "Only in America does pissed mean angry. Everywhere else it means drunk."

Nikolo wore his usual jeans and a t-shirt, but this time one sleeve was pushed far up. Bulging around his left shoulder was a massive, bloody bandage.

"Aha!" I cried. "You did it!"

Nikolo smiled craftily. "You bet I did."

The Croatian proudly peeled back the tape holding the bandage, wincing as it pulled his hair. He wore a huge new tattoo of a roaring tiger's head, brilliantly lit in fiery red and orange. I whistled in surprise at the audacity of the image on an arm that I thought would never see ink at all.

"Let me see!" a voice called from behind us. I didn't need to turn to recognize Dylan: the odor of his words preceded him. He eagerly rushed in to join us.

"That's huge, Nikolo!" I exclaimed. "Did it hurt?"

"Hell yes."

"Well," I said as I fished inside my beach bag, "it is worthy."

"Worthy of what?" Dylan interrupted keenly.

"The sacred sauce," I declared. Dylan silenced and watched with envy as I handed over the purple jar of Tattoo Goo. Nikolo took it up with delight.

"With Leo's kind permission, I now dub thee...the Other Other Sexy Bitch!"

I patted him on the back and then took back my nachos from Leo, who had greedily snatched them up. As Nikolo read the instructions on the jar, there was a moment of quiet. I glanced at my companions and realized that, though it was a moment of joy, each of us had brought issues with us this day. It reminded me that while I was dealing with my own turmoil, everyone had their own demons to deal with.

Camilla had dropped into sullen silence again, but tried to hide her emotions by casting fawning glances to Leo. Dylan, too, regarded Leo with admiration. It was obvious he wanted nothing more than to be in the man's good graces, and it was equally apparent that he had not yet achieved this. Leo was yet again piss drunk and oblivious to everything but my nachos. I wondered how he would get back on board without a shirt: no one was allowed to cross the gangway without a shirt. Nikolo was a quiet man of self possession, and I sensed that he was the most content of us all.

I sipped from my margarita, upset that I had perhaps over-analyzed the moment and therefore ruined it.

8 *Something Sweet at Midnight*

I LOVED THE GRAND GALA BUFFET, BUT NOT FOR THE same reason as most people. This superlative of midnight buffets was the only opportunity for me to display my organizational skills and prove I was worthy of being an assistant maitre d'. Oh, and it was pretty and stuff.

Most ships on most cruise lines presented some sort of once-weekly Grand Gala Buffet, a culinary masterpiece wherein the chefs craft every morsel into a work of art. Such extravaganzas were usually held at night because they required hundreds of additional man-hours to present. Further, it was assumed that few folks would have a scheduling conflict at, say, 1 A.M. The event was strictly formal and so very important that even the captain himself felt honor-bound to leave the crew bar to host it. As if all this were not enough incentive for the guests, *Conquest* took the additional step of combining the Gala with the wildly popular chocolate buffet.

Of course, additional diners meant additional staff. Being kindhearted, ships generally did not force employees to work from breakfast to lunch to dinner to midnight buffet to breakfast to lunch to dinner all in a row. Management grudgingly acknowledged that someone working more or less straight from 7 A.M. one day to 11 P.M. the next night had difficultly being cheery to demanding guests. Therefore waiters doing the Gala Buffet earned a breakfast off in there somewhere.

Traditionally only team waiters worked the midnight buffet. Their numbers were designed to maximize the breakfast buffets and we could ill afford to lose any of them for an extra shift. Therefore in order to pull in several dozen extra employees, we had to dip into the pool of head waiters. This is what led me to stare at my motley collection of four dozen head waiters, spread throughout a corner of the Lido because they numbered too many to fit into the break room.

While team waiters were more or less obedient, head waiters were hard to handle. They were privileged to be probably the highest paid group onboard, and behaved like it. Few cared to be present and even fewer cared to obey the simple commands they were given. Head waiters volunteered for the Grand Gala Buffet because it was the *only* way to get six hours of uninterrupted sleep, short of being quarantined.

While waiting for everyone to settle in, I took one last glance at my roster of names and where I had assigned them. A lucky few were allocated to crowd control and had only to ensure a smooth flow of bodies. Others were dispensed behind the buffet line with the chefs, refilling depleted items and such. Woe betide the head waiter who abused chefs during breakfast or lunch, for here the chef was supreme. The majority of extra waiters were simply glorified busboys, clearing tables and bringing coffee.

"O.K.," I said, rising to my feet. "Everyone looks here. Let's do the roll call and then…"

I trailed off as we all watched Leo stroll casually through the crowd to stand beside me. For a moment he stood tall and handsome in his formal evening uniform, but slowly he tilted like the Tower of Pisa. Just as he was about to fall, his arm shot out to the counter in a move that he no doubt thought was smooth in his obviously inebriated state.

I stared at Leo, amused.

Leo blinked at me, confused.

Both of us waited for the other to say something, and the awkward moment lengthened comically as everyone waited.

Then Leo hiccupped.

Laughter exploded from the crowd, and Leo smiled loosely, obviously trying to figure out what the joke was.

"Leo," I snapped. "Just go to bed, man. Every senior officer and manager onboard will be here in the next ten minutes."

Leo wobbled away in sloppy ignorance, without having ever said a single word.

As funny as the moment was, I was inwardly furious. The first hour of the Gala Buffet was easily the most stressful, and I had counted on Leo to assist me. Despite this abhorrent behavior, Leo was *still* on the fast track to getting his stripe and I was not. I had busted my butt to get to my cabin and don my whites before work because head waiters would not follow orders from anyone in their own uniform. During this time Leo had been hammering shots in the crew bar!

Finally I got everyone off to their duties, and made a few rounds to ensure they actually performed them. Because the Gala Buffet was on the Lido deck, there were no dining room doors to bar any guests from interfering and snooping and sneaking food. We had to rope off the area and assign guard waiters. This was when the head waiters were sure to disappear for a cigarette.

Even though I cruised through the entire dining room and did not see anyone missing, I knew that could change in a mere moment. As soon as I turned my back, head waiters scattered like cockroaches when the light came on. Part of my usual rounds was to swing through the hallway below the break room. The steps leading down to the hall were a usual haunt of the smokers, evidenced by hundreds of improperly snubbed butts littering the floor like leaves in autumn.

With my footsteps clanging loudly ahead of me, wayward waiters were warned of my approach. Down at the bottom of the steps, not far from where my friend Aric had passed out cold on the steel floor, was where I usually captured trouble-makers. They had nowhere to escape to, unless they ran through the guest areas of deck ten. Such areas were significantly taboo to waiters and the penalty was such that it was preferable to have a rebuke from me.

To my surprise, I did not find any head waiters, but a sole team waiter. It was Dylan!

"Come on, man," I chided. "You know this is not the time."

"Screw you," he retorted point blank.

"That's nice. What's *your* problem?"

In an effort at escalation, Dylan took a long drag of his cigarette with exaggerated calm. He tried to blow smoke in my face, but it backfired when he started coughing. Anyway, the acrid stink was an improvement over his usual breath.

Of course, I knew exactly what his problem was. He was upset at his exclusion from the "sexy bitch" club, despite his tremendous efforts to that end. We allowed him to trail along on the periphery of our group, as little as we cared for his presence, until this cruise. Just one week after Nikolo's tiger tattoo, Dylan had rushed off to get ink done like Leo's and mine. Because he had no pattern to draw upon, he had described it to the artist...badly. Instead of his tribal tattoo being subtle and smooth, his was vicious and sharp, like his nose, his pompadour, and general attitude. While Leo and I had said nothing, it had been Nikolo who denied Dylan use of the Tattoo Goo.

Obviously embarrassed at his pathetic attempt at coolly snubbing me, Dylan smashed out his cigarette and headed toward the steps.

"Enjoy your next few nights working the burger line," I called after him.

"What?" he protested. "Why would you do that? Give it to someone black or brown."

I ignored his racist remark.

"You claim you were an AMD, Dylan. Would you let someone disrespect you like this? A few days dealing with the cow animals will do you some good."

All I wanted was for things to go smoothly, and even the people I socialized with were causing me delays!

Unlike a normal buffet, the first hour of the Grand Gala Extravaganza was for photos only. This ensured that even those at the rear of the line could enjoy the untrammeled ice carvings and chocolate sculptures, cakes, tortes, and little chocolate canapés and parfaits. Dozens of extra tables had been erected to accommodate the feast and a system of ropes directed the flow of awed humanity to the climactic head of the display. Here stood the captain himself, splendid in his evening formals, with a retinue of senior officers in descending order of importance: the hotel director, the head chef, the food and beverage manager, and finally the senior maitre d'.

More than one thousand passengers lined up for their turn to walk past the amazing display of edible art. Because the lights were low, flash bulbs punctuated the dark like lightning and reflected off the great dragons and other mythical sea creatures carved from blocks of ice. The very air of the Lido was hushed in respect for the marvel, droning with the admiring murmur of the throng.

I was surprised that *Conquest* did not have some sort of narration during this part of the event, explaining to the guests what they were seeing and the extraordinary lengths the chefs took to bring such beauty to life. Because I had done voice work in the past, I offered to create a tape for this purpose. Senior maitre d' Ganesh had merely shrugged and said that if the chef was inclined to help, I could do so. So I had arranged for later this cruise to meet with the head chef in order to work out the script. Despite my efforts to keep Ganesh informed, he had remained indifferent throughout the proceedings.

My job during this first hour was crowd control. I had to

push, prod, and poke the head waiters into complying with their duty, which was to push, prod, and poke the guests into complying with the rules. The lines had to keep moving at a slow but steady pace, and anyone pausing too long had to be urged forward politely but firmly. Because the head waiters were not dealing with their own gratuity-paying guests, they sometimes snapped like drill sergeants, "Come on, people, move it!"

I worked in and out of the lines to ensure that no one snatched up a chocolate-dipped strawberry or some other delightful morsel before it was time. Because such a formal event was rare in America, I think that most parents were intimidated and kept their children on a tight leash. Making the adults behave, however, was not so easy. Only the grownups snuck food and needed a wrist slapped. Finally at two in the morning everyone had taken their photos and the hush was broken as the buffet was opened for dining.

To my surprise, the captain himself came charging through the guests directly at me. Captain Banducci was an incredibly handsome fifty-something Italian with a rock-solid jaw carefully shaded in designer stubble. His features were large and bold, as was his behavior and even voice. He towered above me somehow, despite my greater size.

"Why are you not in formal attire?" he demanded angrily in his deep, thickly accented voice.

"I am not allowed any, sir," I replied.

"Why not?"

"Apparently the F&B manager doesn't think I am worthy of the formals, but only the regular whites."

"Absurd!" he snapped. "Either you are officer or you are not."

"I agree, sir."

But he was already gone, having spun on his heel and departed. He rushed through the crowd, trailing bridge officers and awed guests alike, directly toward Gunnar. With a sharp word and equally pointed stabbing motion, he gestured for

Gunnar to follow him. Like a beaten dog with its tail between its legs, Gunnar humbly trailed after.

Yes, I sure did love the Grand Gala Buffet for reasons different than other folks!

9 *Showdown and Breakdown*

I WAITED FOR THE BAD NEWS WITH OUTWARD CALM.
This meeting of the restaurant heads was undoubtedly going to be rough. I sat with a simple, erect posture and tried to reveal as little emotion as possible. Beside me Ferrand sat uncomfortably, obviously wanting to be elsewhere, and Gunnar took great pains to ignore us both until Ganesh arrived. The tension in the air was suffocating.

I was here to finally establish my rank. That morning Leo had met with these three men and departed with a full stripe and a half. That was a whopper of a promotion, allowing him to skip the onerous Lido duties for the usual few years before ascending to the dining room. The reason for this unheard-of generosity, Gunnar had said, was because Leo was so very charming to the guests during dinner.

Finally Ganesh arrived, apologizing with his usual shrug. He sat on a chair beside the F&B manager's desk. He avoided my gaze. Even if I hadn't figured out months ago what the outcome of this meeting was to be, the behavior of the MDs certainly made it clear. The silence lengthened as we all waited for Gunnar to begin.

"So," Gunnar finally said. "I have decided not to promote you."

I was not exactly flabbergasted.

"Why?" I asked tightly.

He did not immediately respond, and eventually looked to Ganesh for assistance. With obvious surprise, Ganesh began stalling. He cleared his throat and unhurriedly leaned forward to speak.

"Well, I had expected more, uh, more reports from you." He seemed almost proud of himself at such quick thinking.

"Really?" I pounced. "I did not receive any acknowledgement of that report for nearly a month after you got it. You indicated you would like to discuss it, but cancelled our appointments to do so...*twice*."

"Well, it's your responsibility to follow up."

"What, for infinity? How many reports did you get from Leo? Or from any full AMDs, for that matter? From anyone?"

I had pondered for a long time how I would handle this conversation if it went south, as it clearly was doing. After months of constant badgering, I was through with complacency. I was getting screwed, and I had no intention of letting Gunnar get away with it without a fight.

"Gunnar, we agreed to the unnecessary, additional three month training to satisfy *your* worries that I was legitimately here to work. I have worked an entire contract in the dining room now. How many other Americans have done the same in Carnival's thirty-year history? Oh, *none*? Certainly Mladen and Cedric couldn't think of any, but here I am after eight months. Eight months!"

I looked straight at Gunnar and finally asked tersely, "Now, name *one* concrete reason to deny me the promotion I was *already promised*."

Gunnar did not respond for a long time. I waited, staring at him with all the force I could muster. When he finally answered, he spoke with a tone of admission, rather than rebuttal.

"I don't know why you are here," he said quietly.

"That's not an answer," I retorted.

"It's the only answer."

I leaned back and repeated his words with incredulity. I couldn't believe he actually confessed the obvious. "You don't know why I am here...meaning why *an American* wants to be here?"

Gunnar stared at me as his shoulders drooped.

"So, let me get this straight. I have ten years of restaurant experience and have worked for eight months in the ship dining rooms, from the restaurant college to dishwasher to team waiter to head waiter, provided reports that no one else was inclined to do, *and* I was promised the promotion by your predecessor and two MDs. Now compare that to Leo, who has never worked in a restaurant in his life, did *not* attend restaurant college, was *not* a waiter or anything else, and who repeatedly misses entire shifts because he's too drunk...and you give him *a stripe and a half*? Am I the only one who smells the bullshit here? This room stinks of it!"

"I don't want my name on your record," Gunnar replied sourly. "You will quit someday and I will not have my name on an American. If you want your stripe, get it somewhere else."

"That's it, then? You are actually denying me my promotion based on my nationality?"

"This meeting is over," Gunnar said.

"Oh, no it isn't!" I insisted, my dander up. "I'm not leaving here until we have a plan. I was hired to be an AMD, and I *will* be an AMD."

"On another ship," Gunnar finally acknowledged. "You may get a different answer. Your contract ends when?"

"A cruise and a half."

"That's fine. On your next ship, do another few months of training. If the F&B there wants to, he can promote you then."

"*Another* few months? You already put me months behind. One month."

Recognizing that he was soon to be rid of me, Gunnar apparently had no desire to barter.

"Fine, four weeks then."

"So I will return as a *full* assistant maitre d' trainee for four weeks, and then be reviewed there. None of this half-waiter crap."

"Agreed."

"We are all agreed on that?" I asked, eyeing the maitre d's. I had learned already that no officer ever offered anything in writing. I didn't trust Gunnar at all, and wanted witnesses, even though I knew they were patsies. Everyone was in accord regarding the next course of action, and therefore nothing remained to be said. I turned my back on Gunnar and marched out of his office.

I warred with various emotions. It was actually difficult to be angry because this situation had so obviously been in the making for months. Just before returning to the I-95, both Ganesh and Ferrand pulled me aside, gesturing for me to come closer almost conspiratorially.

"Look," Ganesh said. "You won't find what you want here. Just go to another ship and get your stripe. You'll have my support if you need it there."

"Yes," Ferrand added quickly. "Anything you need."

"On some other ship," I clarified blandly, "but not here?"

"Well," Ganesh demurred. "He is in control here. Go to another ship. Get your promotion there."

I was getting squeezed from every angle: my friends and acquaintances were causing me headaches, management was out to get me, and my dinner guests were a nightmare, this cruise especially. I dreaded every first-seating dinner, knowing that both Camilla and I would be chewed up and spit out before the guests even put down the menus. Tonight I just wanted some tranquility. As fate would have it, this night was to be far, far worse than I could have ever imagined.

My station was filled to the maximum with a family huge in all respects: there were eight children and eight cousins present ranging in age from about six to sixteen, each fatter than the other. How these kids could be so morbidly obese before hitting puberty I did not know, but the 700 pounds shared between their mother and father was a clue.

Just walking past the group was a hassle because their chairs were pushed far back from the tables to accommodate their fat bellies. But even more so, both parents and even two of the children rode huge electric scooters because they were too heavy to walk. These were parked before our service station like a line of hogs at the Harley Davidson rally in Sturgis. The combination of bodies and scooters clogged up the entire port entrance to the dining room. It was a fire hazard, but Ferrand had allowed it. The first day he had apologized, explaining lamely that they couldn't get the wide scooters deeper into the dining room.

"I swear to God," Camilla muttered under her breath, "If I have to watch that kid in the glasses eat more than six entrees again I will throw up right here."

She hurriedly placed an extra half-dozen overloaded butter dishes on the tables. Because the butter dishes with the little lids were so highly coveted on *Conquest* by guests and employees alike, most of ours had been pinched. We were required to stack butter onto numerous saucers to placate our guests.

"Ugh, don't remind me. I may be hungry, but after watching him I couldn't eat if I wanted to."

"He had two prime rib dinners, Brian!" she suddenly shrieked, "*After* eating four lobster tails! That makes six! Six!"

I shushed her soothingly. "I know, I know. He's probably only about twelve years old, too. Look, what can we do about it? Nothing but deal with it."

The family was named Rondell, but of course we called them the "Roundells." Many guests figured that if they had already paid for the cruise, it was their obligation to maximize their money. Being surrounded by high-quality dishes that were perhaps too expensive at home, some tended to eat massive quantities whether they wanted to or not. In the Rondells' case, however, they most definitely wanted.

They had standing orders for dinner rolls to be waiting for them on the table when they arrived, rather than have them served individually. This suited Camilla fine, because they consumed triple the usual amount and she did not have time to accommodate them. She was too busy running into the kitchen for their second or third appetizers, or their fourth or fifth entrees. Mercifully they always skipped the salad course.

"They make me sick, Brian, do you understand?"

"I know, Camilla. I know. They'll be gone in just a few more days."

"Sick! And they stink, haven't you noticed?"

"You know I have no sense of smell. I haven't smelled anything since I started smoking cigars. Well, except Dylan's breath."

Camilla had been behaving a bit strangely today, rambling on a bit too much about trivial things. As much as I had wanted to share with her the outcome of my meeting this morning, I remained silent. Instead I watched her extra closely, sensing something was wrong. Unfortunately the Rondells were in full force, and we were far too busy to communicate anything other than our frustration.

I handed out the menus with as much cheer as I could muster, while Camilla had already left for the kitchen. Though they had not ordered yet, it was obvious that they would each order two or three appetizers, especially anything fried or with melted cheese. Each trip to the kitchen was a tremendous drain on our time, and since only twelve plates were technically allowed to be carried on a tray at once, we needed the head start. Any appetizer that she brought that was not ordered would surely be eaten anyway.

Yet luck was finally on our side. Invariably each member of the Rondell family tripled up on the meat entrée, regardless if it was New York strip, filet mignon, or prime rib. But tonight, to our tremendous relief, was something they would not like. Camilla and I had been gleefully anticipating the horrified looks on their faces all cruise long.

"Tonight's special," I boasted as smoothly as possible, "is the wonderful beef Wellington!"

Both Camilla and I had learned that, other than stuffing their faces, the Rondells enjoyed nothing more than making our lives hell. So I bragged about the joys of beef Wellington with gusto. I knew they would take the bait and enjoy "disappointing" us by not ordering what we so obviously adored.

"This British classic features a filet smothered with goose liver pâté and coated with duxelles." I continued in my best game-show host voice. "Duxelles, of course, is when you take finely minced mushroom, onion, and shallots and sauté them in wine. The whole thing is then wrapped in puff pastry. It was named after the first Duke of Wellington, of course."

"Oh, uh, no pâté for me," Momma Rondell said crassly. "I want a few of them jumbo shrimps."

My good humor fell to the floor, shriveled up, and blew away as mere dust in the wind. I pulled my flaccid jaw from the floor and tried to act nonchalant as Camilla returned with the appetizers. In our excitement over the beef entree, we had overlooked the obvious seafood item.

"Just the shrimp," Momma repeated. "None of that other stuff. I just want a pile of them shrimps."

"The honey glazed jumbo shrimp come with a mushroom risotto, ma'am, and mixed vegetables."

"I don't want none o' that," she said. "You jus' tell the chef to make me a big ol' plate of them shrimp. Yeah, you tell him to just pour that honey glaze all over."

"I'm sorry ma'am, but that I cannot do. With several hundred items going out in mere minutes, they cannot special order anything. I would be happy to bring you two shrimp entrees if you like."

"How many shrimps on a plate?" she asked in her husky voice.

"Four."

"Four? What you talking about, boy? I want at least a *dozen* on my plate."

"They are massive shrimp," I defended, fishing for a way out. "They're like the size of a hockey puck."

"I'm from Alabama. I don't know 'bout no hockey pucks. Give me five of them shrimp plates then. Don't you go givin' me none of that rice, now, neither."

"Risotto," I corrected painfully.

"I got rice at home. Just scrape all that stuff off somewhere and gimme a plate full o' them shrimp. Yeah, *honey glazed* shrimp."

Camilla mechanically set the first round of appetizers on the table, trying to hide her fear of what was to come. She had difficulty reaching the center of the table from so far back in the aisle, and began muttering unprofessionally beneath her breath.

I added the numbers in my head. If the Rondells ordered three or four entrees each, that required far too many trips to and from the kitchen than we had time for. Even if Camilla broke the rules and carried fifteen entrees on a tray, *and* if she filled two trays and I came to the kitchen to assist, we would *still* run out of time. Just getting to the kitchen line and back empty-handed required almost ten minutes, and waiting for the entrees required easily half an hour more.

"And you hurry now," one of the chubby children yelled as I gathered the menus and tossed them into the service station. "I'm hungry! You want your tip now, don't you? No tip unless you bring me food fast!"

After a lightning-fast powwow, Camilla needed to run for the next round of appetizers while I would clear the plates and handle the numerous guests requests. Camilla hesitated before she left, giving me a pleading look. I patted her on the back quickly and searched for comforting words. I said the only thing that came to mind.

"We'll get rip-roaring drunk tonight!"

Time became a blur. Camilla brought the second round of appetizers and, before I had even served the end of the table, Momma Rondell demanded her shrimp.

"I'm ready for my shrimp now. Where are my shrimp?"

The whole table took up the chorus, the children gleefully pounding the table as they screamed for all to hear, "Shrimp! Shrimp! Shrimp!"

Camilla yet again ran to the kitchen, leaving me alone with *them*. Fortunately Ferrand himself soon took over quelling the mob so I could help Camilla bring back the trays. I had ordered her to stack one tray with a whopping eighteen entrees. It was extremely risky carrying such a load through a crowded dining room, but I was tall enough and strong enough to pull it off. On my way out of the kitchen, the chefs hurled insults at me, furious that I would risk so much of their sweat and labor.

We delivered the entrees and our worst fears materialized. Even though the shrimp were a hefty four ounces apiece, the Rondells devoured them in a single bite. They dropped the tails onto the tablecloth, ignored the remaining food on the plate, and haughtily demanded another round. After slaving for thirty minutes and suffering the indignation of the chefs to bring all this food, it was gone before we even got to the end of the table!

So we repeated the maneuver again. This time, however, I handed out the dessert menus with each entree, hoping to take their mind off another impossible round of shrimps. The hot line was already changing up, and Camilla would have to wait extra long for even a single tray of orders. I sent her back one last time to gather all that she could on one tray, while I tried to hold back the flood of protesting.

I was in the service station when I heard the tray crash. I rushed out to see poor Camilla standing amidst a mountain of shattered china and lost risotto, vegetables, and shrimp. One of the children had been so impatient that he actually labored up onto his chair in order to pluck a plate from her loaded tray. The unexpected change threw Camilla off balance, and the entire tray fell…with all fifteen entrees. I experienced a momentary flashback of shrimp continuously revolving on an escalator.

The Rondells laughed like some cruel chorus line, and Camilla began to shake. She began panting, and I suddenly feared she was hyperventilating. I ran over to her and put my arm around her, leading her out of the detritus and toward the service station. She sobbed violently and her entire body shuddered with each convulsion. I suddenly realized this was something serious.

Camilla was suffering an emotional breakdown.

With my arm around her shoulders as reassuringly as possible, I led her away from the vulgar family. She collapsed in my grasp and I had to physically carry her into the service station. I cleared off a place for her to sit by kicking a mass of napkins and menus from a stack of glass racks. Camilla wept uncontrollably and the tears fairly exploded from her eyes. She began babbling almost incoherently while her body shivered savagely.

"What's going on?" a voice demanded from behind me. "Why haven't you cleaned up your mess?"

I didn't turn, but recognized the voice as Catalina's.

"Get someone else," I snapped. "We're busy."

"Th-three d-days," Camilla whimpered, dribbling the words out between choking sobs, "They t-told me not t-to bathe for three days!"

"What's she talking about?" Catalina asked from behind me.

"Will you get the hell out of here?" I yelled. "Go get someone to clean up the mess, and give us a minute, for Christ's sake!"

"I t-told them it wasn't the w-w-water," Camilla continued with a bit more clarity. She stared at the ceiling behind me. "'Fara douche pentru tre zile,' they said. No shower for three days. Now I stink like these cow animals! They are so gross…I'm so gross…everything here is so horrible!"

I hugged her and whispered whatever reassuring words I could think of. I had never before witnessed an emotional breakdown, but seeing Camilla's was far worse than I had imagined it would be. I wanted desperately to help, but felt powerless.

"Ha ha! She said '*douche*'!" an obnoxious child's voice called out. One of the Rondell children was peeking around Catalina's round behind to view the drama.

"That's it!" I cried furiously. "Camilla, I'll be right back."

I rose, ready to give the entire Rondell family a piece of my mind. To my surprise, however, Catalina beat me to the punch. She whirled on the fat child and chastised him viciously.

"That means *shower* in our language. You think that is funny? I think only knowing one, easy language is funny! And what's wrong with you, anyway, don't you have any manners? You're behaving like an animal! Now get back to the table and finish your dinner in silence! Animals, I say, ever since you got here. Yes, I mean all of you!"

I was still glowering, but Catalina pushed me back into the station.

"Now," she said, "you need to stay cool and let *me* be the bad guy. I doubt you'll make a penny this cruise, but maybe there's still a chance. I'll help Camilla to her cabin."

I gave Camilla another reassuring squeeze as she was led away. I was glad Catalina had discovered some character when it was needed. She just went up a notch in my book.

"Hey, Cat!" I called out to her. She turned and I thanked her earnestly in Romanian, "*Mulţumesc*."

After a few calming breaths, I returned to the battlefield.

10 *Jamaican Deep Blue*

I FOUGHT DESPERATELY TO SEE CAMILLA BEFORE SHE disembarked. The hassles of signing off are tremendous, from handing over your luggage to security by 8 P.M. the previous night, to having a manager O.K. the cleanliness of your cabin, returning uniforms, obtaining your passport, to hours of waiting in immigration lines. Once all these trials were undergone, the exhausted crew would then have to wait for the guests to sign off.

I had difficulty being released from the Lido even for a few minutes because home port breakfast was always insane, as people crammed every last penny's worth of food into themselves. I finally escaped at eleven o'clock, and rushed down to the lounge beside the gangway. Here people rested on luggage or luggage rested on them. Bodies were haphazardly scattered all over, barring the marginally organized crew-only corner. I worked my way past the throng of bored bodies, seeking distinctive blond Romanian hair in the crowd. Instead of finding Camilla, however, I met a different woman who had played a substantial role in my ship life.

"Liezle!"

She had been half asleep and nearly jumped when I called her name. I sheepishly apologized, but she beamed up at me, pleased.

"Brian, I was hoping to see you."

"I didn't know you were signing off today! I hope you have a great vacation, you've earned it."

"Yeah," she said, retying her black hair into a tighter bundle. "I'm ready to go home. When are you leaving?"

"Next week. Are you going home, or traveling somewhere?"

"I miss my home. I will just barely get some nice weather before the rains come."

"Me, too, though I won't have any rains. I noticed that fall in Europe means rain, whereas where I'm from it's in the spring."

"Usually," she agreed.

Even though I thought it should affect me, I felt little emotion about Liezle leaving. We had survived some crazy upheavals in our lives; from being teammates in the restaurant college, to Jacuzzi nights in Miami, to finally making a life on *Conquest*. For the last few months she had worked for me as a midnight dessert girl. We were never apart, though once settled into our routines we had rarely socialized. While not actually a friend, Liezle was a milepost along the road of a significant personal journey. We had some great memories, if not really good times, if that made sense. In fact, she was the first person I noticed at the beginning!

"So these are your traveling clothes? I remember the very first time I saw you. You wore that tight black sweater and painted-on jeans."

"You remember that?"

"How could I forget such beauty? It was the most memorable first meeting I had. Well, except for the foreign couple shagging in my room. Or the naked Thai. Or the naked Indian. Anyway, I was praying to be sent to whatever ship you were going to!"

"I see some people haven't changed. Camilla asked me to tell you that she was on the early sign-off list. I guess they got her an early flight. She says goodbye."

I had already figured she was gone, but it was disappointing anew.

"That's too bad, I wanted to see her before she left. On the bright side, however, I have to give all the goodbye kisses and groping to you."

"You wish."

"More than ever. Do you know what ship you are returning to?"

"Not yet. I'll find out in Miami."

I grabbed her hand and gave it a squeeze. "Yeah, me too. Have a safe trip, my dear. I hope we'll see each other again."

"Oh, I'm sure we will," she replied. "I hear that you'll follow women anywhere."

My friends organized a going-away party for me in Montego Bay, Jamaica. There, within walking distance of the *Conquest*, was an all-inclusive resort called Sunset Beach. This remarkable facility courted crew members by granting $20 day passes, which provided unlimited food and drink. Considering my situation, it was the perfect choice!

My friends Leo, Calypso, Rhonetta, Nikolo, Lorena, and Rasa formed the core of our group, though there were a number of tag-along acquaintances, too. Dylan, needless to say, was not invited. A shrubbery-lined road was the only way to access the resort. Fortunately cars only rarely traveled past, because our small herd dominated the street. The bay was to our left, granting spectacular views of mist-shrouded mountains and marshes. To our right, however, was the filth of an undeveloped nation. Many of the prettiest tidal flows and streams were choked with mounds of garbage. We crossed a narrow neck that connected the peninsula to the mainland and entered a paradise of palm trees.

"Nikolo," I asked, "why are you bringing that heavy backpack?"

He wore his usual jeans and t-shirt, but labored beneath a bulky bag slung over his shoulders. It didn't look heavy, but was very large.

"You'll see," he replied with a smile.

Sunset Beach was perched center stage on a peninsula that sat right in the middle of Montego Bay. The beaches were on the glorious Caribbean Sea, where the waves were unbroken until they reached the shores of Cuba ninety miles distant. The resort offered all sorts of ways to get wet: they had beaches, Jacuzzis, pool bars, and every form of rental imaginable, from snorkeling to jet skiing to parasailing. As if this were not enough, it also had rain.

Clouds smothered the northern horizon, but the air was wet, warm, and filled with joy. As soon as we arrived, Calypso and I waded directly into the pool, intent on the underwater seats by the bar. Within moments we were surrounded by splashing friends, all ordering shots to get the party started. We had an unbroken four hours today, and planned to maximize each and every one!

After the shots I relaxed in the Jacuzzi with everyone. This was a communal Jacuzzi that sat no less than twenty people, and even offered some depth in the center for anyone inclined to dive below. When Rasa arrived in her bright red string bikini, I noticed a great many men began doing just that.

"What are you drinking?" she asked, sliding up close. The water was hot, but I began to sweat for an entirely other reason.

"This," I boasted proudly, "is a Yellow Bird: the finest blend of gold rum, Galliano, triple sec, and lime juice you'll ever have. Have one, they're refreshing."

"I'll have yours," she said, pressing up against me. Trying to pay attention to anything other than her pressing her sizable breasts against me, I noticed the males watching with complete absorption. Rasa took the cup from my limp grasp and brought it to her mouth. She slid the straw along her wet lips seductively. Another guest groaned from somewhere nearby.

"Oh, you weren't finished yet?" she asked innocently. "You can have it."

She eased back, pulled open her top, and slowly poured the contents over one of her breasts. The gold liquid flowed over her body and into the Jacuzzi, but somehow I don't think anyone cared about fouling the water. I watched her nipple grow firm under the icy shower.

"Yes," Rasa purred, "Very refreshing."

I gulped in anxiety.

Nikolo gasped in awe.

Leo whistled in admiration.

Calypso muttered in disgust. "Ai yai yai, get a room, why don't you?"

"A great idea!" Rasa exclaimed.

But the clouds were moving in, and we all felt the need to move before the rain came. Well, almost all of us. Leo commented that we had better snorkel before we got too drunk, which I thought was a stellar idea.

Few people were on the white sandy beach, fearing the impending rain. So we marched right up to the snorkel shed and gathered our fins. Nearby a rubber garbage can filled with soapy water held the mouthpieces. Within minutes a cluster of us were stroking out into the sea, led by the lithe Rhonetta.

I had little experience with swimming in waves, having grown up some two thousand miles from the nearest ocean. I was pleased to find the salt aided my buoyancy. The sea was so enchanting, however, I felt like I was floating on cloud nine, rather than merely in the water. On my work break I had first discovered the joy of snorkeling in the Red Sea with Bianca. Yet as amazing as that experience had been, it was merely the first, tentative step into a new world. Now I wanted to explore.

The water was less than five feet deep for the first fifty yards, and with the surging tides we frequently pulled ourselves along by grabbing lichen-covered rocks. Funky sea fans of some sort tickled my belly as we swam farther and farther from shore. After a while the water dropped to perhaps fifteen feet, and the swelling rise and fall of the approaching storm was lessened.

As soon as I began to feel more comfortable in the snorkeling gear, I focused on the amazing colors beneath me. The sun suddenly pierced the clouds and spears of light shot into the depths to illuminate brilliant colors of lichen, coral, plants, and fish. I was a lifelong student of art and formerly a professional artist, yet I could never have imagined the dazzling palette exploding around me. Every glance in every direction became a masterwork seared in my memory. Yet the very next moment it was different as orange fishes popped in and out of crevices, or larger, lazier fish of a dozen colors floated by. When the sun disappeared the world was plunged into fascinating blues. I had never seen such an array, from brilliant baby to cobalt, and everything in between.

I was only able to keep track of the signature creatures I saw, because there were simply too many animals around me. Just below me a three-foot sand-colored snake with white spots wriggled through the water with mesmerizing grace. Then I nearly ran into a puffer fish! He floated off slowly, ignoring me.

We swept out over deeper waters, and I became nervous. The bottom was thirty feet below me, but the clarity was such that I felt like I could reach out and touch it. Within minutes I had overcome my uneasiness and felt shackled to the turbulent, bucking surface. Below was cool, relaxed, and inviting. I watched with awe as Rhonetta dove deep, kicking her legs powerfully to reach the topmost peak of a coral some fifteen feet down. Soon Calypso and Leo followed.

I felt like I was watching a movie, with these attractive people diving into such a wonder world. I wasn't sure if I should join them, or even if I was capable. Could I handle the depths? While twenty or so feet of depth was not particularly far, I had rarely been able to pass six in my youth. My ears were chronically sensitive to water and I had rarely swum at all. I was used to being the weakest swimmer of anyone around, and memories of insecurity washed over me.

But that was a long time ago and, if I had learned anything on the ships it was that *we* were the only thing holding us back. Comfort was overrated...just do it!

Turning sharply, I dove straight down and kicked my fins like mad.

The sensation of being an observer melted with each foot I descended, and I became completely absorbed by the sea, one with the corals and the fish. Within mere seconds I reached the peak of reef that had seemed so elusive, so far away. I tentatively tapped its rough pinnacle, then shot back up to the surface.

I nearly shrieked in triumph as I blew through the snorkel to void the water inside. Treading water, I struggled on the surface because it was so choppy. Clouds rolled above, dark and menacing, and it began to rain. We were easily 200 yards out to sea! I had never been so far from the shore in my life, not in a lake and *certainly* not into the ocean!

Regardless of the rain in the world above, we spent another hour in this place. With each dive I progressed, from first coasting above crevasses splitting into untold black depths, to finally cruising between towering cliffs of rock and reef, brother to crabs and crayfish. Eventually fatigue crept into our perspective, and it was time to return to shore. I followed the others, my mind still wandering the nooks and crannies of coral.

By the time we entered the fifty yard barrier near shore, the tide had changed. I watched Calypso before me slide above the rocks and fans with ease, while I fought to keep from hitting my knees on everything.

I noted with alarm that we passed beside some sort of green blob that defied identification. Suddenly the blob blocked all exits to my left, and I grew very uneasy. I was still a ways from the beach and, though the water was only a few feet deep, the utter jumble on the sea floor made walking impossible. The horrid green sea thing crawled toward me faster, and I fought my anxiety.

What the hell was this thing? It wasn't sea grass or a fan or any kind of plant at all. It billowed and flared, like laundry hanging in a strong wind. It was a brilliant yellow-green that almost glowed. It was not from this world, and it was swooping right at me!

I frantically clawed at the rocks and reef, surging forward with panic just below my own surface. The edges of the alien cloud reached for me, I was too far from the shore...!

I burst into the air like a geyser. My heart thumped from the rush, but instantly the world returned to normal. The water was only two feet deep, yet a mere moment ago I had been on another planet! But just ahead my friends calmly trudged toward the beach, holding their fins above the water.

I blinked and tried to identify the strange green cloud from above. I could see the thing swelling out as far as I could see. Was I glad to be back ashore! I couldn't imagine how I would have reacted had I met this thing farther out. With a shrug, I picked my way painfully to the beach and decided I had earned several more Yellow Birds, with or without Rasa's unique decoration.

After snorkeling we were all hungry, so we devoured as many burgers, hot dogs, and spicy jerk chicken as we could handle. I was enthralled by the superb blend of bizarre, pungent, and wonderful spices in the jerk. Truly one could never appreciate a foreign food without trying it locally. Near the buffet lines we stared in awe up at an entire twenty-foot wall depicting all the different drink specials. After downing eleven rum specials I began to lose track, but was sure I left no drink untried.

The rain came down in force, and the remainder of the afternoon was a blissful, drunken blur. Between its two towers, Sunset Beach had a wonderful open-air space shielded from the weather. The roof was easily thirty feet above us, making us feel completely outside, yet was so protected that over-stuffed cushions and couches lounged everywhere. We all wandered in and out of this perfectly tropical hospitality.

Suddenly Leo and Nikolo ran through the lounge, screaming and soaking wet from something more than the rain: they both brandished huge water guns the size of grenade launchers.

So *that's* what Nikolo had hauled in his backpack: two Super Soaker 8000s!

I chased them and we all ran circles around the outdoor pool tables, dashed into the dripping bushes, and nearly slipped to our deaths near the ping pong tables. A small horde of local children gleefully ran through the complex after us, and if someone managed to hide, a dozen small black arms would reveal us with a giggle. After a while we tired and let the kids play with the squirt guns, to their incredible delight.

For the last hour I settled into shooting pool with Calypso. Leo tried to join us and honestly thought he was capable in his inebriated state, but he never quite made it. He leaned upon his chosen pool cue beside the rack, eyes closed and very near catatonic. His other hand rested upon the counter, open and holding a small cube of blue chalk at the ready. Whenever needed we took it from him, but always returned it out of sheer perversity.

We shot pool and enjoyed the rain pouring down just six feet from us. After all the spent energy and imbibed drinks, we needed some quiet time. Between my turns I watched the rain pummel the beach into pockmarks and listened to it tap on the lush, jungle vegetation.

"I can't believe our time is up," Calypso finally said, looking at her watch.

"The time has come," I replied with some gravity. Neither of us was actually referring to the afternoon's end.

"We should gather the troops," she said. "I think Rhonetta is napping on the divan. I see Rasa over there surrounded by drooling idiots, and Lorena is with most of the others in the restaurant."

"Nikolo is playing ping pong with Beau," I added. "And Leo..."

We both turned to look at Leo, asleep on his feet.

She smiled one of her incredibly generous smiles as we hung up our cues. For some reason we hesitated, both sensing that this was probably our only real chance to say goodbye alone. Under the unseeing eyes of unconscious Leo, we embraced deeply. As we pulled back, our lips met for a surprisingly enjoyable goodbye kiss. It lingered just a bit longer than it should have. Then a bit more.

Just right.

Several days later I sat on a bench near Jackson Square in New Orleans, overlooking the ponderous and muddy Mississippi River. I quietly smoked a wonderful locally rolled cigar I had purchased just after signing off.

As an American, I was the only crew member able to spend a few nights in the French Quarter before flying home. I found it reprehensible that most crew members were forced out of the country within mere hours of signing off. Though a huge mall was literally feet away from *Conquest*, no one was allowed to shop for even fifteen minutes, nor could they purchase a meal anywhere. Most wanted to drop a few hundred dollars on a hotel and shop for a few days, eating out and spending money. Yet America insisted that they take their U.S. cash and depart overseas immediately. How that helped our hurting economy was beyond me.

I had dropped off my belongings at a hotel, but I still felt encumbered by baggage. This hot, humid evening at the very end of August was ripe for reflection. My stomach rolled from all the emotions swirling through me. I was watching something that I had spent the better part of a year trying to avoid: the ship leaving without me onboard. The great white beast pulled directly away from the dock sideways, churning the ugly brown waters of the Mississippi. The river was so wide here that *Conquest* could leisurely spin around to face downstream.

I heard the cheering of the guests from afar. They were so tiny up there on the Lido deck, so far away and so high up. Even though to them I was a mere speck on the shore, I waved as the ship passed. There was something about a departing cruise ship that was irresistible, one simply *had* to wave.

I felt like I was missing out on the action. As I relaxed in the heat and reassurance of a long, well-earned rest before me, my friends were readying for boat drill and the crushing first evening in the dining room. Rasa and Tekin were probably folding napkins, as were Calypso and Nikolo in their dining room. Leo was probably swearing, having just discovered that his new roommate was Bogo.

And Bianca? Where she was I had no idea at the moment. She was in the Caribbean, somewhere. Her affection had brought me to this place, yet it was the others I left behind who currently occupied my thoughts.

"Life is what happens while you are busy making plans," I said aloud to myself with no little ceremony.

After the last eight months, I had learned just how true a statement that was. I was deeply affected by this, my first contract on ships. I had done it. I was the first American in Carnival's thirty-year history to finish an entire contract in the dining room without quitting or transferring. Not a single ambition of mine had been realized, yet in *every* way the experience had been more profound than I ever could have dreamed.

I was closer to enlightenment, but no closer to Bianca.

PART IV

The *Legend*
(Destruction)

*The dominant primordial beast
was strong and under the fierce conditions
of life it grew and grew.*

—JACK LONDON,
The Call of the Wild

1 *How to Fix an American*

THE HISPANIC RECEPTIONIST SMILED BROADLY AT ME as she checked her computer on my behalf. I was at the Miami Marriot once again, but was considerably less fatigued or nervous than the last time I was here. Of course, I was still the only American anywhere in sight.

"Dare I ask," I queried, "with whom I am rooming?"

She frowned as she scanned the screen. "Mr. Bruns, we have you down in your own room. Were you expecting someone?"

I beamed back at her and said, "Oh, no, my dear, not at all. Just checking."

My understanding was that Carnival's management did not share their hotel rooms. After taking my room key, I fairly leapt to the list of ship assignments with a skip in my step. This was a whole new contract, a whole new ship, a whole new world! After two months off I was fully rested and, more importantly, fully fed...*and* I had my own room. My days of surprises were over, and, one way or another, I was on my way to Bianca!

I bobbed up and down on my toes, trying to see over the heads of the numerous others checking the list. There was no point in returning later in hopes of a lesser crowd because people arrived every minute of every day from every continent around the world. Within minutes of arrival they *all* congregated here. My name was not on the list, but this was hardly unusual. Standard procedure required a two-day wait before calling Carnival, should your name not appear in the meantime.

I was extremely anxious to see what ship I would be assigned and what my ports would be. I knew only that *Glory* with my elusive Bianca was impossible, as was *Conquest,* of course. That left only about twenty others to choose from, going all over the tropics! Was I going to Hawaii, or perhaps Aruba? It was very exciting.

After impatiently waiting the necessary two days my name had still not been added to the list. While I enjoyed Carnival's hospitality immensely, soaking in the Jacuzzi after a run or a lazy afternoon of reading by the pool, I was impatient for action. During that time dozens of Carnival crew came and went. No less than four separate people greeted me, none of whom I recognized. Each admitted that we had never actually met, but had seen me on the ships. I also enjoyed a surprise encounter with Jordan of Bulgaria, the storeroom Adonis from *Fantasy*. He asked if I had ever been able to capture my girlfriend. I asked if Anjana had ever been able to capture him.

When the time elapsed I eagerly called Carnival for my assignment. The gum-chewing receptionist who answered my call disinterestedly told me I was going back to *Conquest* as a head waiter. So much for "no more surprises!"

"Obviously a mistake has been made," I protested over the payphone. "I am not supposed to go to *Conquest*."

"Your name is on the list," she dismissed with a smack of her gum.

"Well, what am I supposed to do now?"

"If you have a problem," she answered tiredly. "You will have to go to your assigned ship and ask your senior department head to handle it."

"But my senior department head *is* the problem!"

Her manager was about as helpful as she was. His knowledge extended so far as to who actually made the list, but he claimed to not know how to contact this person or persons. Such a request was most unreasonable, he assured me, with indignation that I would even inquire about it. Frustrated with my lack of progress and everyone else's apparent lack of information, I demanded some recourse, *any* recourse, other than going to the ship first.

"I'm in Miami!" I finally snapped to the manager. "Carnival's headquarters are right here! Why shouldn't I be able to speak with someone about this?"

"I doubt they have time for you—er, uh, *your* situation." His lackadaisical effort to avoid saying "time for *you*" was pathetic.

I hung up and resolved to find a solution myself. Carnival was a huge corporation with some thirty thousand individuals. I assumed those in Miami were somewhat specialized and, if I could not find the proper contact, I was hopeless. I asked around to the many Carnival employees at the hotel, but all were traumatized that I would actually argue my ship assignment. With no help from the sea of crew and only the 1-800 number to the company, I resolved to e-mail the one person I knew for sure was in Miami.

Next afternoon I was in a taxi on my way to meet Mladen.

The small, neat man reviewed me quietly from behind his desk. I waited for Mladen to respond to my story, curious how he would react. His office was simple, orderly, and nice. I was impressed by his working environment: he obviously did not have time for affectation. Indeed, I had been pleasantly surprised to see Carnival's massive office complex also was simple, orderly, and nice. They reserved their profits for their business, their ships, and their employees.

I had done my best to present my story to Mladen as impartially as possible, and tried to balance my sincere gratitude for his time with my indignation at being abused. Mladen, for his part, had listened attentively to my every word and appeared concerned by what it perhaps represented.

He finally said simply, "I had warned you that it would not be easy."

"Yes you did, but not because of such blatant discrimination. I mean, he didn't even bother denying it."

"Well, let us see if he does now."

Mladen picked up the phone and asked for a call to be connected to *Conquest*. I watched this move with alarm. I had figured he would simply put me on some other ship...there were twenty others, after all! Was he choosing to not just handle the situation, but resolve it?

Conquest was somewhere in the middle of the Gulf of Mexico, but that did not concern Mladen. I listened with fascination as he cut through the various layers of personnel simply be stating his name. Within mere moments he had Gunnar on the line.

"Gunnar," Mladen said neutrally. "I am here on speaker phone with the American, Brian. He claims there was some sort of disagreement. I want both maitre d's on the line and we will find out what is going on."

"Yes, sir," Gunnar's tired voice answered. "Ganesh is in his office, and I'll get Ferrand on the line in just a few minutes."

No one bothered with small talk while we waited, and the tense, silent minutes stretched painfully. Finally Gunnar said that Ferrand had joined him in his office. Only then did it finally occur to me what was being set up. My stomach flopped like a fish out of water.

Mladen said, "Brian claims that there was a meeting in which you all agreed that he would be an assistant maitre d' under observation for four weeks on a ship other than *Conquest*. Brian, is that correct?"

"Yes," I replied.

"Ganesh, is this true?"

Ganesh thought over his answer slowly. Eventually he answered with a cautious, "I don't really remember it that well."

I nearly burst out in anger, but managed to control my tongue.

"And you, Ferrand, do you recall this agreement?"

Ferrand, standing in front of Gunnar, did not hesitate. "I do not remember any such agreement."

"So what *was* agreed upon?"

No one answered, and I nearly filled the silence with angry accusations. I knew I should have fought for something in writing, but Carnival simply never allowed it. This was why! When Gunnar began to explain, Mladen interrupted him. "No, I would like Ganesh to answer."

"Well, I don't exactly remember," Ganesh admitted. "That was between the food and beverage manager and the employee."

"Ferrand?"

"Oh, I do not remember any details. Gunnar had a plan for Brian, I remember that much. I do not think Brian was very happy here."

I shook my head and motioned defeat. "Look, I can see where this is going. Thank you, Mladen, for indulging me in this call. Let's move on."

Mladen shrugged, and then hung up the phone. He gave me a penetrating look.

"It's obvious where this was going," I repeated. "I am *not* some disgruntled employee. I enjoyed the challenge of *Conquest* and I returned for a second contract to prove it. Any other *Americans* do that?"

"Well, Brian, what can I say? I was not present, and I must believe my officers in the field. None of them remembered such an agreement."

"Oh, come on! Ganesh and Ferrand were on the phone with their *boss*. You think they would risk their careers over me? What angers me is that they both promised me support not ten seconds after we left Gunnar's office. Jeesh, they could have at least pretended or something."

"There are levels of command," Mladen continued. "You skipped several in coming to me."

"The three tiers above me were in collusion," I protested. "How can I compete with that? All I wanted was another ship, *any* other ship, to be judged on my performance. I am very good at what I do. If I go back through *Conquest* it will take months to get another ship. I was already held back half a contract for no reason, and I am supposed to go back there and do it all over again?" I sighed. "What would you recommend, Mladen?"

He paused thoughtfully. "Take the slap on the wrist. You will not go to *Conquest*. I will send you to another ship. In a few months, if the maitre d' agrees you are worthy, you may seek formal AMD training at that time. If you really want this, it is the only way."

I nodded mutely. My months of excitement and hope during vacation all vanished in a puff. Bianca seemed farther away than ever now.

Mladen picked up the phone and asked, "Where is *Legend* now? Oh, that far away? Hmm. Well, which ships are in home port tomorrow? No, *Destiny* and *Inspiration* will not work. No way on *Fantasy*. What is in home port in two days? No, not those. *Legend* will not be back for six days, you said? When and where is its next port?"

Mladen clearly had a plan, and apparently nothing was conforming to it. It was obvious he wanted to send me to *Legend*, but was hesitant to spend the extra money to get me there. Eventually he hung up the phone with mild annoyance.

"O.K., Brian, you are going to *Legend*. You'll fly to Puerto Rico immediately and sign on this evening in San Juan. It's mid-cruise, but that cannot be avoided. It does eight-day cruises out of New York. Just give your paperwork to Ken and he will get the airline ticket."

"What paperwork?"

"The paperwork you received when you signed off *Conquest*. The packet with your hotel reimbursement form and medicals and all that."

"Hotel reimbursement form? I have no idea what you are talking about."

Mladen frowned, for the first time outwardly irritated. "You did not attend the debarkation meeting on *Conquest*?"

"No. Gunnar had me work a double shift that day and wouldn't let me go. He said there was nothing there for me anyway."

I had difficulty identifying the focus of Mladen's disgusted look. I suddenly feared that he thought I was lying about everything. I could only imagine how much of an aggravation I was at this point. Not surprisingly, it immediately got worse.

"So," he said pensively. "You did not turn in your hotel reimbursement form? You have been at the hotel for several days...you will have to pay for that."

"Are you kidding? I didn't do anything wrong, and now I am paying for the hotel, too? How much is it a night?"

"Three nights is almost $500."

My stomach wriggled when I realized this explained why I had my own room: they thought I was a regular guest!

"Look, I feel like I'm blaming everyone else for all my problems, but it's not like that. Really! I should not have to pay for the hotel. Gunnar probably figured I would not return to the ships once I was demoted. He has gone to remarkable lengths to make my life miserable, as if it is personal or something."

"Well, work out the details with Ken. See what he says. I have things to do now. You will get your other ship."

The flight to Puerto Rico was fast and tense. My two days of relaxation and hope were so far away that I forgot they ever happened. Had Carnival not in the end paid for the hotel, I would have remembered them next time I checked my wallet! When I arrived in San Juan, the airport was surprisingly empty and dark, yet it was only about seven in the evening.

From the moment I stepped off the plane I felt like I was in a dream...which rapidly descended into the stuff of nightmares. Everything looked *almost* normal. The signage was only a bit off, but the lights were almost entirely off. I strode through the shadowed and vacant airport to the baggage area. I felt oddly exposed waiting for my baggage entirely alone. Though the flight had been half full, it was obviously loaded with daily commuters because I was the only person with check-in luggage.

Ken said that someone would be waiting for me with a car, but I saw no one at all. Had it been four in the morning I would have expected such emptiness, but in the early evening? I waited uncomfortably for fifteen minutes, but the driver never came. I wandered the dark terminal, seeking someone in a uniform. The handful of travelers I passed stared at me with strange intensity. Their unusual focus reminded me that *I* was now the minority. Once the last few men disappeared into the dark, I truly felt like I was in the Twilight Zone.

After another twenty minutes I finally found the help desk, or rather, after my third pass someone had finally staffed it. He was inclined to merely shrug off my plight, but I pressed him. He instructed me to find the travel office and said they would help. I asked him where it was, but he only vaguely gestured to the vast, empty, and dark airport as a whole.

At this point there was only me and the echoes of my own footfalls. In time I found my objective: a small door hiding beneath a stairwell, labeled with a handwritten sign in dubious English. Needless to say, no one was in the office.

Greatly annoyed, I resolved to get a move on with finding my own ride to the pier. I walked over to the taxi stand, but it was abandoned. I retraced my steps and headed toward the bus terminal. It, too, was devoid of people. My shoulders began aching from hauling my luggage all over the airport. Needless to say, there were no rent-a-carts for my baggage.

Outside I found an old man sitting on a bench smoking a hand-rolled cigarette. He wore dark glasses and a full beard. He reminded me of a blind, elderly Bob Marley.

"You needin' a taxi, amigo?" he called to me.

"Yes, sir, I do. Any suggestions?"

"There ain't none, amigo. Taxi drivers on strike. *Grande* mob is block the airport."

"What's the strike about?"

"Locals ain't getting no business from airport. Bosses hire rich-man cars. You know, suit-men is hold signs? Ain't none is acting that today, amigo. No way. Things is bad."

"I see. Well, is the cruise ship pier far? If it's close, I could walk."

"Nah. Get ride from local. But they'se probly too busy."

"I have to be on a ship soon."

"You ain't going nowheres, amigo."

"Well, I certainly can't remain here all night!"

He said nothing, but puffed casually on his cigarette. I thanked him for his assistance and headed toward the mob.

The air was wet but cool, and it was uncomfortable. Sure enough, a large mob of people blocked the road to the airport and I headed toward them. Clusters of Hispanic men shouted back and forth, some rushing forward spontaneously to wallop another.

This strike was not some organized protest or union-induced action: these were disgruntled men who had coagulated into an angry, pulsing mob blocking the street. I could not tell at all which side represented what, and it just looked like a dangerous free-for-all. Tension crackled through the air as the masses swung closer and closer to all-out violence. The numerous little flare-ups of shouting and pushing had not yet ignited the entire crowd, but it was obviously not far.

On the outskirts of the throng a large, middle-aged man noticed me approaching with my luggage. He hopped forward eagerly and asked conspiratorially if I needed a ride. I was nervous about jumping into the wrong side of this argument I didn't understand, but I did need a ride. I said as much to him.

"Is O.K.," he said soothingly.

"I need to get to the cruise ship pier."

"Is O.K. I am local. You ride from me." He emphasized his last word menacingly, "*Understand?*"

Soon we were driving slowly through the crowd in a large, dirty van. I was the only passenger, of course, and my discomfort increased as we edged through the swarm. Hands slapped the sides of the van and fists rapped on the windows. I felt like Frankenstein's monster being harassed by the local villagers. All that was missing were pitchforks and torches!

"Door locked, no?" asked the driver nervously.

"Hell, yes!"

The knocking and jostling intensified, and I retreated into the center of the van. It seemed that any moment someone was going to bash through the window. I hugged my backpack to protect the valuables inside, ready to sacrifice my suitcase if need be. I watched warily as men jostled the locked doorknobs. After ten apprehensive minutes we cleared the mob and sped into the tropical night.

When I arrived at *Legend*, it sat gloomy and forlorn in the clammy air. The gangway was empty of people, though at this hour guests were most likely either in the dining room or in the city. Security directed me to the purser's office and called over the radio that "the guy finally arrived." It would be a few minutes, they said, while the purser came to the office.

At about a quarter after seven the purser appeared. Like every other crew purser I had ever met, he was Filipino. He was not in uniform and was not happy at my unusual arrival. He reeked of smoke and had obviously been in the crew bar. He muttered constantly about how my mid-cruise arrival would have to alter this list, that posting, and a whole slew of other inconveniences. Only after he finished handling my extensive paperwork did he look me in the eye for the first time.

"So, you really are American. Did you lose a bet or something?"

"It's a long story."

"You have your uniform?"

"Yes."

"Good. You will be serving second seating."

"What? Are you kidding? It's, like, seven thirty and I'm a nasty, sweaty mess and I just arrived!"

"Dinner starts at eight o'clock, so you better get going. Your cabin is A632. Welcome aboard."

"Wha- wait! Which dining room?"

"There's only one, papa."

"Is this ship anything like the *Conquest*?"

"You wish. And by the way, when you quit will you please *not* do it in the middle of the cruise after hours? It's a pain in the ass."

I rushed through the alien hallways of the *Legend*, completely lost and completely stressed. The layout was fundamentally different from both the *Fantasy* and the *Conquest* class ships, but at least I knew what I was looking at. I managed to find my cabin in a short amount of time, intense as it was. I hurled my luggage onto the empty top bunk, muttered my thanks to every deity I could think of that it was not filled with Bibles, and prepared for work. My uniform was wrinkled from the travel, and unfortunately my lightning-fast shower did not create enough steam to help. Rumpled and frustrated, I wandered deck three in search of the maitre d's office.

Even as I arrived the guests began filling the single, massive dining room. The air was nearly as electric as that of the mob outside the airport, and I was very tense. I asked around for the maitre d's office, but everyone merely grunted and moved on. Finally I rudely interrupted someone and demanded to know where the office was. Annoyed, the head waiter snapped, "Atlantic deck."

"What's that?"

"Upstairs. Where you from?"

So I rushed upstairs and finally found the office. Behind the maitre d's desk was a very solidly built, handsome Turkish man. He rose hurriedly and boomed, "Welcome to Truffles dining room!"

"Thanks," I panted.

"*Oui*...you're cutting it close! Your section is right in the middle of Promenade deck."

He showed me on a diagram of the dining room which three tables I had: three round tables of eight.

"Twenty-four? That's a huge section!"

"Of course! Americans say 'more is better,' don't they? They are here already, and you know New Yorkers don't like to wait. Get going!"

I rushed down to my station, pushing through to the center of the dining room packed with guests shouting and laughing. It was incredibly disorienting, and I felt like I had blundered into the crowd in Pamplona's Running of the Bulls.

A middle-aged Filipino man rushed forward and shook my hand with a huge smile. "I'm Made. Here's the first order. I'll get the hot appetizers, but you need to get these soups and salads from the kitchen."

"Uh, O.K. I'm Brian, by the way. Let's go!"

He handed me an oval tray and we split to attack our respective duties. I spent five minutes wandering in complete confusion before finding a side station with the soups. Truffles was unlike anything I had seen on *Conquest* or *Fantasy*. I hurriedly ladled up my soups before I realized the salads were nowhere to be seen. I grabbed the nearest waiter and finally demanded an answer.

"Where the hell is the galley on this damn ship?"

The skinny Jamaican looked at me like I had sprouted a horn from my forehead.

"On Riviera deck," he answered as if I was stupid.

"What's that?"

"Downstairs. Where you from?"

2 Legend

"SO, I HEAR YOU REALLY ARE AMERICAN," THE PRETTY blonde asked me as we folded napkins. I could barely see her face behind the hedge of candlestick-folds we created between us. Her accent was very strong and I had difficulty understanding her when I could not see her lips move.

"There seems to be little doubt."

"Did you really have a confrontation with Mladen?"

I paused in surprise. "Where did you hear that?"

"Oh, we all know, Brian. I just wanted to know if it was actually true."

I had been on *Legend* for less than two weeks and already people were talking! I guess with my exceptionally odd mid-cruise start and supremely unique nationality it was inevitable.

"I had a meeting with him, yes," I replied carefully. "It was not a confrontation."

She set down her napkins and regarded me carefully, obviously ascertaining if I was lying or not. "You *really* did, didn't you? You met with Mladen! My God, you really *are* American!"

"Oh, come on, Juci. Have I no free will? Why does my nationality explain everything to everyone all the time?"

Juci was my neighboring head waiter, a petite Hungarian with a mildly rough complexion and an athletic physique. Her hair was marvelously blond and her eyes the brightest frosty blue-gray I had ever seen. Juci (pronounced JOO-Kee) was her name, the Hungarian equivalent to Judy, but to her eternal annoyance guests and crew alike read her nametag as "Juicy."

"Only Americans are so bold and demanding," she continued. "You Americans always get what you want because you do what it takes to get it. If that means busting of the balls, you do."

I chuckled at the unlikely colloquialism coming from an eastern Hungarian village girl. Her opinion was overwhelmingly shared by nearly everyone I had met overseas, and it was difficult to refute. On my return to the States for vacation I had discovered the public was staggeringly uninformed about our nation's activities on the global stage. After some introspection I realized that our culture applauded the idea that not only anyone could...but everyone *should*...claw their way to material possession. Merely accepting any situation was wholly un-American.

"Well, don't advertise it, O.K.? I don't want a reputation to follow me. I want people to judge me on what I do here."

Though neighbors frequently worked together, Juci and I in particular had much in common. There were very few Hungarians onboard, despite a plethora of former Soviet-bloc nationals. Hungary had successfully managed the transition away from Soviet rule, unlike many others, say Romania, Bulgaria, Croatia, Poland, or even the Czech Republic. A great deal of jealousy was directed at her and she shouldered it alone. We found refuge in each other's acceptance of our nations' actions.

But really, Juci was hot. *Of course* I hung out with her.

After surviving the remainder of my first cruise on *Legend*, I was happily ensconced in an upper back corner station. My other neighbor was Ramona, a Romanian with an entirely too-large behind and gypsy blood. Other than the constant threat of Ramona's thievery, it was a quiet corner where we all worked together to make our lives easier.

The 88,000-ton *Legend* ran eight-day cruises from New York City to the Virgin Islands. This long trek meant four brutal days at sea every cruise. Sea days were the bane of all crew and with such demanding passengers more people quit on *Legend* than any other ship in the fleet. To accommodate this, a larger percentage of the 930 employees hailed from lesser-developed nations. Carnival knew that Indonesians or Costa Ricans, for example, had a higher tolerance than Czechs or Poles because they had more to lose should they walk out.

This explains why Mladen had fought so hard to place me on *Legend:* he figured I would quit in no time.

Legend was an eccentric ship in many ways. New Yorkers tended to be an extremely forceful breed of human, with loud and fierce demands. While dining they maximized the menu nightly in a barrage of curt orders and curses. They knew what they wanted, they demanded it fast, and they paid accordingly for it. Even when away from home, the residents resonated with the saying "if you can make it here, you can make it anywhere." *Legend* had the highest rate of payout, as well as the highest rate of dropout.

Legend was a *Spirit*-class ship, which was unusual among Carnival's fleet in that it had but one dining room to accommodate over two thousand guests. Truffles dining room was simply huge, with a gaudily decorated balcony circling its entire length. The front and back ends boasted mezzanines for musicians. It was here that the maitre d' presented himself nightly to the people from on high. This was generally the guests' only opportunity to meet the reclusive Englishman, Ian.

"Where are you from, Brian?" Juci continued.

"Chicago," I answered semi-truthfully. I had learned that explaining Iowa to foreigners was not worth the trouble. They either knew American geography better than Americans, or not at all. Yet everyone on earth seemed to know the Chicago Bulls and Al Capone. Since I grew up only a few hours away, I adopted Chicago.

Juci's and my conversation dropped off as music overwhelmed the dining room. The charismatic Assistant Maitre d' Duman (pronounced Du-MAHN) gobbled every spare minute for his unique brand of entertainment. Nightly he inflicted a monologue on us, invariably opening the act with a Turkish song or two. The Turkish dance music was, to everyone's surprise, universally adored. His monologues were not.

Duman was the huge Turk I had met in the office on my first night. He was a very flamboyant man who loved the sound of his own voice. Duman always emphasized specific people and where they were from. He loved the cultural diversity of the ship, and stressed it with every rambling speech. With the microphone's volume at the same overwhelming decibel level as the music, he began to speak.

"GOOD EVENING, LADIES AND GENTLEMEN! IN TODAY'S NEWS WE HAVE THE ANNIVERSARY OF...*RAMAN FROM INDONESIA*! HE IS CELEBRATING HIS TWENTIETH YEAR WITH CARNIVAL. HE DOESN'T LOOK 100 YEARS OLD BECAUSE OF CARNIVAL, FOLKS, IT IS BECAUSE HE HAS FOURTEEN CHILDREN TO FEED. *Oui...*"

Juci and I shared a glance and rolled our eyes.

"AND THIS JUST IN, CIVIL WAR IN AMERICA, *BRIAN FROM CHICAGO* IS TRYING TO TAKE OVER MIAMI! *Oui...*"

After my first full cruise ended, I had finally met with the maitre d'. Unlike on *Conquest*, maitre d' Ian remained primarily hands-off and avoided the dining room until the very last minute. This gave Duman a greater sense of authority and, unfortunately, more airtime. Ian was an experienced maitre d' and was not out to impress anyone. If not in his office, he could always be found in the crew bar.

I arrived one afternoon and closed the office door in a futile attempt to soften the intruding Turkish music. Ian was a very tall, slender man in his early forties with a thin mustache and dark hair.

"Thanks for seeing me, Ian."

"Indeed!" he greeted heartily. We shook hands and he gestured for me to sit.

"Look," I said, easing into the chair. "I can imagine what you're thinking."

"Indeed?" He glanced over an e-mail relaying my situation and murmured, "Ai yai yai..."

"I am not here to make your life difficult. I am just a waiter for a while. Then, if my performance is worthy, I intend to get back into the AMD training. I am here to keep things simple. I've had enough of politics for a while."

"Indeed," he agreed.

"I only ask that if there is any opportunity to distinguish myself that I am unaware of because of my lower position, please let me know."

"Indeed," he said with dismissal as he rose. "Good, then!"

We shook hands again and I was outside in the Turkish music once more, after perhaps sixty seconds with the man. I couldn't recall if he had actually said anything or not. Before I even had a chance to reflect on Ian's singular vocabulary, I was assailed by the remaining AMD, Lutfi (pronounced LOOT-fee). He was a small man of sharp features and a prominent perma-grin. His hair was short, jet black, and curly in a very Mediterranean manner. He was from Tunisia.

"Brian!" he called to me. "I was hoping to run into you."

"Hi Lutfi. What's up?"

"Don't worry about being late yesterday; it's all been taken care of."

"I wasn't late yesterday."

"Well, there is an e-mail circulating that you were. I'm here for you, though, and I took care of it."

"Uh, well, thanks then."

Lutfi appeared very nice, but there was definitely something fishy about his kindness. I sensed he was working something.

"You know, Duman doesn't like you." He tapped his temple and added emphatically, "I know!"

"I haven't done anything to Duman. He seems all right."

"He doesn't like you," Lutfi pressed. "But I do."

"Uh huh," I said noncommittally.

"I know!" he said as he grabbed my arm and conspiratorially pulled me aside. "Paisano business can sink anybody. I read the e-mail to Ian from Mladen. *I know.*"

"Look Lutfi, I am not here for any funny business. I just want to do my job and try to move on."

"I assure you that Gunnar was not the only one who fixed you. Ganesh was equally responsible and ugh, the damned *Frenchman!* I would proceed with caution if I were you. Be careful who you confide in, and avoid those with paisanos. You may have a friend in Ian because he's English, but he's hands-off. I tell you, be wary of Duman. I know, man, I know! The paisanos are jealous that you are American. Indians or Euros band together because they are stronger that way. You have advantages they never will, and they can only cut you down while you are weak."

"This I know," I said.

"But you will skyrocket to the top!" His arm swooped up in emphasis. "When you get your feet back under you. I know! I have no paisanos, but I am smart enough to know which side to be on. You got fixed by everyone, but you are still here. You even challenged Miami! You will go far, my friend. *I know!*"

"Thanks for the words of encouragement, Lutfi."

"You are alone. I know! I was, too. For some reason Carnival keeps me with the Turk. I guess they think all Arab countries are the same. I am as alone as you are. We can help each other. I promise nothing, but time will tell. I go now."

With those final words he disappeared, leaving me again alone and confused. Already people were conspiring and politicking and I wanted none of it!

I headed toward my cabin to reflect upon my new situation. I just wanted to do my job well for a few months, then reapply for management and get going again. I knew it would be difficult on *Legend*, but I was prepared to go to great lengths at this point to protect my chosen future. Ship life suited me on many levels. While I made little enough money at it, I was traveling and meeting people from all over the world. The best part was that I had several months a year to live in Transylvania with Bianca.

When I arrived, my roommate Best was shaving. Our cabin was so small, and we were both so large, that when one stood the other was required to lie in his bunk. I jumped up to my bed and said hi, earning an inarticulate grunt from him.

Dunham Best was a very large islander who had a staggering resemblance to a gorilla. His physique was dense with powerful muscles and he weighed significantly more than I without a spare pound on him. His skin was ebony black and his hair was tightly curled to his head. His features were distinctly primal in appearance, from the heavy forehead crowned with bushy eyebrows to his exceptionally wide, flat nose. As if his looks were not enough, his every movement was lumbering and heavy. I was just waiting to see his knuckles drag on the ground. Even his English was unintelligible, sounding like nothing so much as an irate primate.

It was strange living with a man with whom I could not communicate, despite repeated efforts. Just the other day he had proudly showed me photos of his family with a jumbled commentary that honestly intimidated me. I had absolutely no idea what he was rambling about, but nodded with enthusiasm because I was scared of his unpredictable, violent temper. Sometimes it popped up for no apparent reason, such as when he nearly spit with rage at his pants while folding them.

I reflected as I lay back. I had finally been introduced to all the players and was gaining familiarity with the stage. I tried to be cheery and optimistic about why I was here, but inside I was not pleased. It wasn't just the demotion. Bianca had managed to get Christmas off with her family and we had always planned on me having a work break to join her. Because *Legend* ran for eight days, however, Carnival only allowed two cruises off instead of the usual three. This meant I would miss Christmas and get 30 percent *less* of a break for my troubles, assuming it was even granted.

But life was full of disappointments, and you had to just keep reaching for the good stuff. There had been a million wonderful surprises for me on *Conquest*, perhaps there would be on *Legend*, too. I just needed to keep focused on my goal, which was to find a way to be with Bianca and balance that with a practical life at sea. That meant returning to management. I could do it; I just had to weather the storm.

Whether I liked it or not, one way or the other, *Legend* was to be a crucible for me.

3 *Tongs over Escalators*

A FTER A TIME *LEGEND* MERCIFULLY REPOSITIONED away from New York City. I had averaged working well over eighty hours a week and had only breathed fresh air for a total of forty minutes in the last sixteen days. My fatigue was emotional to a larger degree than physical. Because my labors were not in the context of learning or advancing, they felt particularly demeaning to me.

I was also disappointed and a bit disgusted that I had not been allowed to visit the Big Apple while in port. One day I halved my five hours of sleep in order to squeeze in a little free time, but to no avail. Even though it had been over a year since the tragedy of September 11th, America was still too scared to move on. None of us "foreigners" were allowed to set one foot ashore.

Changing home ports was an interesting process. Our final stop in New York City did not entail the usual swapping of passengers, but rather merely the unloading of them. The weather was chilly and the wind carried bitterness, but the sun tried to peek through every now and then. For being Halloween, the setting was perfect as we left a gray, dreary

New York harbor on a ghost ship.

But the open deck was not empty for long, because on this special afternoon few were working. No staterooms needed cleaning; no buffets needed stocking, and no guests needed refreshments. Why, there wasn't even a boat drill! Men and women from all over the world trickled into the chill to share their wonder at the unimaginably huge skyline of New York City. I saw my first Navy aircraft carrier in person, the U.S.S. *Intrepid*, which was surprisingly smaller than *Legend*!

We all chattered in wonder like children as each direction offered something else famous and exciting. We searched the spiky skyline for the Chrysler Building or the Empire State Building. Some pointed out where the Twin Towers once stood. We moved farther away and it appeared the magic would fade, but suddenly a shaft of glorious sunlight blasted through the firmament to strike the Statue of Liberty. She was much more impressive than I had anticipated. She was magnificent!

Lady Liberty grounded me, however. She reminded me that I was already getting bitter about being on *Legend*. My first opportunity to see her a few days ago had coincided with a home port breakfast, where I had been assigned first station in the dining room. I recalled vividly checking my watch, checking the window, and then checking the door in rapid succession. As fate would have it we passed her at the very moment the doors opened. I saw a flash of her iconic green seconds before I was bowled over by two dozen impatient and demanding guests shrieking like hungry infants.

Later that evening there was a crew party to celebrate *Legend*'s recent successful USPH review. *Legend* had scored a 98: a nearly impossible benchmark rating for a ship several years old. Just like driving a new car off the lot slashes its value, smashing that champagne bottle on the bow loses an entire, crucial USPH point. The corporation was extremely pleased with the rating and spared no expense. Carnival was always generous with their crew parties, but with no guests to handle this party was special.

The party was in the vacant Truffles. I sat at a table near the front with a mixed guest list: Juci was by my side but Duman had wedged himself in between us. Ian and Dutch F&B manager Kevin also sat with us, along with a few hosts and mixed waiters. To my surprise I knew one head waiter from *Conquest*: Tekin the Turk bellowed and spat in tipsy reverie.

Ian rose and took up the wireless microphone. He was tall enough that everyone could see him. He spoke a few soft words into the mic, but no one could hear anything. He tried again, then rapped it lightly against the table.

"Duman!" he snapped. "Your goddamn babbling burnt out the batteries!"

Duman grinned mischievously, and laughter filled the dining room. Kevin took over, hauling out his guitar. He entertained everyone while we fished about for batteries. Ian threw the mic at Duman and demanded sarcastically, "You got any double D's?"

"No, more like Cs, eh Juicy?" Duman answered playfully, giving Juci a squeeze.

"Juci," she corrected.

"Whatever."

"No tit jokes, please," Ian chided with a strained look.

"I have some batteries in my cabin," I offered from across the table. "I'll go get them."

"Indeed, that would be wonderful."

I rushed off to complete the errand. When I entered the cabin, I was surprised to see Best in his bunk.

"Best, why aren't you at the party? There's free food and, more importantly, booze!"

With grave sincerity he replied, "Awga ama ta diyerd for a datamuh kina fun."

I solemnly agreed and, after hastily grabbing the batteries, fled.

When I returned to the party, people were already drunk. The habit of getting as drunk as possible in as little time as possible at crew parties took its toll. Kevin had just finished a surprisingly virtuoso Spanish guitar song when I handed the batteries to Ian. He traded me a fresh beer for them.

I sipped my beer as Ian gave a short speech commending the performance of everyone. Unlike Duman, he was a man of few words. With great fanfare he cut his speech short in favor of music. There was an awkward moment, however, when no sound came through the speakers.

"Duman! You blew out the goddamn speakers, too? Ai yai yai! All right, Brian," he said. "In for a penny, in for a pound."

"I beg your pardon?"

"You want to be management? How will you handle this situation? There's no music and this crew deserves some entertainment!"

"What do you want me to do?" I protested in surprise. "Recite a Shakespearean sonnet?"

"You do that and I guarantee you a stripe."

I hastily rose to call his bluff, but he merely laughed. "Indeed! Kevin just played guitar. I just gave a speech. Lutfi is as charming as a toad, and Duman isn't going to touch the mic ever again. It's your turn!"

Reluctantly I took the microphone, not really knowing what to do. I stood up and looked over the crowd of about two hundred. As soon as I stepped forward, recognition rippled through the mass.

"All right," I said. "I want all the Filipinos to stand up."

There was a pause while everyone tried to figure out if I was serious or not. Finally about two dozen men stood up. "O.K., this is your moment of glory! Who wants to prove he is the king of karaoke by singing a cappella, that is *without music,* in front of half the ship?"

"After you!" the crowd howled. "After you!"

I looked to Ian pleadingly, but he was obviously enjoying himself as he downed not one, but two shots of Jägermeister liquor. With an apologetic shrug, I acquiesced to the mob's demands.

"All right. Any requests?"

"*Just a Gigolo!*" Juci shrieked, receiving many cheers. For a moment I almost blushed. Well, not really.

"Who wants to hear me sing 'Just a Gigolo' a cappella?"

I downed my beer ceremoniously, then reached over and downed Ian's to the roaring approval of the audience. With as much over-the-top showmanship as I could muster, I sang. I strutted during the opening, I pleaded during the refrain, and nearly even hurled my shirt off during the climax. By the time I sat down several minutes later, the crew was deep into party mode and I was more than ready for some of Ian's Jägermeister.

"Indeed!" Ian said approvingly as he slapped me on the back. "If they didn't know you before, they sure as shit do now!"

The morning after our unprecedented night off found us in Philadelphia. Here we began the first of two special cruises, both boasting a whopping three days docked in Bermuda. These were one-way cruises with home ports changing from Philly to Baltimore to Fort Lauderdale.

In Baltimore I had no opportunity to get off the ship because I was given special duty. For some strange reason I was assigned to assist the embarkation staff. It was a very chilly, damp November day and my duty was to stand outside the cruise terminal, coatless, and sort through paper tickets by hand. After six hours of standing in one spot without moving an inch, not even for a five-minute break to sit or use the rest-room, I was a wreck. My hands were stiff and numb from the chill and my only warmth came from the burning in my eyes. My contact lenses blazed like embers and blurred my vision.

Then, as if debarkation night was not difficult enough, that evening our dining room stations rotated. I took over Ramona's former station, which meant that absolutely none of the appropriate supplies were present. She maintained nothing because, as an expert thief, she could produce anything in a pinch. So I added stress to my stiffness and soreness and general misery.

Ironically, just as I took over an ill-prepared station I was given VIP guests: the family of some Miami big shot. Duman panicked at having such guests in the dining room and hovered around. He was horrified to see my station critically bereft of the necessities, and chastised me roundly for it. I mentioned that I just inherited the station, but he did not care. Then even Ian himself deigned to leave his office to ensure all was well, giving me a second round of criticism. Despite my lack of materiel, I could easily have taken care of the guests had I not been constantly slowed by the hindering bodies of Duman, Lutfi, Ian, and even Kevin. I was waiting for the captain himself to appear and interfere.

By the end of the night I was mentally, physically, and emotionally drained. I could hardly see straight. As if all this were not enough for one day, my side job had also rotated. Thus began the worst period of my entire life.

Every waiter was assigned a side job. Usually they were simple tasks, such as ensuring menus were accounted for, or bringing all the bread baskets to the pantry. My side job since arriving had been to gather all the tongs used to dispense the dinner rolls. Twice a week I would swing through each station to collect the utensils. It took maybe ten minutes all told.

"Your new side job," Duman instructed, "Is to clean both sets of starboard escalators. Daily."

"You mean the ones I take from deck three up to the balcony?"

He grinned evilly. "Oh, more than that. You have to do everything from the galley on deck two to the landing on deck three, and finally up to the balcony on deck four."

"But deck three is part of the pantry there. That's covered by the kitchen staff."

"Not anymore. Oh, and don't forget that it's more than just sweeping the steps. You have to sweep *and* mop the floors, *and* scrub the metal sides of all the escalators, *and* polish the metal walls all the way up to the ceiling. I want Three Bucket System every night."

"You've got to be kidding! Where do I get the equipment for all that?"

"From the kitchen staff. You'll have to wait for them to finish with the bleach, the buckets, the hand towels, the mops, and the mop extensions. They usually finish after midnight."

"*After* midnight before I can even start? That adds, let's see, about two hours to my shift. Every night! I work at 6 A.M.!"

"These are the new rules. We used to assign the tough jobs to the troublemakers, but now side jobs are linked to each station permanently and we rotate the stations. Lucky you, this will last at least two months."

"Lovely. So that will take, what, at least forty minutes to go from the back of the galley to the balcony..."

"No, you don't get it. You do *all* starboard escalators. The back two escalators *and* the front two."

"Wh-what? There are forty waiters that use the front escalators...and I'm not one of them! What the hell is that?"

Duman's answer was only a malicious grin.

After the AMD left, Ramona waddled over to me. Her hair was dyed absurdly red and she wore a cherubic smile. She was a pretty woman though round as a tomato. I had recently learned she was from Sibiu, Romania, a medieval city not far from where Bianca lived.

"Ah, just who I wanted to see," I said acidly. "Thanks for a station with only five friggin' water glasses."

"Brian," she soothed. "I'll make it up to you. I have a secret."

"A cache of coffee cups?"

"You can hire the kitchen to do your side job. I've had it a number of times, and I just pay one of the cooks. They spend the last hour of their night cleaning the galley like that anyway: floors, walls, ceiling, everything. They have all the equipment ready and waterproof boots so they can do the whole thing in twenty minutes. Just pay one of them to do it. I

assure you that for twenty bucks a week they'll thank you for
it. That's what we all do."

"Oh, well, I guess that's not so bad, then. Thanks."

"LADIES AND GENTLEMEN, THIS IS YOUR FRIENDLY TURK.
AS YOU ALL KNOW, EVERYONE HAS NEW SIDE JOBS. ALREADY
YOU *MAMAGAYOS* GIVE ME HARD TIME. THERE WILL BE NO
TRADING OF JOBS, NO RAMBO, NO MAFIA. ANYONE NOT DOING
THEIR OWN SIDE JOB CAN START LOOKING FOR A TICKET
HOME. *Oui...*"

4 *F r o g   a n d   O n i o n*

THE MIDNIGHT WIND BLEW HARD OVER THE ISLAND from the black ocean. Palm trees thrashed, waves thrashed, and so, too, did my temper. I seesawed between irritation and excitement. My attitude was becoming a real problem. I hated working breakfast and lunch so much that it soured my entire being. The perpetual, pointless labor I endured was actually the least of my problems. I felt like I was rotting from within.

I challenged myself with introspective questions such as, "Do you think you are too good for this job?" But I became even more aggravated when I acknowledged the answer. I had been on *Legend* for only three weeks and I was already desperate to escape. I knew my strengths and my talents, and I could not utilize any of them here. My natural enthusiasm was already forced and the strain was breaking me. How many more months could I deny who I was...and for what?

My mood finally blushed warmer by the humid night air, and fed off its electricity and exotic, tropical power. I enjoyed a flashback of the air on Paradise Island, in the Bahamas, with the girls from Restaurant College. I could bitch all I wanted, but tonight I was in Bermuda!

Legend was docked on the northwest tip of Bermuda's fish-hook-shaped cluster of islands at an area called Dockyard. Ahead of me loomed a dark open-air museum showcasing the practical needs of British fleets past. Before being a museum, the Keep overlooking Dockyard was a bastion against Nazi U-boats. Before that it guarded a harbor packed with inhumane convict ships, and for entire *centuries* before that it was the home base in the war against Caribbean pirates.

Tonight I was not here for history, for this spit of windswept land was still very much alive. I was here for a blonde. Juci had invited me to join her at the Frog and Onion for a drink and a dance.

Nestled amongst the stone buildings that composed the Dockyard and the Keep was a nightclub called the Frog and Onion. Though *Legend* had already been in Bermuda for three days and two nights, only at midnight on night three did I have a chance to get away from work. I was averaging over fifteen hours a day at work now.

Though overwhelmed by the present, I was nonetheless a student of history and was profoundly affected by the massive, silent remnants of it looming above me. The huge Storehouse Building with its dark towers shouldered a grassy courtyard that once held supplies for the fight against the likes of Captain Kidd and Blackbeard. Some structures had collapsed ceilings, while others were in perfect repair. The limestone was damp and splotchy, illuminated by an eerie green from the humidity-cut gas lamps.

The Frog and Onion opened into a great room made of stone walls thick enough to withstand naval bombardment. The place was dark and damp and filled with wrought iron grillwork and stacks of cannon balls. Six-foot irons held candles that had melted into strangely stirring, lumpy figures. They drooped all the way to the floor, having dripped through two world wars, dripped during Napoleon's invasion of Russia, dripped during America's Revolution, and even as far back as when the pilgrims landed.

Though ancient, the place was throbbing with life. Every corner was filled with a smoking, drinking, laughing, or dancing crew member. I marveled at how many other waiters had arrived before me. I nodded to Ian as I passed by, but he was too drunk to recognize me.

I worked my way through the crowd into the next room. Here the dance floor was modern wood and the lighting and sound equipment were all state of the art, though housed neatly in the ancient limestone. The fireplace, an incredible twelve feet wide and eight feet tall, held the DJ booth. Amazing cross-cultural trance music boomed all around, and bodies from all over the world gyrated together in ecstasy. The energy was awe-inspiring.

The strobe lights, the pumping music, the scenery, and my intense fatigue all combined to make me extremely high. Through this haze of bliss I finally saw Juci. She looked incredibly sexy in tight jeans and a red spandex shirt that exposed her trim waist. Her platinum hair flashed madly as she rocked, and her tight figure pulsed with the music.

Before I even realized it, I was dancing with her. My self-confidence always vanished while dancing, but this night I did not care. Juci and I became one with the music and each other, shaking and dropping and moving. Time flew and so did we as the music spun, taking us higher and higher. The mob moved provocatively, damn near pornographically on the dance floor in the electric Bermudan night. Juci and I worked it for all it was worth. As the music rose to crescendo, everyone descended into an all-out orgy. The room whirled, or we did, completely rapt by the energy, the moment, the sexuality.

Then through the heady haze, everyone slowly realized the music had eased off. Bodies slid into each other with exhaustion. A blend of Spanish guitar and hot gypsy jazz reverberated as panting couples embraced, melted, or groped each other. Juci and I, too, crashed into each other. Lips that had been tantalizingly close through so much heat raced toward each other, but I suddenly pulled away.

With a reassuring squeeze to Juci's hand, I fled. Outside the sea breeze blasted me and the rush of fresh air forced me to drop to my knees. A palm tree above me pitched and bucked in the wind, distorting the eerie gaslight into peculiar shapes. I ran my hands through the thick grass and breathed in the cooler, salt air. My heart still pounded and my head still swam from fatigue, alcohol, and emotion.

What the hell was I doing?

I was reacting, that's what I was doing! I was not following my plan, and I had hardly noticed my first steps off the path. On *Legend* I was so overworked that any pursuit of joy seemed justified.

What was I hoping for by this chase? If I had merely wanted sex, I would have cheated on Bianca a thousand times already. I hardly knew Juci and, though she was attractive, I adored Calypso far more, and had never fallen to temptation with her. Was the Bermudan night air really that powerful?

No, I was simply losing my rationality and becoming an unthinking, impulse-driven being. After all I had been through to be true to Bianca, why would I throw it away now?

I rose slowly and stumbled back to *Legend*, desperate for my bunk. I could only hope that I would be more clearheaded after a good, long sleep. About three hours would have to do.

5 Ice Pirates

LIFE SETTLED INTO A ROUTINE OF WORK, WORK, AND work. Keeping track of my unending fifteen-hour days was easy because there was no break in them. I honestly did not mind the hours as much as I despised the type of work I did. Half my day was devoted to Pancake Darwinism, and I was obviously an evolutionary dead-end.

My new breakfast and lunch partner was Ramona. She lied, cheated, stole, engendered a universally selfish attitude and complained constantly. With no willpower whatsoever she was also exceptionally fat, a real rarity on ships. Our work ethics were completely incompatible, yet I secretly coveted her Rambo abilities to shave five minutes of labor here or there. And we laughed. Oh, how we laughed!

In such an outrageous environment I stopped analyzing things and just existed. I began to enjoy my time with Ramona, and we somehow found humor while polishing silverware, scrubbing pantries, scraping half-eaten food off plates, and even mopping floors. After such long and stressful days, sleep was surprisingly elusive, so we frequently downed a quick nightcap in her cabin. My cabin was completely off-limits because Best was an animal and I believed in the adage of "let sleeping dogs lie."

As I knew would happen, my late-night visits to Ramona's cabin provided evidence enough to the crew that we were sexually intimate. I was amused by the general confusion over my assumed behavior, from "obviously scoring with sexy Juci" to "wildly shagging fat Ramona." Soon to add to the mix was Ramona's new roommate, Xenia.

"So," I said to Xenia on her first night aboard while she unpacked her suitcase. "Where in South Africa are you from?"

She dropped what she was doing and whirled on me. "You must be American because you know nothing about the world. South Africa *is* a country."

"Whoa, slow down there, tiger. I know it is. I meant what city?"

"Oh! I'm from Cape Town."

Xenia was very tall and slender, with long hair and bright blue eyes. Like so many women Carnival hired, she could have easily been a model. Ironically, there was a great shortage of women working on *Legend*. Perhaps by my subconscious design or perhaps just dumb luck, I found myself surrounded by the few pretty ones.

"I love Cape Town," the bubbly blonde continued. "I'll show you pictures of my dad's restaurant. They're on my laptop. I love my laptop because it's purple."

"I see."

"Xenia doesn't have a boyfriend," Ramona offered suddenly. "Neither does Brian."

Before I could respond, Xenia pulled from her suitcase a miniature pink cowboy hat. She squealed with delight and, all in one blurring movement, placed it on my head and snapped several photos.

"My first cowboy," she giggled with a charming Afrikaans roll of her words.

"Not exactly. I'm from Iowa."

"Well, they eat potatoes in Texas, don't they? Now don't

you try anything, cowboy, I have a boyfriend."

"Good!" I replied. But Ramona was already chipping away at Xenia's credibility.

"You mean Graeme? Are you kidding me? You said you broke up on your last ship!"

"We did," Xenia replied as she propped her cowboy hat onto a small teddy bear she had brought. "But he's signing on here next cruise to be with me."

"You said security separated you on *Inspiration!*"

"Yes, yes. But we'll still shag. I mean, at least he's familiar."

"Well, ladies," I hastily interjected. "It's been real, but I must be going."

"That still gives you both eight days to have some fun," Ramona pressed. "I won't tell Graeme."

"That's good," Xenia added, "because he's insanely jealous and gets violent."

"Uh oh. Guilty by association," I muttered to myself. I knew I was headed for rough seas, but was just too tired to head off the potential trouble.

"Ugh, I hate him so much!" Xenia suddenly shouted. "And he's so bad in bed! Simply disgusting. I wonder if he slept with that Portuguese bitch when I left *Inspiration*? I'll bet she even liked it. She would, the whore."

Ramona and Xenia were perfect roommates for each other. Both were gossipy, funny, and spontaneous. Neither had any self-control whatsoever and could only think of what they wanted at that moment. Ramona stole at least five desserts daily, adding to her monstrously wide hips, while Xenia played people against each other with her considerable charms, adding to her cluttered list of sparring admirers. Both women were incapable of surviving life on their own: they clung to others not so much for emotional support, but as distraction from themselves.

I sank deeper and deeper into disillusionment as time rolled on. With the exception of an occasional meeting with Juci, my only friends on board were Ramona and Xenia. *That* spoke volumes about the quality of life I led. A part-time teenager working at McDonald's made roughly the same money I did, and I was unable to see any of the fabulous places we visited. *Legend* began alternating its cruises to even more exotic locations, from Barbados in the east to Costa Rica in the west and Panama in the south. I missed them all because I only had three hours off every eight days. My cabin was a pigsty and the bathroom smelled like urine. Best pissed on the toilet seat because he was apparently unaware that it could lift up. My fingers had split open from the daily bleaching and became ravaged by some sort of rash that blistered and burned.

I longed for a work break to see Bianca. We had scrapped our long-held plans when we discovered we could not be together for the holidays. Via e-mails we had been trying to build a concrete plan to keep us together more permanently, but it was a long and nearly impossible process. She trekked through the snow at all hours in Transylvania to the internet café in hopes of chatting, because my only hours off were so wacky and we were at opposite ends of the earth.

I was in real danger of losing sight of my goals and desperately needed to see her. A single hug of reassurance was all I needed to keep me going.

Once every eight days I was freed from having to mop the escalators, coinciding with the Grand Gala Buffet. On *Legend* the event was held in Truffles, so no one had time to deal with the soapy floors. Needless to say I was not given a reprieve, but was forced to work even later at the buffet.

On one of these special nights I was in a particularly bad mood because I had been arguing with everyone I met. For whatever strange reason, Ramona's and my lunch station had been filled *after* the end of lunch by Duman. Initially he sat only two people in our section, but they expected either two or ten more guests to join them at some unknown point during the afternoon. Duman happily informed the guests that, while the kitchen was closed in the afternoon, the "special American waiter" could remain to serve them whatever cold items were available at their convenience.

My partner was stuck with me and Ramona, of course, had blamed me.

"Brian, why didn't you tell Duman to shag off when he sat those bastards?"

"What, argue in front of the guests? What could I do?"

"You could have grown a penis and told the guests to F off.'"

"I see. So *your* silence was due to lack of a penis?"

In the end the situation created drama between me and Ramona, Duman, and also the kitchen staff. Instead of taking my very necessary nap in the afternoon, I spent the whole time kowtowing to the arrogant guests who trickled in over the entire damn afternoon. So not only was I angry with everyone, I was to work twenty-one hours straight that day.

I finished up my dinner duties with Luis, my Filipino assistant. We knew that there would be snippets of down time during the Gala Buffet where I could catch up on preparations for the next shift, and I was folding napkins when Ramona approached me. She had a smirk on her round face and her cheeks were red, which meant mischief. I was sure she had simply forgotten about a bitter exchange we'd had earlier in the day. She was unable to hold a grudge because I don't think she was able to remember anything for more than a few hours.

Luis and I watched with amusement as she tried to pinch a slice of cake, but an Indian slapped her hand away.

"Hey, Ramona," Luis chided loudly, "how fat is your ass now, anyway?"

"That's none of your business!"

"Of course it is. I have to look at that thing all the time!"

"You like big women," Ramona snapped. "But you'll never have a piece of me."

"Thank God for large favors."

"Brian!" she said conspiratorially. "You need to be careful. Graeme knows you're shagging Xenia."

"I'm not shagging Xenia," I replied tiredly. "I'm too tired to brush my teeth, and you think I have the energy to please *her*?"

"What man cares about pleasing the woman? Besides, everyone knows you are. You are both so out of place here: from leading nations, good English, tall and good-looking...of course you are shagging. You know we all want to watch."

"Maybe I'll charge a fee for it. Cat knows I need to supplement my income somehow."

My eyes strayed to the broad-shouldered white South African with a shaved head crossing the chaos of Gala Buffet setup. Graeme was a fairly big man, almost six feet tall and fairly well-muscled. While I suspected a percentage of his bulk came from heavy drinking, his demeanor indicated that he was a rough individual not to be dismissed. Since his arrival we had nodded politely a few times, but I knew he kept a wary eye on me. My nightly trips to Ramona and Xenia's cabin had not gone unnoticed.

"I NEED THE FOLLOWING WAITERS TO COME TO THE FRONT," Duman's voice boomed via the speakers. "JOSÉ FROM NICARAGUA, BRIAN FROM CHICAGO, AND TEKIN FROM THE GREATEST OF ALL NATIONS, TURKEY."

At the hostess station, a small gathering of waiters surrounded Duman. I recognized Tekin from *Conquest*, and my roommate Best. Also present were the seven-foot Petek from Croatia and tiny Sasko from Macedonia.

"Ice carvings," Duman ordered to us curtly as he walked by. Petek and Tekin nodded with understanding, but the rest of us were confused.

"We need to bring the ice carvings from the freezer on deck two," Tekin explained. "Find two carts somewhere and grab as many dirty table cloths as you can find."

"Dirty table cloths? Why?"

"Hurry, go!" Duman yelled back, when he realized we had not yet departed. "Chef's waiting! And if you break anything like the idiots did last cruise, you can count on special cleaning for a month."

As we rushed off, Duman intercepted me and pulled me aside.

"I know you," he said with a sly grin.

"What do you mean?"

"You love those blondes. Like California girls, eh? First Juicy—"

"Juci."

"Whatever. Now Xenia. The only two blondes in Truffles! *Oui*...very nice. Now make sure no one breaks any ice sculptures."

I departed, not really sure why Duman had said that to me. The six of us raced through the kitchen, tiny José and Sasko pushing the carts and us remaining four lugging armloads of dirty table cloths. Only Tekin knew where we were going, and he enjoyed being the man in charge. He teased the whole time about how Turks should naturally be in charge. Sasko and Petek, both of whose nations had been dominated by the Ottoman Empire for centuries, rebuked him with good humor. In response Tekin merely gave them his sinister "*Bwah-ha-ha*!"

After ten minutes of rushing maniacally through the kitchen, we were all feeling good. Our task was something different and, surprisingly, refreshing. We opened the stainless-steel door to the walk-in freezer, when suddenly José stopped up short.

"Whoa, I'm not going in there!"

"Why not?"

"I'm from Nicaragua, papa! I'll die in there!"

"You guard the carts, then."

With José as sentry outside, the remainder of us rushed into the frigid, vapor-filled air. The temperature was approximately five degrees Fahrenheit, and our sweaty polyester conducted the chill directly to our skin. Shivering and laughing, we found the ice carvings all the way in the back. Rising from the floor like some sort of Ice-henge were monoliths carved into fanciful fish, cruise ships, and cornucopias overflowing with frozen bounty.

"O.K., little Macedonian," Tekin bellowed to Sasko, pointing to the fish. "Wrap it in the dirty tablecloths and carry it out to the cart."

"But that's huge!" Sasko protested. "I'm only sixty-five kilos, man. Why am I even here?"

"Bah, no wonder we conquered you so easily!" Tekin reached over and pulled the four-foot tall carving off the floor. He waddled out of the freezer lugging the frozen fish.

"Let's go, people!" he thundered triumphantly from outside.

Working together the six of us hauled out a full load of ice carvings, taking the easy ones first. With affected ceremony we delivered them to the chefs and returned to the freezer for the last load. Remaining was a small baby dragon and its mother, the latter in three massive sections. Tekin immediately hefted the lightest dragon section and declared, "Check this Turkish power!"

Left were only the two heaviest of the sculptures and the baby. The strongest of us all was obviously Best, but he had disappeared. This left the heavy loads to the very tall but also very skinny Petek, and me.

With a loud grunt, Petek heaved on the dragon's curling tail and struggled to get it out of the freezer. Sasko trailed, boasting, "That's European power!" The ice began to shift beneath the wrappings and they fumbled comically to grip the slippery body. Finally José had to rush in and hold up the tip of the tail. Only with tremendous effort did Petek manage to deposit the load onto the cart.

Not missing a beat, José declared triumphantly, "¡Mira, papa! As always, Central American power makes it happen!"

We all started ribbing each other and laughter cut through the icy air.

"Say, where is Best? He's the biggest and he hasn't lifted anything yet!"

"Are you kidding? He can't even lift the toilet seat!"

We heard his angry reply from somewhere beyond the hanging slabs of meat, "I aina gotta takemunga dat crap from muckybrain lak do!"

We scanned each other's faces in confusion, then all burst out laughing. "Brian, you're the only native English speaker. What the hell did he just say?"

"Cat only knows," I replied. I was pleased the heaviest sculpture was left to me. Not to be outdone, I taunted, "Now children, let the world leader show you how it's done."

"Children!" Sasko rebutted. "Your country is, what, five years old? Alexander the Great was conquering the world when you were still monkeys!"

"Eh, papa, monkeys are in Central America, not North."

"Bah!" Tekin bellowed. "America has been a leader for only sixty years. My country ruled for centuries!"

"Yeah!" José jeered. "Everyone knows gringos don't like hard work. Let's see how a fat Yankee does!"

I slowly wrapped the dragon's head section in multiple dirty tablecloths and hunkered down to lift with my legs. One massive heave later and I had the thing in the air. As I struggled to get it out of the freezer, I nearly dropped it from laughter at everyone's commentary.

"Whoa, look at that! Americans aren't weak after all!"

"Carrying all that money takes strength."

"So *that's* why Schwarzenegger moved to America."

Flush with the exertion and laughter, we stopped up short when we saw what was left. Though only the baby dragon remained, we all whistled in unison when we realized the challenge that lay before us.

Baby was frozen to the floor.

Apparently the sculpture had been set into a puddle of water, for it was now stuck fast. Unlike all the monolithic sculptures that were four feet tall on a narrow base, the baby dragon had a wide, flat footprint that created the maximum surface contact with the floor. As if that were not enough, the dragon itself was very delicate and offered nothing strong enough to wrestle with. We all stared at it, wondering what we were to do.

From the deep recess of the freezer, Best drew near. We heard his rumble before we saw him, not unlike King Kong approaching through the dense jungle. Entire sides of meat swayed as his massive bulk pushed through them. He bellowed like a wounded animal when he saw the ice-locked sculpture.

"AWGA HATTA THE MUTHA FURCKRA SCREWEDA UP!"

His roar was deafening in the enclosed freezer, and he followed it up by wordless, irate jabbering. Despite our best efforts, Best's anger made us howl with laughter, which made him even angrier. He began stomping around the freezer, slapping aside hanging sides of meat with his huge fists.

"Whoa! Slow down there, Best!"

"The beef's already dead, Best, calm down!"

"Yeah, don't hurt the beef! Americans cannot survive without it."

Only too late did we realize what Best's rage was leading to.

"Wait, Best, no!"

"Don't kick the baby, Best!"

"Baby hasn't done anything to you, papa!"

He kicked the baby dragon with his heavy boot. The delicate sculpture smashed into shards that spun across the floor to rebound off the walls with a clatter. We all yelled in a heady mixture of desperation, resignation, and fatigue.

"You killed the baby!"

Tekin, looking for all the world like an ogre, brutally parodied a mother in distress by bellowing in falsetto, "My baby! My baby!"

We watched the shards slow their rotation and finally come to rest. I panted in the frigid air and suddenly realized this was the happiest moment I had experienced since joining *Legend*. The international camaraderie was wonderful. In ship life, you just never knew where you would find yourself. Here I was, suffering from mind-numbing fatigue and shaking in a five degree freezer, but I was having a blast.

I foolishly thought for a moment that maybe, just maybe, I had hit bottom. Maybe this was as bad as life would get, and I had learned to find the joy.

Nah, not really.

6 *The Boatyard*

THE ROCKING BENEATH WHERE I LAY WAS FROM A life raft.

After living on the sea for nearly a year, I could differentiate easily between the sizes of ships based on the waves they produced, barring any structural anomalies. Some guests who had never been on a megaship worried about being seasick, but the majority of vessels rocked about as much as a shopping mall, albeit during Christmas season.

No, I was definitely on a life raft. Had I finally escaped *Legend* in the middle of the night? All was dark, but I knew I was being tossed about and I was unbelievably happy and relaxed. This obviously indicated that I had escaped, or perhaps had died.

Now there was light, and I was lying with a gorgeous woman by my side. Together we lay on a raft, pitching and bucking in the great ocean. Her hand slipped into my pants, and my relaxation began to give way to something else. Dolphins swam around us, squeaking strangely. They began spitting in my face....

I woke up with a start.

I really *was* rocking as if on a raft, though I was actually on a floating trampoline. It surged with the waves below me. Rain dropped into my face, and it was cool and cloudy all around me. Lying face down beside me was a strange woman in a string bikini. Her hand was in my shorts, but she was unconscious.

Blearily I listened to a strange squealing sound in the distance. Some fifty yards away was a white sandy beach and a bar, both loaded with partying, drunken revelers. In the parking lot behind was an outrageously painted bus, furiously honking its customized horn. A line of crew members surged toward it.

Where in the hell was I? The last thing I remembered was working breakfast and getting yelled at by some morbidly obese woman because I did not have Coca-Cola readily available to pair with her Frosted Flakes. I checked for the time, but my watch was missing. The thick clouds hid any hint from the sun.

I followed the slender forearm resting on my navel, seeking her watch. I gently pulled us apart and looked at the time. With horror I realized that I had to be in the dining room within an hour! I had to get on that odd bus immediately.

"Wake up!" I called urgently, shaking the woman.

Groggily she raised her head from the trampoline. Her cheek was imprinted with the mesh pattern, making her appearance very amusing. She winced as the rain washed down her face.

"We have to go! The bus is leaving!"

With painful casualness she reviewed her watch. She squinted a moment through the rain, then shrugged. Finally she said with a thick Russian accent, "I have three more hours."

She returned to her sleep. I had to fight every nerve and muscle in my body not to join her. We had obviously not simply taken a nap out here: we had passed out from alcohol. We both reeked of rum and who knew what else.

Again I frantically looked to the beach, some hundred and fifty feet away. Behind us, perhaps two hundred feet away from the white sand, was a floating, inflatable climbing mountain. We were on one of two trampolines, and there were a few other indescribable, inflatable shapes bobbing in the rough sea. I recalled that a tropical storm was approaching the Caribbean, and I deduced that we were in Barbados. This was the easternmost of the Windward Islands, almost jutting out into the Atlantic.

"I have to leave right now, and I'm not leaving you out here!"

"Go, then," she mumbled.

I hauled on her figure, which was very sluggish. "I'm not leaving you out here. Together we go, *right now!*"

She squealed in protest, but I dumped us both in the water. The waves hurled us toward the beach, for which I was extremely grateful. After splashing in the salty water and being slashed by the rain and wind, I was beginning to sober up. Apparently she was not.

"Brian, let me go!" We lurched onto the beach, and she settled into the sand like an octopus hiding at the sea bottom. "You need to go, I understand. I stay here."

"Hey!" a voice called from the nearby bar. A Russian man trudged out into the rain-beaten sand, oblivious to the storm. For a moment I feared he thought I was molesting this strange woman. Finally he said something long and slurred in Russian. I'm not really sure how I knew it was slurred.

"Can I leave her with you?" I asked desperately, seeing the bus nearing capacity.

"*Da, Amerikanski!* Olena no problem, I watch. Go!"

Soaking wet, sans towel or watch or clue, I rushed onto the bus. I was terribly disoriented, but managed to find a seat in the overcrowded, noisy bus. Ordinarily I would have been thrilled that the seat was next to a beautiful woman, but under the circumstances I would have preferred a bouncer from a strip club who could carry me if I passed out again.

"Let's get this show on the road!" she shouted impatiently at the driver.

My sense of alarm slowly went off in my head. It took me a few moments to recognize it, and I looked at her for a while as I tried to figure out what was wrong. My lengthy scrutiny obviously made her uncomfortable, but she said nothing.

"Aha!" I said eventually. "You don't have an accent! You are American!"

"Yeah."

"Oh my Cat...this isn't a crew bus? Are we even going to the *Legend*?"

"Yeah. You're dripping on me."

I sheepishly slicked my hair back and wriggled my bottom to give her more room. I could only imagine how obnoxious I must have appeared to her.

"But you're not crew," I protested.

"I'm the new singer," she answered curtly. After a moment she obviously decided I was harmless and taunted me, "So, you recovered from your fall?"

I frowned, trying to figure out what she was talking about. She started laughing in my face. "You don't remember it, do you? Are you *that* drunk?"

A blurry fragment of a memory clarified in my addled mind. I had awakened on the floating trampoline, but I seemed to recall that I had originally swum out to tackle the large inflatable climbing mountain. It had been a rough swim against the current as the tropical storm pushed toward the island.

The mountain was fifteen feet tall and almost vertical the entire way up. The wind and the waves made it buck like a bronco, and I had difficulty even getting my hands on the first rungs, which were above the water in which I tread. The handholds were placed sporadically along its flank, though the easiest ones had long since been torn off from overuse. It was a tremendous challenge to pull my bulk up against gravity, rain, fatigue, and inebriation. The surface was slippery and because the mountain was low on air, everything was smooshy and awkward. I straddled the slick surface and clung onto the sides with great difficulty, but finally worked my way upward.

Near the top both handholds had been torn off. I refused to give up at this point, however, and tried desperately to grip the top. It was just too wet. I remained there, motionless, trying to figure out a way forward, when my watch popped off my wrist. By pure, insane luck it fell between my body and the mountain, slowing it just enough for my reflexes to catch it. I gripped it between my teeth because there was no way to re-latch it or reach my pockets.

After great deliberation under the elements, watch between my teeth, I finally lurched clumsily onto the top. A particularly strong wave struck the mountain just as I reached the pinnacle and the peak collapsed in. I was flipped upside-down and pitched over the far side in a heartbeat. I tumbled the fifteen feet and had landed badly into the sea.

"So that explains where my watch is. Bottom of the Atlantic."

"Cool," she said. I could tell she was greatly amused by me, which probably explained why she was not annoyed. "Yeah, we all cheered for you when you decided to tackle that climb. None of us thought you would make it."

The woman beside me had bouncy, natural red curls. She was attractive, though her features always seemed for some reason ready to spring into a frown.

"I don't recognize your *lack* of accent, either," I said. "Where in the States are you from?"

"I'm from Iowa."

"Yeah, right," I replied sourly. "Where are you *really* from?"

Her face instantly wrinkled into a frown. "Why would I lie about that? Why does everyone make fun of Iowa, anyway? I am from Des Moines, so kiss my ass!"

"Whoa, tiger, slow down. I'm from Iowa, too."

"Look, I'm not going to sleep with you, zit-face, so you can drop the lies."

"Hey! What's your problem?"

"You have an accent, dumb ass. You're a bad liar."

"I'm from Cedar Rapids. I picked up the accent in the dining room. Everyone on board seems to know me, so I figured you were mocking me. Sorry."

"Oh, so you're the one! Brian had told me there was another American onboard in the restaurant."

"Who's Brian?"

"He's the new guitar player. He's from Pella."

"Are you trying to tell me," I asked incredulously, "that of the *only four* Americans on board, two are Brians from Iowa?"

"So it would seem."

I settled into silence for the remainder of our journey, trying desperately to remember what had led me to this beach bar. I assumed we had been at the Boatyard, because that was the only bar the crew referred to. I had never had a lunch off in Barbados before, and I knew that lately I had felt the need to get wildly drunk. Apparently I had achieved my objective.

On top of my negative thoughts and general dissatisfaction with my current situation, I had contracted some sickness from my guests. I had been fighting a sore throat and sniffles. Passing out in the rain would help fix that! Adding to my annoyance in life was my new face-full of pimples. These were not merely little red spots, but deep wells that ached with every rare laugh and each repeated frown. I blamed the pimples and the ill health on my continual diet of fried chicken. It was either that or fish-head soup on rice, which did not particularly appeal to me, either. Like everything else about *Legend*, the crew food was criminal. But after starving on *Conquest*, I would be damned if I went hungry again!

So my lame attempt at distracting myself from misery by chasing a woman in Bermuda failed, and then I thought alcohol might be the answer. While I loved a drink or three, I rarely depended upon such a distraction to better "deal with" my life. With horror I realized that life was so bad on *Legend* that neither women nor alcohol could improve it. I might as well have joined my watch on the sea floor!

As the bus rumbled back to *Legend*, I fiercely tried to recall who that woman was with her hand in my pants!

Still drunk out of my mind, I meandered through my first seating at dinner in a daze. My assistant Luis saved me countless times by being on the ball and working extra fast. Apparently I had forewarned him of my agenda that day, and he had come in early to be extra prepared. I resolved a thousand times to reward him for his efforts.

By the time second seating arrived, I was actually able to walk without a stagger. This was fortunate, because Ian was waiting for me when I returned from the kitchen with my silverware.

"I'd polish that extra carefully if I were you," he quipped.

"*Would it were not so, you are my mother,*" I quoted from Shakespeare for some inexplicable reason.

"Hamlet, to Gertrude," he smartly answered. "And might I add that you seem to be floating through the evening much like the Ghost of King Hamlet."

"Dude, you are cool."

"Indeed. The hotel director and his entire family are in your section tonight. His brother is a cruise director for Royal Caribbean, so I want you to put on a good show."

"I am nothing if not entertaining. A veritable barrel of friggin' monkeys."

"Indeed."

"*Yet I have of late, but wherefore I know not, lost all my mirth.*"

"Hamlet, to Rosencrantz. You'll have to start doing the dances, mate."

I was too drunk to even attempt to hide my disgust. "There is no Cat! Come on, man, the dances? The stupid babaloo dances Carnival makes us do with the sole purpose of denigrating and humiliating us?"

"Yep, those would be the ones."

"What's tonight, the Hokey Pokey or the frickin' Chicken Dance?"

"Indeed," he replied smugly. "It's Macarena tonight. Enjoy!"

As I set up my station, I railed against fate for sending me such VIP guests when I was so thoroughly inebriated. It was just like karma to do this to me. All I had wanted was one afternoon of mind-numbing bliss away from the ship, and I had been prepared to pay the price during dinner...but this was ridiculous. I had never heard of such a thing, the highest-ranking man onboard, the hotel director, having dinner in the dining room.

When the guests arrived, I stared at them with nothing short of vitriol. Daniel the hotel director was exceptionally handsome in his crisp, white formal attire. All around the table were arrayed exceptional people: exceptionally well-dressed, exceptionally gorgeous, and undoubtedly successful. On Daniel's left was his exceptionally beautiful wife, Lisa. A jarring oddity was the unlikely, gangly man wearing a bright red shirt with huge orange polka dots.

To my great surprise, the evening turned out to be a gem. Daniel was a very genial man from Ohio. Though soft-spoken, he had an excellent sense of humor. It was obvious he was thrilled to be seeing his family again. In particular he was pleased to meet up with his bizarre cruise director brother Randy, who reminded me distinctly of Shaggy from *Scooby Doo*.

All night Randy and I traded jibes and insults that were completely spontaneous and painfully unprofessional. The dinner took far longer than expected because we spent so much time talking and laughing. Ian and Duman hovered on the edge of my station in constant stress at the elapsing time, but were assuaged by the sound of continuous mirth. By the end of the dinner all of us were gasping for breath and complaining that our sides hurt.

"Brian," Randy finally asked me. "What are you doing here? I'm a cruise director and you are funnier than I am."

"No, I am merely drunker than you are. If I remember it, I will no doubt be horrified at what I thought was funny here tonight."

Daniel suddenly looked at me with gravity. "You know, Randy's right. What *are* you doing here?"

"Chasing a woman."

"Of course!" Lisa blurted enthusiastically. "Is she a mysterious beauty from some exotic corner of the world?"

"Transylvania," I answered with a smile. I added slyly with a knowing look, "She's the second most wonderful woman I have ever, ever met. Third, if you count Mom."

"Whoa," Randy cried, "That was so smooth, it *had* to come naturally!"

"Of course it did!" Lisa snapped. "Maybe you could get a woman if you said such things."

"Alas, she's not on *Legend*," I continued. "The great evil of corporation has temporarily parted us. That's why I am drunk. Fortunately for us all Randy's shirt has sobered me, though I fear for life."

Lisa clung to Daniel's side and pleaded, "Danny, help this poor man in his noble pursuit."

"Yeah, Dan," Randy jibed. "If you can't help me get laid with all your power, at least help my brother-in-arms."

"O.K., O.K.!" Daniel surrendered. Cheers rose from around the table. "Swing by my office some time. We'll see what we can do."

7 *Lost in Panama*

M Y NEXT SHIFT OFF, NINE DAYS AFTER THE Boatyard affair, was an ugly, rainy day in mid-December. I had resolved to see the Panama Canal as a Christmas gift to myself, and knew that my next few hours off, though closer to the holiday, would be in god-awful Limón, Costa Rica. I had arranged to start work at 5:30 A.M. in order to be off the ship as early as possible. By 9 A.M. I walked off the gangway and entered exciting, exotic Panama.

A small complex of nondescript shops embraced the pier at Colón. Many of the crew would hop off the ship for a quick drink at the Iguana Café or a sandwich at Subway. A little farther from the ship was the famous Zona Libre, or Free Zone. This tax- and duty-free zone was at the center of trading throughout the Western Hemisphere. It was difficult to purchase one pair of jeans, but you could get 2,000 for about the same price.

Taxi drivers hovered near the Subway, knowing Americans congregated there because it was familiar. I shopped around for a personal tour of the Canal. After a few false starts I found that forty U.S. dollars would get me a cab for several hours and a personal guide. This was about one-third of what most non-bartering ship guests would pay. Then I shopped for a companion to split the fare, being an incredibly cheap man.

Eventually I met up with Radka, a very shy and petite red-head from rural Lithuania. I knew her vaguely from the ship and had always assumed she was Irish, based on her looks. I easily sensed her disappointment at ship life. She was quitting the ships after one contract and was fighting tooth and nail to see something, anything, of the world before returning to peasant life back home.

The famed Panama Canal was not far, and quite simply exceeded all my expectations. The engineering achievement would be impressive by today's standards, and to think that America made it happen a century ago was simply astounding. The list of superlatives and firsts the canal claimed was lengthy and, when the entire history was learned, almost unbelievable.

We spent some time at the famed Gatun locks. A lock is a huge, water-filled chamber that rises and falls in an operation like an elevator for ships. Each gargantuan tank filled with millions of gallons of water so fast that the naked eye could easily follow the progress. Though over nine hundred feet long, the lock actually filled up faster than a bathtub, and pulled up a 300,000-ton tanker along with it. This astounding feat was routine here, happening some forty times a day.

After collecting our satisfaction and our photos, we returned to the ugly entrance to the Zona Libre. I had planned on parting with Radka to get some much-needed rest, but she had a different idea. Nothing would deter her from roaming the streets of Colón: not the wretched poverty, splattering rain, nor the chilly wind. She seemed oblivious of the danger of being a lone, tiny woman in one of the worst slums in the Western Hemisphere.

"You want to wander around in *there*?" I asked, incredulous. Before us opened a network of garbage-filled streets lined with decaying buildings. The very concrete, of which everything was constructed, was crumbling and moldy. Graffiti was the only uniform decoration.

"Yes," she said simply.

"Are you crazy or just stupid? Man, have I always wanted to say that to somebody! All right, I'll go with you."

I was curious to walk around myself, though I had planned on waiting for another day, preferably sunny and surrounded by NFL linebackers. I entered the rotting neighborhood with tense shoulders and wide eyes, but Radka seemed oblivious of any potential danger. Within a block we were completely surrounded by ruins inhabited by the most desperately poor I had encountered since the Cairo slums.

Colón was constructed by Americans a century ago. Unknown to most, the United States had created a socialist society to build the canal, so each building was identical to the next. Unfortunately, not one had seen even a lick of repairs since being abandoned in 1914. Moss and other growth sprouted from the moldering concrete walls.

Dark, dank stairwells between the buildings provided access to upper floors by meeting up with each level's front balcony. Doors, invariably missing, opened into thin air because most balconies had long since fallen to the earth. Haphazard planks bound together by chicken wire reached from the landings to the thresholds, allowing access.

We continued down the widest street we could find, at my insistence. Most of the streets were one-lane or even narrower, and even then filled with mountains of garbage. To my surprise, a wonderful smell emanated from an alley roofed with limp laundry dripping in the rain. To indicate a restaurant a handful of tables poked into the alley, pushing aside the rubbish. While I knew the best food was usually to be had in unlikely corners, we opted out of lunch in that alley.

We passed a cross-street that I deemed sufficiently wide enough to offer at least a modicum of safety. Turning down it, we were suddenly intercepted by a youth in a yellow rain coat. He rode a bicycle and charged us so quickly that I nearly struck him in self-defense before realizing he was merely a child.

Stopping directly before us, exhausted, panted a black youth. His hair curled tightly to his head and his smile, though missing a front tooth, appeared honest.

"No, no," he said, gesturing for us to avoid the street. I reviewed it again at his behest, and noted that large groups of idle men had materialized on each side.

"Gracias, amigo," I said, and we moved on.

The young teen followed us, though remaining at a respectful distance. I kept one eye on him, but the other was very occupied with the amazing array of sights. From the balcony of a green building a sad, tired-looking grandmother watched us. Her black skin sagged along with her posture, and her hair had long since turned snow white. I gave her a smile, but she never raised her head.

We passed another interesting, decrepit structure with thick iron bars on the second-floor balcony. Behind the bars was a tough-looking young man wearing a bandana. He sipped from a can of beer and stared at us with menace. Beside him was a young boy who openly stared at Radka's red hair and emerald eyes. He grinned with glee.

Finally we were about to turn on another street, when the youth on the bicycle again rushed up to gesture us off. He pointed farther down our street and indicated in Spanish what I understood as "three more blocks." Suddenly I wondered if he was part of a plot to lure us into the wrong area where we were easier prey.

"What do you think," I asked Radka, "should we follow this kid?"

She looked up at me and shrugged. She was not nervous at all, and I wondered if I was just another American projecting my own homegrown fear of the unknown onto the rest of the world. I knew the lack of diversity in America, coupled with corporate branding, had created in our society a fear of anything not immediately recognized. This was manifested both profoundly and subtly, from fearing other races to not trying a new restaurant. Europeans, on the other hand, frequently grew up surrounded by different languages and other cultures. They were far more likely to take it all in stride.

All that having been mulled upon, I resolved that Radka was a naïve peasant girl from a small village in the country and had no idea what to expect from a third-world city slum. To aid my decision, I reviewed the boy again. I realized he was riding a new, expensive multi-gear bike.

"*¿Quién es?*" I asked in Spanish, meaning "Who are you?"

He grinned at me with pride, and pulled open his yellow raincoat. The t-shirt he wore underneath read in bold letters, "Carnival."

It all began to make sense to me. Carnival had quietly arranged to protect stupid tourists like us from wandering down potentially dangerous streets. This local boy knew better than anyone where to go and where not to. He rushed off ahead as the drizzle turned to rain. We followed along, and finally turned on a perpendicular street that promised to lead us back toward the pier.

Somewhere in the deepest part of this slum, more wretched than anything I had seen since watching the homeless living in open Egyptian sewers, I witnessed a wonderful moment. Three little black girls sat cross-legged, bunched together behind a screen door with an elaborate grill. Opposite them were three young chickens. The girls poked their little fingers through the grill at the chicks, who peeped quietly. Each regarded the other with intense fascination, the girls hunched so low that they were almost eye to eye with the chickens.

It was a moment of discovery and wonder for us all. There was something amazing about that moment, something pure and transcendent. I reached for my camera, but a violent scream from far away shattered the serenity.

Only then did Radka become aware of a possibility of danger. When she began urging me to return with her to the ship,

I did not argue. It marked the first time I was actually satisfied to see *Legend*.

Amazingly, the next port in Panama I was scheduled to work at 5:30 A.M. again. I hastily arranged to see more of the country, this time with Juci and her new assistant, Martina. I knew Martina from restaurant college and was thrilled to see her again. They had already seen the canal, so we aspired to visit the Pacific Ocean instead. We thought it would be noteworthy to visit two oceans in one day.

While the ladies readied themselves for our half-day out, I rushed outside to arrange the taxi. Using a painstaking mix of English and Spanish, I managed to barter successfully with a driver. I haggled the price down to $80, from $120, for three of us in a taxi that would take us entirely across the isthmus to Panama City and back.

"O.K.," the driver said to me as he gestured to a man in a tiny, dirty sedan. "Here is Bob. He will take you."

"Wait wait wait," I said. "I deal with you. I never agreed to this. He probably doesn't even speak English."

"Sure he does. Ask him."

I ducked my head into the car and looked over our proposed driver. He was a small man in simple clothing with a shaved head. He was not black but apparently some sort of local native Indian. Bob my ass, I thought acidly.

"So you speak English?"

"Yes," he answered enthusiastically.

"You understand that we are not going to the canal, but want to see Panama City and the Pacific?"

"Yes."

I was not yet satisfied, but my companions arrived ready for action. Juci bounced up wearing her non-work uniform: a tight red shirt pulled up to reveal her trim middle. Her platinum hair fairly glowed in the tropical sun. Despite being

Czech, Martina had dressed surprisingly American by wearing a t-shirt, blue jeans, and tennis shoes.

"Everything ready?" Juci asked.

"Well, sort of," I reluctantly agreed. "I am not so sure."

"Quit being American," Juci teased. "It doesn't have to be air-conditioned car. It will be fine."

The ladies got into the back of the sedan, so I sat in the front. As the driver pulled away from the curb, I looked him over more closely. I was getting a bad vibe about Bob.

"What did you say your name was again?"

"Yes!" he replied earnestly.

We drove like lightning across the Isthmus of Panama, enjoying the weather. It was exactly as we had pictured it: hot, humid, and sunny. The jungles were lush and omnipresent, and even from the highway we saw large birds and strange shapes pushing through the foliage. We joked and laughed and exclaimed at every glimpse of the fabled canal. It was fascinating to watch a 200,000-ton barge sailing beside us, only to disappear behind a hill.

Our first sign of trouble came when we neared the huge Miraflores Locks of the Panama Canal. This set of multiple locks was very impressive and picturesque, marking the beginning of the gargantuan man-made lake that filled the valleys. At the time Gatun Lake was the largest man-made lake on earth. Bob pulled up to the parking lot, turned off the engine, and smiled with pride.

"What are we stopping for?" I asked.

He merely grinned at me. I exchanged a concerned look with the ladies. Finally Bob read aloud the huge sign that rose before us.

"*Esclusas de Miraflores.*"

"Uh, Bob," I said rather testily. "I know these are the locks of Miraflores. Why are we stopping?"

"Canal!" he boasted.

"We don't want to see the canal. We want to see Panama City."

His grin finally lessened and confusion clouded his features. "No canal?"

"I knew it!" I exploded. "You don't speak any damn English at all, do you?"

His blank look answered my question. Juci groaned from the back of the car, but Martina just laughed.

"Panama City?" I repeated. "¿*Ciudad de Panama?*"

Slowly recognition crossed his features. "¿*Ciudad?* ¿*No Canal?*"

Undeterred, I grabbed my map and showed him where we wanted to go. Smiling once again, Bob drove onward to Panama City.

Panama City anchored the canal on the south, and was in all ways the opposite of the northern city of Colón. All the immense profits from the canal were surely funneled directly to the capital, because it was truly magnificent. We stared around in awe, stunned that such a monstrous city lay at one end of the canal while such wretched poverty held down the other. Panama City, the financial and cultural capital of the nation, boasted a skyline that rivaled Miami!

The traffic leading into the city was extremely thick, and we followed a miles-long line of buses and dirty Volkswagen Beetles belching black smoke.

Using the slow traffic to our best advantage, I tried to communicate with Bob. I knew a modicum of Spanish, understanding "stop, right, or left." For a precious half hour we drove in circles in the colossal city because Bob had obviously never before been there, and he did not understand what we wanted. Even I figured out the strange traffic system faster than he did, but was unable to communicate it to him.

Bob drove onward as if he knew exactly where he was going. Foolishly, but also partly out of curiosity, we waited to see where we would end up, squandering our precious time in the process. Eventually we found ourselves outside a massive, ugly, concrete shopping mall.

"Shopping!" he boomed with pride.

"Brian," Juci begged, "will you please talk to him?"

"No shopping, Bob. Downtown. Palace. Museums. *Centro de ciudad.*"

He looked at me blankly.

"Brian," Juci begged, "say something in Spanish!"

"What do you want from me? You speak seven languages between the two of you, for Cat's sake! You want me to sing a Marc Anthony song to him?"

"I am hungry," Martina said. "Restaurant is the same in Spanish, isn't it?"

"Yes it is. Bob, *restaurante, por favor.*"

"Shopping?"

"*No, restaurante.*"

"Canal?"

"Bob," I said slowly and clearly, "*¿Habla español?*"

His blank look answered my question. Not only did Bob not speak English, he did not speak Spanish, either. All crew knew that leaving the ship behind was always done at their own risk, but this was ridiculous! We needed to get back to our ship in just four hours, and we were literally on the wrong ocean!

I pointed toward the sea and said, "*¡El Mar Pacifico!*"

This Bob understood. He revved the engine and we were off. Minutes later we drove along the Pacific Ocean. We yelled for Bob to stop, and after a few emphatic gestures he understood. We hopped out of the car on a very busy road and reviewed with wonder what lay before us.

Bouncing on the waves was a fleet of fishing boats of all sizes, none of which were moored to the land. Far to our left was the skyline of modern high-rise buildings that stretched far out to the sea, looking just like Miami. Frigate birds, with their forked tails, swooped and screamed in massive flocks to obscure the marvel so far away. Only 300 yards to our right was a huge cluster of European-style buildings two and three stories tall. All wore red tiles and bunched right up to the water, shouldering each other for every square inch of earth. Hidden among the clutter of fascinating, centuries-old buildings was the Presidential Palace.

Thrilled, we indicated to Bob that we wished to explore the old town. We had no intention of walking there, fearing that Bob would abandon us in some miscommunication. Unfortunately none of us counted on the complexity of the one-way streets. It was mind-boggling. Every time I thought I had finally figured out where we needed to go to get to our destination, a series of fruit stalls filled the street. We drove for a full hour, circling like buzzards, but never found a way to penetrate the labyrinth.

Time began to run short, and we did not underestimate the difficulty of our situation. Not wanting to take any more chances, we resolved to eat at the first restaurant we saw and to rush back to *Legend*.

To my chagrin, Juci and Martina both grew excited upon seeing a McDonald's.

"McDonald's! Let's eat there!"

"You aren't serious are you?"

"Of course! McDonald's in Panama...sounds fun."

"For the love of Cat, we are in an exotic, foreign country and you want to eat at McDonald's?" I clarified painfully.

"Oh, come on, Brian. All Americans eat McDonald's."

We were satisfied that Bob would not abandon us while we ate. With the promise of a Big Mac, he made it clear he would wait all day. For the next thirty minutes I was extremely self-conscious and displeased. I was well aware of the world's perception that Americans only eat at McDonald's, and I felt like I was playing into a stereotype that I deplored. I hated McDonald's food for innumerable reasons, but finally settled into a chicken sandwich and French fries. Juci and Martina devoured cheeseburgers like, well, Americans. All the locals stared at them, marveling over their trim European bodies, white skin and blond hair.

Only then did I realize that I had not been utilizing my camera. The challenges of communication and getting lost had resulted in not a single photograph of grand, challenging Panama City. With mere minutes left to enjoy the city, I had to capture something, anything, before it was gone forever. Thusly my only picture of that crazy day was of Juci eating a Big Mac.

As we passed out of Panama City, heading for *Legend*, I suddenly realized that nearly everyone we had met was Hispanic on the Pacific coast. On the Caribbean coast the population was universally black. I had never seen such a stark geographical delineation before.

The heat became oppressive, and in the steamy car both Juci and Martina fell asleep. I watched Juci in her slumber for a long time. She was quite attractive, and the sunlight on her platinum hair was nearly blinding. It is strange how watching someone sleep offers such an opportunity for reflection, as if you are finally free to review them unhindered. I concluded firmly that my struggle over Juci in Bermuda had nothing to do with her at all, but was a test of my own resolve. She was a sweet girl and I was glad nothing too silly had happened between us to spoil our friendship.

I struggled desperately to stay awake. I did not trust Bob worth a damn, though I did not particularly fear he would take advantage of us if we were all asleep. Still, I found no reason to take a chance. The jungle flashed by and I wondered why I didn't feel cooler because I had seen two oceans in one day.

Several days later I knocked on the hotel director's door. Though on the phone, Daniel waved me in with a smile. As he finished his call, I reviewed his office. It was very large with two full-sized windows revealing the crystal-blue waters of the Caribbean. Though trite with a typical hotel's décor, it was very warm and nice. Open space was the greatest luxury of all onboard, of course.

"Brian!" he greeted after hanging up the phone. "Finally! Someone I can shoot the breeze with who understands me. You know, there are a number of Canadians onboard, but they don't have a clue what I'm talking about. I made a joke about *The Dukes of Hazzard* and they stared at me like I was an alien. I've long since stopped trying to imitate The Fonz. Dude, there are just not enough of us!"

"Oh, I don't know. There is another Brian from Iowa onboard, a fact which galls me to my very foundation."

"So, you are after your woman. What ship is she on?"

"She's on vacation at the moment."

"Well, not much I can do for you, then! But really, you shouldn't be in the restaurants. You are too funny for that."

"Tell me about being a cruise director, then."

"You know, lots of those guys make a hundred grand a year. I can educate you about everything. If you put in the time at the bottom being a social host, I know you could make it as CD."

"Really?"

"Oh, yeah. Being a social host is a lot of work for very little money, but if you can handle hard work you'll make it to the top. It's just a matter of perseverance. I had heard there was one American who made it a whole contract in the dining room, so obviously you can handle it. I'm proud of you, by the way. Did you meet the Australian couple in the dining room that quit?"

"No."

"They both quit after three days, man. They were forced to work until the end of the cruise because we still fed and housed them. Anyway, if you can make it a few years with almost no money at all, you'll be in big. Then your girlfriend can live with you for free on the ship."

"Where do I sign up?"

"You need a signature from the senior maitre d', the F&B manager, and me to get a transfer. After that it goes to Miami for approval. I can put in a good word for you, shouldn't be a problem."

"I will do anything to be with my Bianca," I said earnestly. "If I could actually start a career path out of it, I won't think twice. At the moment I only seem to get a few months a year with her, but even that is worth all the hassle. I had planned on pursuing the maitre d' spot because it was the most logical way to get me on board and it fit with my experience, but the politics are killing me. You know, I've always secretly wanted to be an entertainer."

"You have a good presence. Randy noticed it right away. But you know, the real shame is that you don't know anything about art."

I leaned in. "Is this where I casually mention I have a Bachelor's degree in art history?"

Daniel perked up. "No kidding? Dude, you should become an art auctioneer!"

"A what?"

"Art auctioneer. Those guys make the most money on-board, even more than the captain, and they work only a couple days a week."

"Keep talking."

"A few days a week they conduct an auction in one of the lounges. You have excellent speaking skills, and if you have a degree in art history, I can't see why you couldn't do it. Now, I don't know exactly how much they make, but, well, look at this!"

He gestured for me to come around his desk. On his computer he pulled up a spreadsheet, but suddenly paused. "Now, you can't tell anyone I am showing you this."

"Mum's the word."

"Our auctioneer, Chester, pulled this in sales last cruise. See that? He sold over eighty thousand dollars of art in one week. Now I don't know what his percentage is, but let's say it is only five percent. That's still $4,000 for one week, dude. I would do it myself, but I don't know anything about art."

I whistled in awe. "There *is* a Cat!"

"Huh?"

8 *The Four Temptations of the Apocalypse*

A PLAN! IT WAS ALL ABOUT A PLAN!

My continuous desire to dive into outrageous situations was surely my rebellion against the perfect suburban dream from which I came. My parents had gone to remarkable lengths to provide unshakeable security at home. Like so many naïve youths, I had wished to cast aside such domestic bliss in favor of adventure. Why go to elementary school to study, when I should be on a spice caravan crossing the Sahara? I didn't want my mascot to be the Hiawatha Little Cougars; I wanted to run with jaguars in the jungles of Central America!

As an adult my extremes naturally shifted to other things, though they were oddly similar. After all, I had crossed a thousand miles of scorching desert in a car with no cash, a manic-depressive vegetarian, and a cat. As if that were merely to whet my appetite, a Transylvanian temptress lured me onto three continents within one month of meeting her. Boy, did I have some stories!

Yet throughout all my seemingly crazy behavior, I always had a plan. After several bitter disappointments with Carnival,

I finally realized on *Legend* how fragile my current plan was. The cure was about to kill the patient. But now, finally, I had not one option, but two!

Having options felt good, and gave my whole turmoil-filled life a meaning. So Plan A, as I began to call it, was to switch departments to the cruise staff with the hopes of someday achieving a cruise director job. This required a number of signatures before the main office could sign off on it, and would involve years of further effort. Though tough, it sounded fun, would pay off well and seemed doable.

Plan B, however, had me most intrigued. I had learned that nearly all major cruise lines worked with Sundance at Sea to supply the ships with art auctions. This was right up my alley. I had been an art dealer before and could actually capitalize on my college education while achieving my goals of life with Bianca *and* a profitable career. Yet there was a tremendous amount about this path I did not yet understand and had little ability to research. I had fought several times already in vain to witness an auction. Plan B was a long shot, but would exceed my expectations if I could make it happen.

The problem with both plans, of course, was my acute lack of free time. Though easier, Plan A did require meeting several high-level individuals. Because I still worked at least fourteen hours a day, this provided me precious little time to accommodate office hours. But with the support of the highest-ranking member of the ship, if I could just meet with the others I was sure to obtain their signatures.

Fueled by ambition and desperation, I stretched my work ethic's tolerance to the limit. I cut corners to shave five minutes off a shift so I could meet with people. During bathroom breaks I rushed to offices with my documentation. I even pretended to take up smoking in order to get a few minutes here and there. As every restaurateur knows, break requests were commonly denied because bosses imagined thirty minutes of rest, whereas a smoke break was considered a benign, quick puff.

Whenever I found myself too tired to pursue the signatures I needed, such as a meeting with the F&B manager or with the highly elusive art auctioneer, I would read my previous day's journal entry. Rather than complaining aloud, I always vented in my diary.

My latest entry, for example, with 231 words, contained no less than 43 profanities. That day I had snapped and began throwing things at work, smashing a cream-filled pitcher in a spectacular display of childish anger that resulted in a twenty-minute clean up. I had railed against everything I could think of, and it was sobering to read how demoralized I was. Raw thoughts were spit onto the page with tremendous aggression.

"I am so f**king tired of fighting every f**king second to keep a positive attitude. I am so f**king tired of being f**king tired of being f**king tired of this shit! When was the last time things really worked out? It never f**king does, or if it does it is overwhelmingly overshadowed by bullshit of all kinds."

Such excerpts were typical of my *Legend* journal entries. As December crawled by painfully, I was more determined than ever to make Plan A or Plan B happen. And, of course, to hide my diary from my mother at all costs.

A Christmas Crew Talent Show was scheduled for a few days before Christmas. It started after midnight, and over a glass of Amarula on ice, Ramona and I debated seeing it. This South African drink was similar to Bailey's Irish Liquor, though it was a bit sweeter and funkier. Xenia always maintained a bottle of it for emergencies, and on this night Ramona found herself in need of the medication.

"I don't feel like any fun," Ramona lamented. "I want to stay here with pictures of my baby and get drunk."

"Sounds like a plan to me," I agreed tiredly.

"Oh, I hear they are putting time cards on the ships."

"I'll believe that when I see it."

"I hear they are already on *Glory*. You should ask Bianca."

"But that will give proof to the world that they work us like slaves. I just don't believe it."

"Maybe they will keep the hours down this way."

"Hmmph!"

Suddenly the door burst open and Xenia swept into the room. She leapt with nervous energy, bumping into us both and rebounding like a rubber ball.

"Oh my God oh my God oh my God," she babbled excitedly. "I've got to get a robe. A robe! Where is my robe?"

"What robe?" Ramona asked.

"For the show tonight. I'm playing Madonna."

Ramona and I shared a glance and rolled our eyes. The phone rang, and Xenia literally jumped with a shriek. I covered my ears and observed silently. I was teetering toward annoyance with her, but I resolved to stay cool. After all, I had not seen Xenia outside of work in quite some time because she no longer spent nights in her cabin.

"Answer it, Ramona! Answer it!" Without ceremony she grabbed the receiver and shoved it up to Ramona's ear. "It's Graeme, I just know it!"

"H-hello?" stammered Ramona. "You want Xenia? Give me a minute to see if she's here."

"The room is five feet by five feet," I said sarcastically. "And you need a minute to see if she's here?"

"Tell him I'm in the shower," Xenia blurted. "No, wait! I'm not in. No, I'm practicing for the show tonight!"

Her voice was loud enough that Graeme didn't need to hear her through the receiver; he could probably just put an ear to his cabin door and listen to the words reverberate down the hall.

"Xenia," I said with irritation, "will you chill out?"

"He knows I haven't been spending nights with only him. Oh my God...Brian! Be quiet. He'll hear you! Graeme is going to hear Brian here! Oh, what do I do?"

Feeding off Xenia's affected fright, Ramona panicked and hung up the phone. Her wide eyes met Xenia's, they shared a girlish scream, and the blonde bolted from the room. I leaned back in Xenia's bunk and silently sipped my drink, worried for some reason that everyone I knew and respected would somehow see me in this odd situation.

The phone rang again, but Ramona did not answer. Instead she suddenly began crying. I stared at her for a moment, wondering if I had missed some sort of segue to her sudden emotional outburst.

"I miss my daughter so much," Ramona sobbed into her glass. "She's only five. Christmas is more special with children."

"Ah," I said. "I see. Of course you miss her. She misses you, too. But think of the opportunities she will have because you are here."

"You think that makes it better? Typical man. Opportunities and money in twenty years? You have no heart, you beast."

"Wow. O.K."

"You should see Christmas in Transylvania," she continued. "It's always white and the mountains are deep with snow, the windows are always frosted and Saint Nicolae is there. Even in the city we somehow roast a whole pig. He's always so beautiful! You don't miss your family or Christmas or any of that, do you, Brian?"

I briefly pondered my situation. Instead of Christmas in Transylvania with Bianca, I was spending it in a criminally tiny cabin with two madwomen, overworked, underpaid, exhausted, unhealthy, belittled, and now in fear of an ambush by a South African I had never met in retaliation for a crime I did not commit.

"I don't know whether to laugh or cry," I replied, trying to lighten the moment.

"Monster," she repeated with surprising venom.

I swallowed my drink, and fought my sudden urge to snap at Ramona.

"Oh, I have a heart, Ramona. Like yours, it's in Transylvania right now. We are both here for our loved ones."

"No. I wonder if you have any feelings. You haven't complained once. You are such a Grinch. Heartless monster!"

"Don't you know?" I finally chided her. "Sometimes it's easier to be a monster."

Ramona and I ultimately decided to watch at least the restaurant's contribution to the talent show. Somehow we found ourselves in the very front row of the huge main lounge. Though able to seat many hundreds, the balcony was empty and the main floor was half-filled with about sixty different nationalities. All drunk, of course.

A long line of waiters sat with us, starting with our Romanian friend, George. While we waited for the skit, George drank heavily from a six-pack of beer he had brought along. He also carried a mysterious towel-wrapped bundle in his lap. Already drunk, he steadfastly and loudly refused to tell us what it was.

"What Madonna song is our Material Girl going to sing?" I asked Ramona. "I hope it isn't 'Like a Virgin.' I don't think I could handle the irony."

"*Like a Prayer*," she answered. "She worked out something with four temptations, like wealth, pride, power, or whatever."

"This ought to be interesting."

Now nearly 2:30 in the morning, we impatiently waited for a Filipino housekeeper to finish his crooning of a Jon Secada ballad. Finally the cruise director announced that the next act was from Truffles. The front row emptied as our colleagues filed onto the stage, leaving only myself, Ramona, and drunken George. What followed was the most pathetic and most hilarious thing I had witnessed on *Legend*.

The lights remained low, and a spotlight faded in to reveal Xenia on her knees in prayer. She wore a blue hooded robe and carried a candle. The opening of the song was respectful and solemn, with all attention on the solitary figure in candlelight. Xenia obviously relished being the center of attention. When the tempo picked up, her melodrama began.

From the shadows came the First Temptation. Leaping into the light was a creepy man wielding a spear capped with feathers. Wearing a white toga that contrasted sharply against his dark brown skin, he rushed around the stage poking at Xenia, who swooned dramatically in response to the danger.

I recognized the First Temptation as Nestor from Guatemala. Not only did his features freakily resemble those of a bat, with ears nearly pointed by some cruel trick of nature, but he was obsessed with the creatures. He had numerous bat tattoos across his body, and he drew them compulsively on his ordering pad and silverware rack. Bat-like Nestor was truly a personification of jungle ferocity.

As Xenia fended off the danger, things began to go awry as the Second Temptation arrived in the form of wealth. A Jamaican waiter, Dominic, danced toward her brandishing a bag of gold. He dangled the gold before her with exceptional grace and worked his hips in a fluid, tribal rhythm. Ramona whispered in awe of his performance and I concurred. Yet apparently Xenia was not so happy he was on stage. While still trying to avoid the sharp spear of Nestor, she lost ground in fending off Dominic, whom she feared was truly trying to club her with the bag.

To tip the scales into chaos came Duman. The huge Turk lumbered onto the stage in an obviously drunken stupor. His toga revealed a massive frame, and all could see just how hairy and apelike he was. He gave Best a run for his money! Because he was so intoxicated, his movements were gross and inarticulate, not unlike an ape.

For some inexplicable reason Duman carried upon his shoulders the wine cellar steward. Few waiters knew his actual name, but we universally called him Spider Monkey. He weighed barely over one hundred pounds, chattered just like the small simian, and with his Indonesian features and brown skin, he even looked like one. There was little doubt that huge, inebriated Duman had no idea that Monkey was riding his shoulders. Together they plodded into the circle, adding confusion to an already spiraling mess.

The main composition of the song ended, but apparently they had obtained an extended remix of it. As the music carried on and on, no one knew what to do and they all began prancing around the stage. Nestor hopped up and down to his own dance, spearing people with wild abandon, while Dominic continued to rhythmically club Xenia. Suddenly Monkey lost his balance and clung to Duman's head for life. He dug his claws into Duman's face and his sharp knees and elbows flailed about, jabbing everybody. Bellowing in pain, Duman pounded about the stage, blindly adding to the mayhem. Screaming at the top of her lungs, Xenia pinged between all the dangers as if in a pinball machine.

Finally Monkey's two legs lifted in perfect unison on either side of Duman's head, and in slow motion the small man plummeted backwards six feet to the floor with a resounding *WHAP!*

George suddenly sprang to his feet, as if the sickening clap were an alarm clock. He boomed drunkenly, "I'm supposed to be on stage! I'm the Fourth Temptation!"

He cast aside the towel that wrapped his mysterious package, revealing a purple teddy bear. To the utter confusion of the crowd, he flourished it before him dramatically before leaping onto the stage. Unfortunately his foot hooked on the edge and he slammed into the floor with a painful THWACK! Moaning pitifully, he clawed toward Xenia like the living dead, brandishing the teddy bear as some sort of talisman.

Mercifully the curtain began to close, hiding the two pained, writhing bodies on the floor, though not before Xenia leapt into the audience with a very real shriek. As the curtain slammed shut, I barely caught a glimpse of Duman snapping Nestor's spear in two over his knee after having been stabbed one too many times.

The cross-cultural chaos was a fable for the ages: a South African princess, a Guatemalan bat, a Jamaican thug, a Turkish ape, and an Indonesian spider-monkey. I looked to Ramona, who had laughed herself into tears. With my own sides aching from the laughter, I resolved to always seek the joy in life. It was always there, I realized, in some form or other. Even at this unCatly hour in the morning, exhausted and bitter, joy was right there in front of me. I just had to put on the right glasses.

New Year's Eve happened to be on debarkation night. With our home port in Barbados, it promised to be a wild, tropical party night indeed! The duties were far from usual during the day, with many waiters assigned to makeshift kiosks set up for champagne sales. Free champagne would be available to the guests, but the kiosks offered higher quality bubbly. There were tremendous rewards for the waiter selling the most.

I was assigned a kiosk back behind the Jacuzzi that was under construction. For five hours I stood in the hot, Caribbean sun, accompanied only by a work crew of three, their exceptionally loud power tools, and a cloud of clinging dust. Needless to say, my sales were low. I did not mind working at midnight, however. Everyone I knew was working and I had spent years in dining rooms celebrating the countdown.

As midnight neared, *Legend* sailed through serene, tropical waters. The lights from Barbados were not far, offering a truly exotic view of tiny palms thrashing along moonlit beaches. Everyone, and I mean everyone, attended the open deck party. Any crew member even remotely related to service was assigned to Lido deck, and certainly every guest attended the party. Huge screens were erected on either side of the pool to show music videos, and a zillion tables were set up for appetizers and champagne.

Like several dozen other waiters, I was assigned to wander

the Lido and offer the free champagne. Because nearly two thousand guests were packed in there, it was truly insane. In all my years, I had never seen such a sight. The guests, fresh and excited at having just arrived that afternoon, were in a party mood unlike any I had seen in landlubbers. The tropical heat made them all crazy, and thirsty, and champagne flowed like the rain in Panama. Some forty minutes before midnight it was apparent that no one would be able to penetrate the crowds with a tray, so I was assigned to hauling cases of champagne to the various bars.

Though I had not had a drop of alcohol, by midnight I was high as a kite. The energy was amazing, as the sweaty masses shivered and gyrated maniacally to the omnipresent European-style dance music. The pool was filled to the brim with shaking bodies, and the screaming, oh the screaming. I was nearly deaf by midnight.

When the magic moment happened, the din took on a fever pitch and the entire ship seemed to rock. Hundreds of bottles of champagne popped by guests and geysers of golden liquid showered all. Dozens of people around me howled that their $100 champagne was lost instantly in the flood, but it was worth every penny.

Only after midnight did I finally catch a breather. I escaped into a pantry for a poolside bar. To my surprise, inside were several waiters of my acquaintance, including Ramona.

Despite the absolute chaos of the party outside, the sailors *still* partied harder. Inside the pantry, empty champagne bottles overflowed from two fifty-five gallon garbage cans to literally pile all the way up from the floor. Stacks of boxes rose from the sticky tiles all the way to the ceiling. With each shift of *Legend* a tower wavered and threatened to collapse onto everyone.

Hardly a square inch of floor was available. Two Jamaican waiters had already passed out and the other waiters had pushed their unconscious bodies unceremoniously out of the way. Sitting cross-legged beside them was a Slovakian couple I knew, Lorenzo and Zusanna. The pantry stank of champagne and every surface dribbled with it: walls, racks, cases, sinks, and ceiling.

"Don't bother with a dry place," Ramona said to me from behind a stack of champagne.

"Oh, hey Ramona! What the hell happened in here?"

"*Miez de noapte*," she answered in Romanian, meaning "midnight."

"We shook the champagne!" a blasted Indian waiter named Sanjay cried from behind yet another pile of empty champagne cases. His head was wrapped in the ribbons that bound the bottles shut. As if we could not already tell, he began shouting, "I'm drunk! I'm drunk!"

Then I noticed a tiny Indonesian curled up in the bottom of a huge, industrial-size sink. Sitting in the other sink beside him was Martina. She drifted drowsily into and out of a stupor.

Ramona scooted over to allow me to join her on a pile of smashed cardboard cases. I gratefully rested my aching legs, having been on them non-stop since 6 A.M., but not before grabbing two bottles of bubbly. Everyone was already completely inebriated in the pantry, so I decided to follow suit. Drinking straight from the bottle, I rested in the relative quiet of the cramped pantry, drinking myself silly.

Various waiters we knew burst through the door in a drunken frenzy, snatched up a few bottles, screamed a few joyous obscenities, and departed. Nearly forty-five minutes passed, and I surprisingly finished off two whole bottles of the cheap champagne myself. Ramona began drifting off to sleep, and Lorenzo had long since passed out on top of Zusanna. We had all enjoyed watching the couple having wild, sloppy sex at our feet. Even as they labored on the sticky floor, we bemoaned that they were too drunk to disrobe because they were·both so gorgeous.

I finally staggered back into the hot, humid night with Ramona and Martina. Immediately a bar manager spotted us and pounced, begging us to help clean up various areas. Ramona slipped away into the chaos of the crowd, but Martina and I gave the obviously overwhelmed and panicking man a hand.

The next thing I remember was being in the crew bar with Martina.

"How about a Sex?" she screamed into my ear over the din of the music. The crew bar was as packed as the Lido deck, but instead of being humid with open, tropical air it was hot and dense with trapped smoke. My uniform shirt was untucked, unbuttoned, and completely open. To my pleasant surprise, so was Martina's.

"Oh, hell yes!" I replied earnestly.

"No, idiot, a Sex on the Beach!"

"Isn't that a girly drink?"

"You'll see!"

We both downed two double Sexes before my attention was pulled away by Sasko. In our inebriation, conversations came and went with various people and no one noticed any incongruity. He shouted to me how badly he wanted to hook up with Martina, and wanted my help to do it. I replied that if he couldn't catch her tonight, when she was already half undressed and wholly drunk, he was hopeless.

Suddenly the swarm parted, and both of us stared in admiration through the distractions. Slithering seductively toward us was a slender, sexy Slavic goddess in a black dress. Sweat and champagne slid off her bare shoulders and into her cleavage, and her mascara ran to give her eyes an exotic, slutty look. A cigarette hung from her red lips with an alluring, dirty self-confidence.

"Oh, my God!" Sasko breathed, awe-struck. "Who is *that*?"

"I don't know," I replied loudly, equally stunned. "She looks familiar! She's not a waitress, is she? She looks Russian!"

"Ukraine," she corrected, sliding right up to me. We both stared as she blew out a long stream of smoke from those incredible lips.

"I love you!" Sasko screamed to her. "Brian's too tall for you! I am just right!"

Her response was a sly smile. She grabbed my drink and with one long, deep guzzle emptied the glass. She then took my hand and pulled me away from the bar.

As she led me through the thick horde of revelers, I barely heard Sasko shout, "What chance of Ukraine sandwich?"

Shouting woke me up. I reluctantly looked around, but immediately clamped my eyes shut against the brilliant light.

"Brian! Wake up!"

The yelling penetrated, and suddenly I perked up, knowing in my gut that I had overslept.

"Wha—?"

At first I thought I was lying in a hammock with someone, but I realized that we had been sleeping on a net that covered the empty Jacuzzi. Passed out on the open deck with me was some woman I did not recognize. She was very pretty, but absolutely filthy. She reeked of an entire crew bar's worth of smoke, as well as being sticky with dried champagne and who knew what else.

I struggled to lean up in the net. Holding me back, I realized, was the woman's hand in my pants.

"I finally found you!" the voice continued with exasperation.

Blearily I looked up and squinted against the bright Caribbean sun. My contacts were glued to my eyeballs, preventing me from focusing clearly. I blinked aggressively and was thankful the brightness hurt enough to make my eyes water. Slowly I recognized the wine cellar steward, Spider Monkey.

"Huh?"

"You were supposed to work hour ago!" Monkey screamed. "I look everywhere for you! Is seven, and guests come."

"Yeah, yeah," I answered ruefully. "I'm coming."

I couldn't recall having ever been late for work in my entire life, and certainly this was the first time someone came looking for me! Figures, I thought bitterly, Carnival couldn't just write you up for a missed shift, but they had to punish you first and *then* write you up.

Finally I was able to review myself. I had no idea where my uniform shirt or vest was, and my work pants were stiff from dried champagne and my shoes were splotched with golden stains. Like the mysterious beauty at my side, I reeked of filth and smoke and grime. Hardened sweat and champagne encrusted my chest hair, making my climb out of the net particularly annoying.

I had no idea how I had gotten here, floating above an empty Jacuzzi. Nor did I know who this woman was or why her hand was in my pants. Yet odd as this situation was, I had the strangest sense of déjà vu.

9 *Toast Master General*

T HE FIRST TIME I SEARCHED FOR THE ART AUCTION-eer's cabin to drop off my résumé, I had been very confused. I did not recognize the cabin number at all, nor even the numbering system. With a wry smile, Daniel had eventually informed me that Chester lived on Riviera deck in a guest cabin.

Chester, the art auctioneer on *Legend*, leaned outside his cabin door. Though nearly two o'clock in the afternoon, he was in his pajamas and had obviously been sleeping when I knocked.

"Sorry to keep you outside," he apologized, "but my honey is sleeping."

I resisted the urge for a voyeuristic peek at his honey in bed. His girlfriend assistant was a Slovakian goddess barely half his age. After finally catching a few minutes of an art auction, and after having studied art for years, I found myself only looking at her.

"I'm just glad for any of your time."

"So," he began, rubbing his bald head in thought. "I e-mailed your résumé to the fleet manager, and she liked it, too. Usually Sundance prefers inexperienced art dealers, but you've never done auctions so it shouldn't be a problem. They like to mold the new ones, you know?"

"Of course. I can be as stupid as they want. Indeed, I'm here, aren't I?"

He chuckled. "Yeah, what *are* you doing here, anyway?"

"Following my woman."

"Well, as an auctioneer she will follow you," he said. "Honestly, it's a great life. You live in a guest cabin, you work only a couple days a week if you're any good. It's lots of money. Don't go around bragging about that, by the way. You'll learn in this job that people come out of the woodwork trying to be an auctioneer because of the money, and none have a clue. I only met you because the hotel director personally asked me and assured me you were qualified. You look all right, understand ship life, and have art education. Yeah, I think you'll do all right."

"Thank you so much for your help. What's the next step, do you think? Is it appropriate for me to contact the fleet manager?"

"You know what? You need to meet her. You look good on paper, but you look better in person. My fleet manager, Amy, will actually be here in late February for an inventory. I'll arrange for you two to meet."

"Perfect!"

"Here's the deal, though. There is a conflict of interest. Sundance at Sea, as a contracted vendor for Carnival and simply out of courtesy, won't hire Carnival employees. You need to finish your contract naturally or they won't hire you. You cannot quit or be fired. When does your contract end?"

My hopes dropped. "Not for another six months."

"Well, after that, you can start. Make all the arrangements first, of course. It takes time, anyway. Meet Amy, charm her, and you'll be in."

"I'll knock her socks off," I promised to both Chester and myself.

My days on *Legend* finally began to change. Instead of just the heartless, impartial pounding of bad news, a hint of brightness appeared. My morale timidly peeked out from the darkness, recognizing a seed of control. Did I want to push harder on Plan A or Plan B? I could transfer soon and save my sanity with Plan A, or I could choose to endure six more months of hell in order to capture the superior Plan B. But could I seriously handle six more months?

As if to squash any hope, *Legend* was out to get me. No matter what happened, life forced me into fifteen hours at work, seven days a week. For example, I *finally* changed side jobs, meaning I no longer ended my long, painful days with hours of degrading escalator scrubbing. Yet, as if on cue, the Norovirus struck. Suddenly we had special cleaning day and night. My fingers were already cracked and split, so the excessive bleaching was simply par for the course.

As if this were not enough, the customer reviews came in. Ratings for guest satisfaction had plummeted to the low eighties. Carnival placed a premium on guest approval and insisted on ratings in the high nineties. Such a drop was cataclysmic, and the corporation scrambled for answers.

In my opinion the drop was indicative of the utter misery of the employees. Waiters were jumping out like rats from a sinking ship. One friend of mine requested a transfer to *Inspiration*, and in the last week two more had requested *Fascination*, while yet another left for *Paradise*. Just that morning I had witnessed Xenia crying from the stress, while Ramona had cried herself to sleep for a month. Everyone was overworked and underappreciated.

The corporate solution, of course, was *more* work.

Because the guests were not having enough fun, waiters were forced into joke and trick training. Though everyone was simply dying for a little rest, we were pressed into hour-long meetings to learn knock-knock jokes and how to fold paper napkins into little birds. Needless to say, no one was amused.

When management exhausted their bag of tricks, they began a two-week intensive training of the menus. They bullied and threatened us with a big test at the end. I offered to take the test on day one, knowing I would ace it, but they refused. I had to attend the monotonous, redundant training like everyone else. Of course they never tested us.

In a nutshell, fate worked overtime with *Legend* to pull in every resource possible to keep me working over one hundred hours a week. But it wasn't just the hours, it was the stress factor that really destroyed me and many other waiters.

A great example of our needless stress was during breakfast and lunch in Truffles. If our section was deemed likely to be empty, Ramona and I were sent to work on the Lido buffet. Because we were ordered to drop what we were doing and go, our station was abandoned, unprepared and ill-equipped. Without fail Truffles would subsequently fill and we would be ordered to abandon the Lido and run to Truffles. We always arrived to a station overflowing with impatient guests and we didn't even have the ability to get them a glass of water, let alone the juice or coffee they demanded. To exacerbate our disenchantment, the AMDs lashed out that anyone unprepared was a *mamagayo*. This was a daily occurrence.

One day Lutfi made my life easier. After a typically mind and body-blasting lunch, he pulled me aside with surprising news.

"Brian!" he said sharply. "You are not happy during breakfast or lunch."

"I hadn't noticed," I replied dryly.

"I know! I have a plan for you. Look, Carnival is horrible at allocating resources. It's the paisano system, and it's a mess. You do a favor to the Turk once, and you get easy life forever. Look at Best. He's working the wine cart, for God's sake. He's a goddamn gorilla and they have him trying to sell fine wine! Then there is you, with ten years of American fine-dining experience, and you are working like a burro bringing cheese-burgers. I know!"

"I couldn't agree more."

"Did you see what happened to Juicy?"

"Juci."

"Whatever. She is working in the office with the Turk because he loves the blondes. He did it to spite you."

"Me?"

"He likes taking the blondes from you. Everyone knows you shagged Juicy. Now he wants to. Don't worry, I'm sure he won't steal the fat Romanian from you."

"That's a relief."

"Next cruise I am putting you on wine cart. You will wan-der the dining room and talk to the guests, educate them about wine, get them to try some! It's hard enough to get Americans to try wine, but you know how! And during break-fast you will be toast master general."

"Lutfi, I love you."

"Please, none of your America-loves-gays stuff!"

"Well, then praise Allah, my friend. Better?"

"Good man! Now, instead of pancakes and cheeseburgers, you will use your talents. In the mornings no hard time. Make toast in peace. That way you are fresh for lunch and can joke with guests naturally."

"You mean no knock-knock jokes?"

"I know! I will get it past the Turk, don't you worry. Did I not say I was on your side?"

"*Noroc!*" I said, toasting with Ramona in her cabin that night. "To the most glorious of all positions!"

"Cheers," she agreed, downing a glass of Amarula on ice. "Toast master general!"

"So I have all the signatures I need now," I said with a relieved sigh. "The hotel director sent in the paperwork today. We should hear back from Carnival soon."

"It won't be the same without you," Ramona said. "You are the only American I can complain to about Americans."

"Chester also confirmed with his boss that she will be here soon. He set up an informal interview over coffee."

"Forget coffee, man. Screw her!"

"I beg your pardon?"

"Shag her! How else are you to get the job? That's the way to go. Forget Carnival, go with art stuff. Think of all that money. I don't care if she has ass like mine, shag her!"

"Well, my cabin is a mess and Best will scare her to death. How about using your cabin, then?"

"Sure, I'll spray Lysol for you and everything."

The phone rang, and Ramona gave me a smirk. "That's one of Xenia's suitors, no doubt."

She picked up the phone and immediately snapped into the receiver, "Xenia's not here!"

I could clearly hear the angry words on the other end. I recognized Graeme's voice. After a few seconds of listening to the shouts, Ramona hung up the phone with concern on her face.

"Brian, leave!"

"Why?"

"Xenia told Graeme that she was going to her new boyfriend's cabin. She came here first and Graeme followed her. He saw."

"Yeah, so? That was five minutes ago. She left."

"Well, he didn't see it. He went to next hall and called from a house phone."

"Why didn't he just knock on the door?"

"Because boys are dumb. He thinks Xenia is here, and he knows you're here, too. He's mad and wants to fight."

"What, fight me because I'm Xenia's latest toy?" I sighed. "I'm not, more's the pity. But you know what, that's fine. I am sick of running around avoiding that idiot. If he wants a piece of me, he's gonna get it. I could kick his ass and he knows it."

"I don't think he knows it. But can I watch?" Ramona gushed. "I love watching men fight. Take off your shirt first, will you? Pants, too?"

Suddenly I realized just how precarious my position was.

"Wait a minute! If he starts a fight, we will *both* be fired...even if I don't fight back!"

"Lucky you," she replied. "Anything to get away from here."

"But if I get fired, I can't become a cruise director *or* an art auctioneer!"

Without a further word I fled the cabin.

I would have done anything to be toast master general, *anything* to get away from serving the guests breakfast and lunch. Working with the public was extremely trying. Because people are people, they come into every situation with their own wants, needs, biases, dreams, chips on shoulders, or what-have-you. Guests angry at their spouse could easily take it out on their waiter, and worst of all were Americans working the system to get something free.

I was ecstatic to become toast master general, where I only had to deal with employees. *That* I could handle because I didn't care about their level of cruise satisfaction.

During breakfast each station had a breadbasket filled with white or wheat toast, some pastries, and maybe a bagel. My job was to work the massive toast machines and continuously brown the bread for the waiters. Most waiters barged into the pantry to stuff a few loaves of bread into their baskets only to abandon it all once they delivered a piece or two. Left unchecked, some fifty stations would have several loaves each of untouched bread every breakfast.

I understood such behavior. Running to the pantry for an extra piece of toast was a phenomenal waste of precious time, and guests were severely demanding for breakfast. Breakfast, more than any other meal, was a matter of habit and routine. Add to this their hangover, or general fatigue from too much activity, and waiters were in for a world of hurt because they took the brunt of the petty frustrations.

Because the toast master was not otherwise monitored, the cruise line could only gauge progress by the amount of bread used. Whether from guests overeating or from food waste, the toast master was judged solely by bread volume.

So like an anti-social penny-pinching accountant in a dark back room, I became a miser. When breakfast began to wane I dramatically curtailed the bread allowance. This forced impatient servers to wait as I prepared toast to order, or to instead search the pantries for untouched toast. Though I suffered a barrage of insults about my nationality, masculinity, and anything else they could think of, I smiled the whole time. Funny, although able to say anything I wanted to in response, I simply smiled instead.

But like everything else in life, there was a tradeoff between good and bad. The toast master was invariably the last man out of the dining room every day because the cleanup was significant. On my way out, I brought all unused toast to the chefs in order to make bread pudding. This amount was always scrutinized by the head chef, who was keen on keeping food costs down. I took great pride in my lean, efficient toastness. Nothing, *but nothing*, was going to take me off this most glorious of jobs.

Except, as it turned out, my best friend.

10　*The　Suicide*

AFTER NEARLY A MONTH OF SUCCESS AS TOAST master and working the wine cart, I had finally found my smile again. I was still working like a dog, of course, but my morale had stabilized. Even though Mr. D, as we called the diarrhea from Norovirus, was sticking around tenaciously, life on *Legend* became survivable.

I was proud of myself, actually. I had documented myself working over one hundred hours a week for ten solid weeks, yet had managed to push both Plan A and Plan B through. Further, I had even created a second edition of a book I had self-published before joining the ships. Over two thousand copies were scheduled to be printed any day. Not bad for a slave!

Hope springs eternal, and I felt like I could handle anything. I no longer judged my life on where I was, but on where I was going. Daniel had informed me that my transfer to the cruise staff had passed all but the very last hurdle in Miami. Even more exciting was my scheduled interview later in the week with Amy, the fleet manager from Sundance at Sea. Things were moving together perfectly, just slow.

"Brian," Lutfi said to me one day in late February. "I have bad news for you. Duman is taking you off the wine cart and the toast."

"Wh-what? Why? I sold over double the wine Best did!"

"I know! But the Turk broke up with Xenia."

"Aha! *He* was the mystery lover Graeme was searching for. But what does that have to do with me?"

"The Turk is mad at Xenia, but he won't punish her. So he blames you because you used to bang her."

"I *never*...whatever. Son of a Cat, does everything have to fall on me?"

"He only let you off the escalator side job because he took the blonde from you. With that victory he felt lenient. When Juicy moved to his side he let me put you on wine cart. But now you go back to the fat one. I am sorry, my friend."

O.K., so things weren't quite so perfect.

My mornings with Ramona were not very successful. She was falling apart at the seams, and it was not pleasant to watch. Having already witnessed one emotional breakdown on *Conquest*, I had no desire to be around another. For whatever reason, Ramona had a whopping eleven-month contract, which was enough to crush anyone.

Ramona began to resent my presence at breakfast because her method of handling stress was to enjoy screwing her partner. But because of our friendship she had to exercise self-restraint, which I knew she had in short supply.

"Ramona," I said one morning, "you only have three cruises left, you can make it."

"What would you know?" she snapped back. "I have a daughter at home who is missing me. You have nothing."

"Yes, you have a daughter who needs you to keep your job. You actually swore at Duman the other day. Did you even know you did that? You are starting to lose it, darlin'. Why don't you take a cruise off? You won't work, except to be on call. That will give you some time to chill out and finish your contract without getting fired."

"I want out of here now. Right now. I don't care if I get fired."

"If you get fired, you can't come back. This may suck, but it's still a ton of money in Romania. Enough to get your daughter into a better school, or buy her a computer or something."

"I don't care."

"You've got to fight, Ramona! Nothing worth anything in this life comes easy. If you just give up then you've been apart from your daughter for nothing. If you want something, you've got to keep at it until you get it. You had to fight to get here, didn't you? I know all about the agent in Romania and the process to join Carnival. It's not easy, but you fought for it and got here. It's been a hell of a long road, but you are almost at the end. Don't throw away a whole year in the last few weeks."

"I want to go home."

"Everyone wants that."

"I want you to shut up."

"Everyone wants that, too."

While my hectic mornings were rounded off by the struggle to shore up Ramona's crumbling resolve, my lunches were absolutely destructive. I was assigned a station with a Jamaican named Roy. He was a slender man with a shaved head and a permanent look of arrogant dismissal on his face.

On the very first day he waltzed in mere minutes before the guests. He had not known who his partner was nor had he cared, he merely assumed someone else would handle things. Because he did not care if lunch was a disaster for the guests, it remained entirely up to me to prepare everything. Every day he found new and surprising ways to infuriate me through his sloth, lies, and arrogance.

I complained, of course, but Lutfi could do nothing. Within six days, my whole month's worth of relative peace was but a dream. Because Bianca was out of contact for a few days to travel to Florida for her new assignment, I latched onto hope for my approaching interview with Amy. Unimaginably, that day of promise was actually the very worst day of my life.

During breakfast Ramona was surprisingly quiet. She had hardly said a word at all during our set-up hour. I, on the other hand, bubbled with enthusiasm and humor. I tried to lure her into conversation repeatedly, but she would have none of it. Finally I let her be, figuring that she obviously preferred solitude. Just before the guests arrived I tried to confirm our plan for the day.

"So, I will leave at 10:15 for my appointment, as we agreed, right? I'll be back in only twenty minutes and take care of everything."

She avoided looking me in the eye.

"Ramona? We've been planning this all week. You know I need your help this morning. I'll make it up to you."

Her only response was to purse her lips tighter.

"Ramona, what's wrong?"

But she said nothing. I began to get a bad feeling, but the guests swamped us and we were too busy to even think. We ran around like chickens with our heads cut off for nearly an hour. Everything came to a screeching halt when Ramona suddenly began yelling at me in front of our guests.

"You did it again! You piss me off every morning!" she shrieked. Standing with two coffee pots, I stared at her dumbfounded that she would shout while among our guests.

"What do you mean?"

"You *basura*! You always piss me off! You are always late, and you always serve those two *bamboclats* outside our station!"

She pointed to the couple right beside us, who stared up with big eyes.

"Always late? I was late once, and that was two months ago! And that couple only wanted a refill of coffee. I had two full pots in my hand, so why wouldn't I?"

"Because they aren't in our station, idiot!"

"They are *guests*, Ramona. It only took ten seconds!"

She dropped the subject, but sulked in overt silence. Behavior like this, of course, was why Ramona did the galley run. She enjoyed the Pancake Darwinism because it gave her a chance to yell and scream at people with abandon. I was better with the guests and the logical face to put forward. So she stormed off to the galley, while I tried to smooth over the guests.

But she took an unusually long time to bring the food. Despite my best efforts, the guests grew restless. So did I. She had been gone over thirty minutes and there were only so many times I could offer pastries and coffee to tide people over. Further, any delay on this, of all breakfasts, was most alarming. Finally I ran to the galley, figuring she needed help bringing back the entrees.

Ramona was not in the galley. I stared at the line of squabbling waiters in shock, barely hearing them as the horrible realization buzzed in my head. She had not left for the kitchen, I realized. She had simply left.

"The bitch abandoned me!" I screamed to no one and everyone.

The remainder of the breakfast was a blur of anger and frustration. I had to retake the orders because Ramona had walked off with it, and none of my lame excuses for her behavior and disappearance mattered to anyone. I was universally harassed for my unacceptable level of service. For whatever reason, every guest latched onto Ramona's crazy comment that I was always late and chastised me for driving her away and leaving them in the lurch. My anger smoldered hotter with each ignorant jab from the guests. I asked Lutfi for assistance, but he had none to offer. Not a single neighbor offered to help because I was surrounded by a bunch of lazy Jamaican friends of Roy.

I fought very hard to get the station into a place where I could abandon it for a few minutes in order to at least meet Amy and cancel our meeting, but fate would not have it. Half the guests were still sitting and bitching when 10:15 rolled around. It was maddening that the fleet manager was a mere four decks away, but I had no way of communicating that I was going to miss our meeting. I tried to send a friend as a messenger, but to no avail.

The very second the last guest departed my station, I fled Truffles and raced to call Chester. He was not in his cabin, nor in his art locker. I had no way of tracking them through the huge ship, so I descended to the gangway and asked security if Amy were still onboard. She was not.

Completely shattered with disappointment and anger, I cleaned up my station mechanically. I seriously considered seeking out Ramona and beating her senseless. I could handle our bickering because we were all human and under stress, but this was different. This was not a poor work ethic or sloth on her part, nor ignorance of the importance of my meeting. This had been a deliberate action designed to sabotage another's success.

I had to accept some responsibility for socializing with a person I knew to be of such low caliber. I knew she was cracking, but what could I do? Abandon her? I never dreamed she would do this! I had never even *heard* of anyone walking away from a full station. No matter which way I looked at it, I could not excuse her for such a blatant act of selfishness. I was a very forgiving man, but I realized at that moment that I would never forgive her.

I needed to calm down, and I had only ten minutes left before starting lunch and meeting up with Roy again. I had to get out of Truffles, even if for just a few minutes. I figured that if Bianca were not there to offer solace, at least her words were.

I ran to the internet café and logged in. I planned on rereading Bianca's last e-mail, sent just before leaving Transylvania, but to my surprise there was an e-mail from my mother.

Happily I clicked on the message, figuring it would be filled with soothing, Grandma-stories about my nieces. While it was about family, the message most definitely did not cheer me up.

There had been a suicide in my family.

I was in a complete daze as I returned to Truffles. I stumbled past the line of waiters checking in like a zombie, and finally sat at a table. Waiters rushed around everywhere, but to me everything seemed to move in slow motion.

I simply couldn't believe that my cousin had committed suicide. Why? Though I tried, I could not picture his face. Instead all I saw was my uncle. I knew full well how much my uncle loved his son, and how he used to drive endless hours to spend every minute of time allowed by the split custody. My uncle was a joyful man, and it was easy to imagine his excitement when arriving at their Texas lake house to meet with his son. Oh, the anguish he must have suffered when not seeing his boy, but a note and a missing rifle. I nearly choked when I read that he had finally found my cousin on the other side of the lake. How long had he searched the woods for his only son, how much pain did he endure?

I really did not know my cousin well at all, and had not seen him in many years. We both grew up a thousand miles apart, and once reaching adulthood life had taken us even farther apart. When he had gotten out of the military, I had left for the West Coast.

Had he gone to college? Had he ever fallen in love? There was so much to do in this world, and so little time...how could he cut it short at only twenty-four?

What could possibly have been so bad that he would give up? How could he be a soldier and not a fighter? Of course life was bad, but you had to just get through that to the good stuff, damn it! I hated my life and was as low as I could have ever imagined. I worked like a slave and every goal I had set for myself a year ago had failed. My health was shattered and my heart ached with separation from my loved ones...but it never even occurred to me to end it.

My smoldering anger flared brighter. I was furious at my

cousin for this act. I didn't care what life had dealt him, there was simply no excuse in my mind for suicide. How could he have put his father through all that pain? Why couldn't he fight for his father's sake as much as his father had fought for him? What was it about this world that people hurt their loved ones so easily?

I looked at the clock and realized over half of my set-up time had elapsed. Whether I liked it or not, I had another mind-numbing lunch to plod through. Roy, of course, had not yet checked in. I rose to my feet, still burning with anger at Ramona, at my cousin, at life in general. I marched over to Lutfi and demanded forcefully a new lunch partner.

"Bah," Lutfi scoffed. "You just miss the cheeky cheeky with the fat one."

"Knock it off, Lutfi," I snapped. "I will not work with that *basura* one more day. He's late every single day, half the time actually arriving *after* the goddamn guests."

As we spoke, Roy came sauntering in smugly. Like everyone else, he heard me shouting at Lutfi. Even though we had both watched his late arrival, the Jamaican absurdly protested that he was never tardy.

"Eh, *rasclat*! Why you give me hard time? You lie!"

I wheeled around and poked my finger at him and yelled, "You shut the hell up!"

"*Bamboclat*, you make drama with boss? I never late, mon! You always late! You the *basura*!"

We shouted at each other as we stormed through Truffles. There was no question that we were mere moments away from a fight. The balcony above filled with spectators and a circle formed around us.

"You bloodclot!" Roy screamed. "I could kick your ass right now!"

He leaned toward me furiously clenching his fists in anger.

I could not believe that he taunted me so. I was several inches taller than he, and easily thirty pounds stronger. Yet he raged on with obscenities that were begging for a violent response. I fought to remain calm, despite all the absurd circumstances and hardships I had endured for so long. Somehow I stopped myself from hitting him.

With seething calm, I gave him a final warning. "If you ever talk to me like that again, you son of a bitch, I swear to God I will destroy you."

With phenomenal self-discipline, I turned my back on him and walked away. I was almost shaking with emotion, be it rage, sorrow, or whatever. I didn't know or care. Something powerful was overwhelming me and I didn't want it to win.

Unfortunately for Roy, puffed up and posturing, he renewed yelling curses at me.

I spun around and pushed against his chest with all my strength. He launched over an eight-foot table. He rolled across it, flailing legs casting aside glasses and plates, only to drop off the far end in a cascade of falling silverware.

Cheers and jeers exploded throughout the dining room. Roy struggled to his feet and immediately rushed back to reengage with me, but I was ready. I grabbed a handful of his vest and brought my arm back to hit him in the face, when suddenly a huge man leapt into the fray.

"Stop it!" Petek shouted as he struggled to keep us apart. The huge Croatian was over seven feet tall, and he needed every inch of his leverage to keep me back.

"You want some, eh mon?" Roy shouted. "I give it!"

"Shut up!" Petek boomed. "Look at his face, man! For Christ's sake, he's gonna kill you!"

Roy paused in mid-sentence and looked me over. Though reluctant, he soon eased off. Petek pressed his retreat further, trying to put more distance between us as quickly as possible. I saw nothing but red and wanted desperately to chase after the Jamaican and beat him to a pulp. My anger flared so red-hot that I felt invincible. Roy limped away panting and shaking his head, and Petek tried to restrain me with both his hands on my shoulders. Finally he looked down at me and said, "Jesus, he was going to run right into it. What an idiot."

Still viewing through a haze, I observed the waiter whose round table we had destroyed. The waiter, also Jamaican, quivered wide-eyed and terrified. He was scared of me, I realized. I sobered up after that. What had happened to me?

Sensing my change, Petek asked, "You cool?"

"Yeah," I answered slowly. "Thanks."

The excitement over, Lutfi reminded everyone forcefully that we were opening soon. Waiters wandered back to their stations, and I shared a long look with Lutfi. I had completely lost my head and could have been fired on the spot. But Lutfi merely smiled his cheesy grin and walked away.

THE NEXT CRUISE SAW RADICAL CHANGES IN TRUFFLES. The rearrangement of stations and head waiters was no doubt prompted by the dramatic events swirling around the troublesome, and now quarrelsome, American waiter. While I didn't believe my presence was the cause of all the drama, management clearly did. Most likely they were right.

Roy was demoted to team waiter and assigned to work the Lido buffets, as was Ramona. The day after our incident she had insulted Lutfi in hopes of getting fired and, thusly, sent home. Lutfi instead demoted her until the end of her contract and kindly enabled her to return as a head waitress. He was far more understanding than any other manager I had yet met, which perhaps explained his difficulties in advancing.

Xenia no longer worked in Truffles, nor did Graeme. I feared some drama had occurred between them as it had on *Inspiration*, where security had been needed. In fact, Xenia was no longer allowed to work because she was pregnant and Carnival instead sent her home. As if her leaving in a few days were not fast enough, the father booted her out and forced her to sleep in her own cabin. I had warned her against sleeping with Duman, but she thought it would propel her career forward with Carnival. It didn't.

And Graeme? Another girlfriend of his had broken his nose with a hairdryer.

So much happened so fast on the ships that little time was available for reflection. After the dramatic events of the last cruise, things moved even faster. Miraculously, Amy from Sundance had not been able to visit *Legend* on that fateful day. I was able to meet with her two days later and our informal interview had gone marvelously. She offered me the job as clearly as she could, asking me four times to call her the minute my contract with Carnival ended. From there she would get me into the very next training class with Sundance.

In fact, my Plan A results came to fruition at the very same time as those of Plan B. Word came from Miami that my request had cleared and I could transfer whenever I wanted. This left me with a debate. Should I transfer to the cruise staff now, in order to keep my sanity for the next six months? When my contract was over I could then join Sundance. That would keep me rolling forward on both plans and get me out of the hell I was living. But did I really want to work almost as hard for the cruise staff for only a grand a month, all while knowing I was leaving for Sundance anyway?

I was heavily distracted those next few days, trying to decide the course my life would take. I was happy because I had found a way to retain control, and had merely to decide what I wanted. My assistant Luis proved an excellent sounding board for my thoughts.

"You are so lucky," he said to me one night. "Everything just falls into place for you Americans. Last cruise you were just a waiter, but now you are going to be an art auctioneer. Lucky bastard."

"Luck," I replied, dumbstruck. "You think it was merely luck?"

"Well, yeah! I mean, you just *happen* to have the hotel director in your section, you just *happen* to have Chester notice you, and you just *happen* to meet with his boss lady. Everything just fell into place with ease and grace!"

"Ease and grace, my ass!"

The miracle happened during lunch set up. I was upstairs in Truffles gathering menus from a pantry when Ian made an announcement that changed my life.

"This is for all head waiters," he said simply into the microphone. "Anyone who wants to shorten their contract and sign off immediately can do so. That means leaving in two days."

I stood in the pantry, frozen in shock. Did he really just say what I thought he said?

"I'll only take the first four," Ian continued.

Vaulting into action, I dropped the menus and ran to the mezzanine so fast that my momentum nearly threw me over it. From on high I shook my fist into the air like a dictator to my people of Truffles. My voice boomed to the far corners without any need of a microphone.

"ANY BASTARD IN LINE BEFORE ME WILL BE BEATEN TO DEATH AND THROWN OVERBOARD, SO HELP ME CAT!"

I sprinted across the balcony and leapt down the escalator four steps at a time. I rushed through the dining room with so much speed that chairs fell into a vacuum behind me. I blasted through clusters of waiters and scattered them like fallen leaves. Waiters saw me coming and clambered over each other to get out of my way.

Ian sat relaxed, casually reviewing his paperwork as I towered over him, panting. He finally looked up and said cheekily, "Oh, Brian. Indeed, I thought you might be interested."

I signed my name in big, bold letters. I was so excited my hands shook and my signature was hardly even legible! Two days later I sat waiting to sign off *Legend*, hugging my luggage and sitting beside Graeme and his bandaged nose.

I watched the water gush across the windshield of my rental car. I was about an hour north of Fort Lauderdale on Interstate 95. Rain pummeled the coast so hard that traffic literally idled on the highway. The last time I had been on this road we had also been idle from traffic enroute to watch the space shuttle launch. Exactly thirteen and a half months ago I had first met Ravi and Gabriella right here on this highway. It felt like a lifetime ago.

The windows steamed and I opened them, happy to breathe in unconditioned air. The last two days had been a stunning blur of activity, and it did not feel at all like I had finally left *Legend* behind. Unlike the previous two sign-offs on *Fantasy* and *Conquest*, I had not celebrated my departure from *Legend*. I did not have the time or the inclination. Most crew did not sleep a wink the night of their sign-off, and my night had been par for the course. After leaving work at nearly midnight, I had to check in my luggage so security could search it and prepare it for customs clearance.

My time was spent online desperately trying to communicate with Bianca. The newest ship, *Glory*, was scheduled to dock that very night in Florida! I had a chance to see her! But it was unclear if Bianca could receive my news because *Glory's* satellite situation was still unknown. It was highly unlikely that on first arrival to America she would have had a lunch free to find an internet café. There was a very real chance she would not know I was coming.

But how could I *not* gamble to see her? Maybe, just maybe, I could see her for a few hours after she worked dinner.

So I frantically arranged for a flight home, rented a car, downloaded maps for the 350-mile drive, and communicated to my loved ones in the wee hours of the night. I left an e-mail for Bianca saying that, Cat willing, I would be waiting for her outside *Glory* after dinner that night.

I said a hectic goodbye to a few acquaintances, gave Juci a hug, shook Lutfi's hand, and gave Ramona a curt nod. There were few enough people I wanted to see, for I never really made a connection with anyone on *Legend*. Indeed, I had nearly lost connection with myself. To think that I had actually gotten into a fight…! Before I knew it the sun was up and immigration was calling. Of course, Carnival expected me to return to Truffles and work until lunchtime, but immigration was so disorganized that it wasted several hours. By the time it was done, breakfast was mostly over.

The rain lessened enough to allow traffic to attain the impressive speed of thirty miles per hour. I pushed north, ever crawling toward Bianca. If I had followed her from North America to Europe to Africa within a month of meeting her, how could a lousy seven-hour drive deter me?

Eventually the hours passed and the sun disappeared. The rain continued and the temperature dropped. The cold was acute, being just days away from March. The cruise terminal of Jaxport was at that time only temporary. I passed miles and miles of wet, dense forest and crossed numerous bridges, seeking signs. I was in the middle of nowhere, without a single business or even building in sight to query.

I finally pulled over and reviewed the maps in depth. A number of the streets I had passed were not labeled, and I tried to imagine the layout from the air, connecting the bridges and rivers into a mental map. As 10 P.M. rolled around, I began to worry that I was lost and would miss my only chance to see Bianca. But then I saw a small guard post with a man inside.

I parked beside the tiny booth and satisfied myself that it was indeed a checkpoint for port security. I ran through the icy, slashing rain and knocked on the door. The booth was almost entirely windows, but the man inside glanced around as if he did not see me. He was an extremely heavy-set African American with a very uninterested look on his face. Obviously loath to leave his coffee and magazine, he took his sweet time crossing the four feet to the door, outside of which I hopped about shivering in a t-shirt.

"Is this where *Carnival Glory* is docked?" I asked the guard through the door. Without answering, he slowly shuffled through some paperwork. After several long, painful moments while the rain rapped against the windows, he asked, "You ain't got no coat?"

"I just signed off *Carnival Legend*," I answered through chattering teeth. "We've been in the Caribbean for months. *Glory's* here, yeah?"

He nodded.

"Thank Cat!" I cried. "And thank you, sir! Have a wonderful night!"

He nodded again mutely as I raced out to the car. I thrust it into drive with tremendous excitement and relief. The road turned a corner and, to my surprise, was immediately blocked by security. I slammed on the brakes and stared at the arm barring my way for a moment, then rushed back through the chilly drizzle to the checkpoint.

Inside the guard slowly sipped his coffee and read his issue of *Guns & Ammo*. I figured bitterly that he was probably trying to qualify for a job with the Department of Homeland Security. After a full year of going in and out of America, I knew that reading *Guns & Ammo* probably overqualified him for the job. I knocked on the window several times before he looked up with a dull, surprised look.

"Oh, yeah," he said languidly. "You can't go in there."

"Why not?" I asked irritably.

"You ain't got no business there."

"I'm going to *Glory*," I replied. "I'm a head waiter for Carnival."

"ID?"

My jaw dropped when I realized I had turned it in that very morning.

"I turned it in this morning when I signed off *Legend*.

Look," I added, "just let me talk to the security chief. Or the purser. There are many options."

"No," he said. "We ain't got no phone."

"Well, a walkie-talkie or radio?"

"Nope."

"You are a checkpoint that cannot communicate with the port? I don't even see it, it's so far away. What do you mean?"

"It's all new," he explained. "Ain't nothin' here yet. Wait a minute."

He left me as a taxi pulled up. He waved the driver through with nary a glance and without a single word. When he returned to his post, he seemed surprised I was still there.

"You let him through!" I cried. "Why not me?"

"He's a taxi."

"Look, I'm here to pick up my girlfriend. She works in the dining room."

"So?"

"What, you think I'm a terrorist or something? I can tell you her cabin number, her ID number, all of it. Terrorists try to get *in* to the country, I would think, not out. I'm from Iowa, for cryin' out loud."

"Don't sound like no Midwest accent to me."

More headlights cut through the dark, revealing another taxi approaching. This time I followed the guard as he glanced over the driver and, just as he was about to pull away, I asked the driver to relay a message for me.

"Please, do me a favor and tell ship security this: 'tell any waitresses they see that the American is outside'. That's it."

"Yes," the Indian driver replied, "No problem."

I was not particularly reassured, but could not do anything else but watch him drive off into the night.

Forty minutes passed, and the hour crept toward midnight. My tension rose alarmingly. I simply could not believe that there was no communication between the guard post and the ship! They had no phone, no radio, no walkie-talkie, no internet, nor even visual contact for flashing lights or freakin' smoke signals. *This* was what the Department of Homeland Security bragged about to reassure scared Americans? Ignorance sure is bliss!

So I shivered in the cold, waiting, wondering if Bianca had gotten my e-mail.

Several taxis departed the port, and I scanned the drivers for the Indian bearing my message to security. I saw him and tried to flag him down, but he had a passenger and ignored me. I was sure my message had not gotten through. No matter what avenue I suggested, the guard wouldn't let me into Jaxport. I offered to leave my car the half-mile away, including all my baggage. I offered to let him search me, I even offered to go to the ship in my underwear just to prove I had no bombs, but it was to no avail.

I couldn't bear to stay in the car because I was required to park it behind a copse of trees and out of view of the road. So I paced along the guard arm, staring down the long, empty road flanked on both sides by dense, dripping forest. Rain splattered chaotically on the asphalt stretching ramrod straight into the distance. Street lamps glowed in the chill night at regular intervals, shrinking as they numbered farther and farther away from me.

Midnight came and went, and I finally leaned against the arm in defeat. I knew it had been a long shot, but I had done some extreme things to be with Bianca. Now, in the end, I finally learned the true answer to the question that had plagued me for a whole year at sea. I was *not* crazy or eccentric or anything else noteworthy.

I was just stupid.

Then, far in the distance, came a flutter of movement. Several hundred yards away I observed someone walking on the empty road. I squinted, desperate for details. The figure passed into each globe of light, only to drop into darkness again. After several painstaking minutes I finally recognized in the backlight a waitress in uniform, and my hopes soared.

Bianca ran the last hundred feet toward me through the icy

drizzle. We crashed into each other and embraced for a long, long time. I could hardly breathe, though from the crushing hug or the emotion I did not know. I didn't care. At that moment we lived a scene straight out of Hollywood, and I learned that magic really does happen. That moment was worth all thirteen months of ship life.

Every crazy, stupid minute of it.

Epilogue

I   F I HAD LEARNED ANYTHING FROM BEING ON THE SHIPS, it was that life was composed of moments...moments to cherish before the tide takes them away.

That night Bianca and I enjoyed ourselves immensely, all the while knowing we were merely proverbial ships passing in the night. We played wildly, like children at recess releasing oodles of pent-up energy while they could, desperate for every second. In the dark before dawn I watched Bianca trudge back down that same cold, wet road which had brought so much vexation and joy just five hours before.

I watched her disappear behind a tree that drooped more wearily than even I, and I mapped the future. *Carnival Glory* was leaving early for a day at sea before docking at Freeport. That left more than enough time for me to drive my rental car back to Fort Lauderdale and fly to the Bahamas for one more glorious half-night. Then I had to rush to training for my new position as art auctioneer.

Only rarely did life transition cleanly from one chapter to the next. When I signed off *Conquest* I had time for reflection. Such was not the case when I found myself spinning from

Pittsburgh, Pennsylvania to Royal Caribbean's *Majesty of the Seas* in the Bahamas, and back to the *Carnival Conquest* all within a month. My next three years as an art auctioneer at sea made my life as a waiter seem serene. My relationship with Bianca deepened as we explored the mystery of our happenstance meeting, falling in love, and finally spending time together. Deeper, too, was the gulf that materialized to separate us. The bizarre characters I met every day continued to plague me every which way...but that's ship life and a story yet to be told.

PART V

Appendices

Glossary of Ship Language

aft. Toward the back of the ship

Ai yai yai! A favorite expression of surprise or wonder

babaloo. Friendly jibe used for all occasions

balona. Overweight woman, or "balone" for a man

bambino. Italian word for "child"

basura. Spanish word for "trash," frequently used as an insult

bomboclat. Jamaican insult, rather graphic

blood clot. Jamaican insult, somewhat lighter

boleta. Late for work

bow. The very front of the ship

bridge. Area where the ship is piloted from

cabina. Few people properly say the word "cabin"

cheeky-cheeky. Sex

comaros. In great quantity, a play on Spanish *con arroz,* meaning "with rice"

comida. Spanish word for "food"

crew bar. Lounge for crew only, usually very small, very crowded, and very smoky

flotsam. Debris floating in the water

fore. Toward the front of the ship

gangway. The portable walkway over the gap between a ship's hull and the dock

I-95. Main crew corridor, also documentation foreign workers carry to work in the U.S.

kaput. German word for "ruined," used constantly on ships

knots per hour. Velocity at sea, one mph equals 0.868 knots per hour

mafia. Nickname for groups within the dining room based on nationality

mamagayo. Someone intentionally lazy on the job so others have to pick up the slack

mooring line. Ropes used to secure a ship into a port

nautical mile. One land mile equals 0.868 nautical miles

like rice. A great amount of something, referring to Asians' appetite for rice

list. To lean

open deck. Any outside deck, though crew usually refers to the crew-only bow area

paisano. Italian word for "fellow countryman," also common is "paisa"

pasta. Money

poop deck. A lower deck that houses mooring lines

port. The left side of the ship, while facing forward

purser. Officer in charge of organization of personnel and guest matters

rambo. A worker who is efficient to the point of destruction and/or theft

rasclat. Jamaican insult, somewhat lighter

sapo. To tattle on someone who is doing something wrong

siesta. Spanish word for "nap"

starboard. The right side of the ship, while facing forward

stern. The very back of the ship

USPH. U.S. Public Health inspection of cruise ships: phenomenally difficult to pass

Where you from? Crew term used to mock someone's ignorance or naiveté

Why you pinch? Common question when caught "borrowing" needed supplies

Provisions for a Cruise

Provisions for an average seven-day cruise on a mid-sized cruise ship with about 2,000 passengers and almost 1,000 crewmembers.

24,236 pounds of beef

5,040 pounds of lamb

7,216 pounds of pork

4,600 pounds of veal

1,680 pounds of sausage

10,211 pounds of chicken

3,156 pounds of turkey

13,851 pounds of fish

350 pounds of crab

2,100 pounds of lobster

25,736 pounds of
fresh vegetables

15,150 pounds of potatoes

20,003 pounds of fresh fruit

3,260 gallons of milk

1976 quarts of cream

600 gallons of ice cream

9,235 dozen eggs

5,750 pounds of sugar

3,800 pounds of rice

1,750 pounds of cereal

450 pounds of jelly

2,458 pounds of coffee

1,936 pounds of cookies

2,450 tea bags

120 pounds of herbs and spices

3,400 bottles of assorted wines

200 bottles of champagne

200 bottles of gin

290 bottles of vodka

350 bottles of whiskey

150 bottles of rum

45 bottles of sherry

600 bottles of assorted liqueurs

10,100 bottles/cans of beer

Stupid Questions

Such lists as this are endless, but these all have truly been
asked of me by guests.

Do these steps go up?
What do you do with the beautiful ice carvings after they melt?
Can you purchase ice carvings in the gift shop?
Which elevator do I take to get to the front of the ship?
Does this elevator go up or down?
Does the crew sleep on the ship?
Is this island completely surrounded by water?
What elevation is this beach?
Why don't you tell people it's hot in Jamaica when they
    buy the cruise?
Does the ship make its own electricity?
Is it salt water in the toilets?
Does the ship's engine run better at sea level than in the
    mountains, like my car?
What time is the midnight buffet?
If the photographer took my picture, how do I know which
    is mine?
Can I water-ski off the back of the ship?
If I fell overboard and no one knew, would the ship come back
    for me?
If the captain is here, who is driving the ship?
Does the captain have any training?
For the right gratuity, will the captain let me drive the ship?
Can you ask the captain to stop the waves? I'm getting seasick.
I see only one button on the coffee machine. Do I push it for
    coffee? (Asked daily.)
This watch is waterproof for only three meters...so I can only
    swim fifteen feet across?
I asked for a sea-view cabin, I want my money back. (Said while
    docked in New Orleans.)
What country is Iowa in? (Asked by an American.)
Are you crazy, or just stupid?

About the Author

After twenty-five years of a staggeringly mundane life in Iowa, Brian David Bruns woke up one day in Reno with an empty wallet and an irate cat. One year later he co-founded a company, secured international investment, and finally placated his pet. Five years after that he had traveled to forty-six countries across three continents, all the while living in Transylvania.

A reborn adventurer, Brian has run desert marathons in Nevada, climbed the highest mountain in the lower forty-eight, zip-lined over jungles in Costa Rica, parlayed with snake charmers in Morocco, entered the pyramids at Giza, consulted the oracle of Delphi, anted up in Monte Carlo, and visited Dracula's house on Halloween night.

Brian is also a professional artist and public speaker. He has delivered his amusing angle on art history to thousands on Carnival Cruise Lines, Royal Caribbean, Holland America, and Windstar Lines. His first book, *Comstock Phantoms: True Ghost Stories of Virginia City, Nevada*, a blend of accessible history and hilarious ghost-hunts gone awry, sold out its first edition in just seven weeks.

Foolishly lured to sea in the pursuit of love, Brian was the only American waiter in Carnival Corporation's thirty-year history to survive an entire contract without quitting. This outrageous experience, both entertaining and enlightening, resulted in *Cruise Confidential: A Hit Below the Waterline*.